lonely

Portuguese

Phrasebook & Dictionary

Acknowledgments
Product Editors Damian Kemp, Bruce Evans
Book Designer Fergal Condon
Language Writers Yukiyoshi Kamimura, Robert Landon, Anabela de Azevedo Teixeira Sobrinho
Cover Image Researcher Gwen Cotter

Published by Lonely Planet Global Limited
CRN 554153

5th Edition – June 2023
ISBN 978 1 78868 0639

Cover Image Sunbathers on the golden sands of Praia da Marinha, Algarve. Sonja Filitz/Shutterstock ©
Printed in China 10 9 8 7 6 5 4 3 2 1

Contact lonelyplanet.com/contact

Look out for the following icons throughout the book:

'Shortcut' Phrase
Easy to remember alternative to the full phrase

Q&A Pair
'Question-and-answer' pair – we suggest a response to the question asked

Look For
Phrases you may see on signs, menus etc

Listen For
Phrases you may hear from officials, locals etc

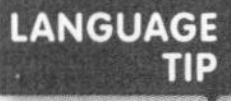

Language Tip
An insight into the foreign language

CULTURE TIP

Culture Tip
An insight into the local culture

How to read the phrases:

- Coloured words and phrases throughout the book are phonetic guides to help you pronounce the foreign language.
- Lists of phrases with tinted background are options you can choose to complete the phrase above them.

These abbreviations will help you choose the right words and phrases in this book:

a adjective
f feminine
inf informal
lit literal
m masculine
n noun
pl plural
pol polite
sg singular
v verb

ABOUT THIS BOOK

Contents

PAGE **6**

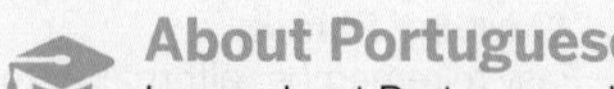

About Portuguese

Learn about Portuguese, build your own sentences and pronounce words correctly.

PAGE **27**

Travel Phrases

Ready-made phrases for every situation – buy a ticket, book a hotel and much more.

Who speaks Portuguese?

OFFICIAL LANGUAGE

PORTUGAL
BRAZIL
CAPE VERDE
GUINEA-BISSAU
ANGOLA
MOZAMBIQUE
SÃO TOMÉ & PRÍNCIPE
EAST TIMOR
MACAU (CHINA)

Why Bother

If it's true that language is the door to a nation's soul, you might get a little closer to grasping the *saudade* – that melancholic longing for something (the 'Portuguese blues'), and its famous musical expression, *fado*.

Distinctive Sounds

Throaty 'r' (similar to French) and nasal vowels (pronounced as if you're trying to force the sound through the nose).

Portuguese in the World

The global distribution of Portuguese began during *Os*

200 **MILLION** speak Portuguese as their first language

40 **MILLION** speak Portuguese as their second language

Descobrimentos (The Age of Discoveries) in the 15th and 16th centuries, when Portugal was a colonial power with huge economic, cultural and political influence. The empire's reach can be seen in the number of countries where Portuguese or Portuguese-based creoles are spoken today.

Portuguese in Portugal

The Instituto Camões (www.instituto-camoes.pt, in Portuguese), named in honour of Portugal's greatest poet Luís de Camões, was created in 1992 to promote Portuguese language and culture worldwide. The most important literary prize for Portuguese language is also called Prémio Camões.

False Friends

Warning: many Portuguese words look like English words but have a different meaning altogether, eg *salsa* *saal*·sa is 'parsley', not 'sauce' (which is *molho* *mo*·lyoo in Portuguese).

Language Family

Romance (developed from the colloquial Latin spoken by the Romans during their 500-year rule of present-day Portugal). Close relatives include Galician, Spanish, Italian, French and Romanian.

Must-Know Grammar

Portuguese has both a formal and an informal word for 'you' (*você* vo·*se* and *tu* too respectively). Verbs have a different ending for each person – like the English 'I do' vs 'he/she do**es**'.

Donations to English

Numerous – you may recognise *albino, port, brocade, dodo, molasses, commando* ...

5 Phrases to Learn Before You Go

1 When is admission free?

Quando é grátis a entrada?

kwang·doo e *graa*·teesh a eng·*traa*·da

Try to plan your sightseeing in Portugal around free-admission days (often Sunday mornings).

2 Can I have a half-serve, please?

Podia servir-me meia-dose, por favor?

poo·*dee*·a ser·*veer*·me *may*·a·*do*·ze poor fa·*vor*

Much Portuguese cuisine is served in massive portions – it's often worth ordering a half-serve, especially if you're on a budget.

3 Can I get this without meat?

Este prato pode vir sem carne?

esh·te *praa*·too *po*·de veer seng *kaar*·ne

Vegetarians aren't generally well catered for in Portugal, and they may need to be creative in requesting their dishes.

4 Where can we go for 'street fado'?

Onde é que há fado vadio?

ong·de e ke aa *faa*·doo va·*dee*·oo

For an authentic, spontaneous approach to music, seek out places where locals take turns singing the 'Portuguese blues'.

5 Where can I find an art exhibition?

Onde é que há alguma esposição de arte?

ong·de e ke aa alg·*goo*·ma shpoo·zee·*sowng* de *aar*·te

There are always interesting cultural happenings in major Portuguese cities, including free fringe-art exhibitions.

10 Phrases to Sound Like a Local

Cool!	**Óptimo!**	o·tee·moo
Great!	**Fantástico!**	fang·*taash*·tee·koo
Sure.	**É claro.**	e *klaa*·roo
Maybe.	**Talvez.**	taal·*vesh*
No way!	**De maneira nenhuma!**	de ma·*nay*·ra neeng·*yoo*·ma
Just joking.	**Estou a brincar.**	shtoh a breeng·*kaar*
No problem.	**Não há problema.**	nowng aa pro·*ble*·ma
It's OK.	**Está bem.**	shtaa beng
Of course!	**Claro que sim!**	*klaa*·roo ke seeng
Never mind.	**Não faz mal.**	nowng fazh mao

ABOUT PORTUGUESE

Pronunciation

Vowel Sounds

The vowel sounds in Portuguese are quite similar to those found in English, so you should be able to get talking with confidence. There are some differences, of course. Most vowel sounds in Portuguese also have a nasal version with an effect similar to the silent '-ng' ending in English, such as *amanhã* aa·ma·*nyang* (tomorrow), for example. The letter *n* or *m* at the end of a syllable, or a tilde (~) in written Portuguese indicate that the vowel is nasal (also see **consonant sounds**).

SYMBOL	ENGLISH EQUIVALENT	PORTUGUESE EXAMPLE	TRANSLITERATION
a	among	maçã	ma·*sang*
aa	father	tomate	too·*maa*·te
ai	aisle	pai	pai
ay	play	lei	lay
e	ten	cedo	*se*·doo
ee	feet	fino	*fee*·noo
o	lot	sobre	*so*·bre
oh	oh!	couve	*koh*·ve
oo	book	gato	*ga*·too
ow	cow	Austrália	ow·*shtraa*·lya
oy	boy	noite	*noy*·te

Consonant Sounds

Most of the consonants in Portuguese are also found in English. Note that the *r* rr is similar to the French 'r' sound.

SYMBOL	ENGLISH EQUIVALENT	PORTUGUESE EXAMPLE	TRANSLITERATION
b	bed	beber	be·*ber*
d	dog	dedo	*de*·doo
f	fit	faca	*faa*·ka
g	gap	gasolina	ga·zoo·*lee*·na
k	kit	cama	*ka*·ma
l	let	lixo	*lee*·shoo
ly	million	muralhas	moo·*raa*·lyash
m	mat	macaco	ma·*kaa*·koo
n	no	nada	*naa*·da
ng	sing (indicates nasalisation of preceding vowel)	ambos, uns, amanhã	*ang*·boosh, oongsh, aa·ma·*nyang*
ny	canyon	linha	*lee*·nya
p	pin	padre	*paa*·dre
r	like 'tt' in 'butter' said fast	hora	*o*·ra
rr	as in French 'croissant'	relva	*rrel*·va
s	sad	criança	kree·*ang*·sa
sh	shut	chave	*shaa*·ve
t	top	tacho	*taa*·shoo
v	very	vago	*vaa*·goo
w	water	água	*aa*·gwa
y	yes	edifício	ee·dee·*fee*·syoo
z	zoo	camisa	ka·*mee*·za
zh	pleasure	cerveja	serr·*ve*·zha

Some consonant sounds can change depending on where they appear in a word. For example, an *s* at the beginning of the word is pronounced like the s in 'sea' – eg *sal* saal (salt). When *s* comes at the end of the word, or at the end of a syllable which is followed by a consonant, as in *está* shtaa (are), it's pronounced sh, but if it's surrounded on both sides by vowels (as in *camisa* ka·*mee*·za), it's pronounced z. Follow the coloured pronunciation guides and you won't have any trouble.

Word Stress

Stress (ie the emphasis on one syllable over another) generally occurs on the second-to-last syllable of a word, though there are exceptions. If a written vowel has a circumflex (ˆ) or an acute (´) accent marked on it, this cancels the general rule and the stress falls on that syllable.

fino	*fee*·no	fine
português	poor·too·*gesh*	Portuguese
cajú	ka·*zhoo*	cashew

Also, if you're reading Portuguese words for yourself, it's handy to know these other exceptions: when a word ends in a written *i*, *im*, *l*, *r*, *u*, *um* or *z*, or is pronounced with a nasalised vowel, the stress falls on the last syllable.

beber	be·*ber*	to drink
calor	ka·*lor*	heat
actuação	a·too·a·*sowng*	performance

Don't worry too much about it when using phrases from this book though – if you follow the coloured pronunciation guides you can't go wrong.

You'll notice in conversation with Portuguese speakers that as in English, when certain syllables are given more stress, others are practically unpronounced. For example, unless the final syllable is stressed, the vowel is pronounced very lightly and in conversation may disappear altogether – so *antes* is technically pronounced *aang*·tesh but in practice sounds more like ants. Again, we've always given the correct pronunciation in our coloured guides.

Reading & Writing

Portuguese is written with the Latin alphabet. For spelling purposes (eg if you need to spell your name to book into a hotel), the pronunciation of each letter is provided below.

~ PORTUGUESE ALPHABET ~

A a aa	**B b** be	**C c** se	**D d** de
E e e	**F f** e·fe	**G g** je	**H h** a·*gaah*
I i ee	**J j** *jo*·ta	**K k** *ka*·pa	**L l** e·le
M m e·me	**N n** e·ne	**O o** o	**P p** pe
Q q ke	**R r** e·rre	**S s** e·se	**T t** te
U u oo	**V v** ve	**W w** *da*·blyoo	**X x** sheesh
Y y *eeps*·lon	**Z z** ze		

You'll notice that some letters, usually vowels, have accent marks. The acute (´) accent and the circumflex (ˆ) indicate stress, the grave (`) accent indicates the contraction of two *a*'s, and the tilde (~) indicates nasalisation. You'll also see the cedilla sometimes used at the bottom of the letter 'c' – *ç* is pronounced as s rather than k (*criança* kree·*ang*·sa).

ABOUT PORTUGUESE

Grammar

This chapter is designed to explain the main grammatical structures you need in order to make your own sentences. Look under each heading – listed in alphabetical order – for information on functions which these grammatical categories express in a sentence. For example, demonstratives are used for giving instructions, so you'll need them to tell the taxi driver where your hotel is, etc.

Adjectives & Adverbs

Describing People/Things • Doing Things

Adjectives are generally placed after the noun. They change form depending on the gender and number of the noun they describe (see also **gender** and **plurals**).

handsome boy	menino bonito (lit: boy handsome-**m-sg**) me·*nee*·noo boo·*nee*·too
handsome boys	meninos bonitos (lit: boys handsome-**m-pl**) me·*nee*·noosh boo·*nee*·toosh
pretty girl	menina bonita (lit: girl pretty-**f-sg**) me·*nee*·na boo·*nee*·ta
pretty girls	meninas bonitas (lit: girls pretty-**f-pl**) me·*nee*·nash boo·*nee*·tash

Adverbs are normally formed by adding *-mente* ·*meng*·te to the end of the feminine form of the adjective.

~ ADJECTIVE ~			~ ADVERB ~		
clear	clara f	*klaa*·ra	**clearly**	claramente	klaa·ra·*meng*·te
slow	lenta f	*leng*·ta	**slowly**	lentamente	leng·ta·*meng*·te

Articles

Naming People/Things

The Portuguese words *um* oong and *uma* *oo*·ma correspond to the English article 'a/an'. If what you're referring to is masculine you use *um*, if it's feminine you use *uma*. The plurals *uns* oongsh and *umas* *oo*·mash correspond to the English 'some'.

	~ MASCULINE ~	
sg	um café oong ka·*fe*	**a coffee**
pl	uns cafés oongsh ka·*fesh*	**some coffees**
	~ FEMININE ~	
sg	uma sandes *oo*·ma *sang*·desh	**a sandwich**
pl	umas sandes *oo*·mash *sang*·desh	**some sandwiches**

There are four words that correspond to the English article 'the'. The form you use is determined by the gender and number of the noun the article is used with (see overleaf).

See also **gender** and **plurals**.

~ MASCULINE ~

sg	o comboio oo kong·*boy*·oo	**the train**
pl	os comboios oosh kong·*boy*·oosh	**the trains**

~ FEMININE ~

sg	a mochila a moo·*shee*·la	**the backpack**
pl	as mochilas ash moo·*shee*·lash	**the backpacks**

Be

Describing People/Things • Doing Things • Indicating Location • Pointing Things Out

Portuguese has two words which can be translated as 'be' in English: *ser* ser and *estar* shtaar. They're both irregular verbs (just like 'be' in English) so you need to learn the various forms they take by heart. Learning to use them perfectly will take some time and effort, but the basic difference in their usage isn't too difficult to grasp.

The verb *ser* refers to states that have a degree of permanency or durability about them.

You also use *ser* to point something out in Portuguese. Just start your phrase with *É* ... e ... (lit: it-is ...) as in the example below. See also **demonstratives** and **there is/are**.

That's a beautiful building.	É um edifício lindo. (lit: it-is a-**m-sg** building beautiful-**m-sg**) e oong ee·dee·*fee*·syoo *leeng*·do

~ *SER* – PRESENT TENSE ~

I	**am**	eu	sou	*e*·oo	soh
you sg inf	**are**	tu	és	too	esh
you sg pol	**are**	você	é	vo·*se*	e
he	**is**	ele	é	*e*·le	e
she	**is**	ela	é	*e*·la	e
we	**are**	nós	somos	nosh	*so*·moosh
you pl inf	**are**	vocês	são	vo·*sesh*	sowng
you pl pol	**are**	vós	sois	vosh	soysh
they m/f	**are**	eles/elas	são	*e*·lesh/*e*·lash	sowng

The verb *estar* generally refers to events which are temporary in nature. It's also used to talk about the location of things that are moveable.

~ *ESTAR* – PRESENT TENSE ~

I	**am**	eu	estou	*e*·oo	shtoh
you sg inf	**are**	tu	estás	too	shtaash
you sg pol	**are**	você	está	vo·*se*	shtaa
he	**is**	ele	está	*e*·le	shtaa
she	**is**	ela	está	*e*·la	shtaa
we	**are**	nós	estamos	nos	*shta*·moosh
you pl inf	**are**	vocês	estão	vo·*sesh*	shtowng
you pl pol	**are**	vós	estais	vosh	shtaish
they m/f	**are**	eles/elas	estão	*e*·lesh/*e*·lash	shtowng

Demonstratives

Describing People/Things • Indicating Location • Pointing Things Out • Giving Instructions

To refer to or point at a person or object, use one of the following words before the noun, depending on whether the person or object you're referring to is close or further away, masculine or feminine, and singular or plural.

	~ SINGULAR ~		~ PLURAL ~	
	m	f	m	f
this (close)	este *esh*·te	esta *esh*·ta	estes *esh*·tesh	estas *esh*·tash
that (away)	aquele a·*ke*·le	aquela a·*ke*·la	aqueles a·*ke*·lesh	aquelas a·*ke*·lash

Is this seat free?
Este lugar está livre?
(lit: this-m-sg place is free-sg)
esh·te loo·*gaar* shtaa *lee*·vre

These words can also be used on their own, without an accompanying noun, meaning 'this (one)', 'that (one)', 'these' and 'those'.

Those are Portuguese.
Aqueles são portugueses.
(lit: those-m-pl are Portuguese-pl)
a·*ke*·lesh sowng poor·too·*ge*·zesh

Gender

Naming People/Things

All Portuguese nouns are either masculine m or feminine f. This determines the endings on any adjectives you use to describe them, as well as which forms of the Portuguese equivalents of the articles 'a/an' and 'the' are used.

The gender that a given noun takes is often arbitrary: there's no reason why, for example, the noun *sol* sol (sun) is masculine while *praia* *prai*·a (beach) is feminine. The dictionaries and word lists in this book indicate gender for nouns, but here are some guidelines for taking a guess at gender if you need to:

» nouns referring to male persons or animals, and those ending in *-o*, *-ema* or *-oma* are usually masculine

» nouns referring to female persons or animals, and those ending in *-a* or *-dade* are usually feminine

See also **articles** and **adjectives & adverbs**.

Have

Possessing

An easy way to indicate possession is to use the verb *ter* ter (have), which has different forms for each person.

~ *TER* – PRESENT TENSE ~

I	**have**	eu	tenho	e·oo	*ta*·nyoo
you sg inf	**have**	tu	tens	too	tengsh
you sg pol	**have**	você	tem	vo·*se*	teng
he	**has**	ele	tem	e·le	teng
she	**has**	ela	tem	e·la	teng
we	**have**	nós	temos	nosh	*te*·moosh
you pl inf	**have**	vocês	têm	vo·*sesh*	*teng*·eng
you pl pol	**have**	vós	tendes	vosh	*teng*·desh
they m/f	**have**	eles/elas	têm	e·lesh/e·lash	*teng*·eng

Negatives

Negating

To make a sentence negative, just add the word *não* nowng (no) before the main verb – in the example below, the verb is *vejo* *ve*·zhoo (see).

I see the market.	Vejo o mercado. (lit: I-see the-m-sg market) *ve*·zhoo oo mer·*kaa*·doo
I don't see the market.	Não vejo o mercado. (lit: no I-see the-m-sg market) nowng *ve*·zhoo oo mer·*kaa*·doo

In Portuguese, the double negative is not only acceptable, but correct:

I can't see anything.	Não vejo nada. (lit: no I-see nothing) nowng *ve*·zhoo *naa*·da

See also **there is/are**.

Personal Pronouns

Doing Things • Naming People/Things

Subject pronouns corresponding to 'I', 'you' etc are often left out in Portuguese, as the verb endings make it clear what the subject is. You only need to use them if you want to emphasise who or what is doing the action. You'll also notice that there are polite and informal versions of 'you' (marked with pol and inf). The polite version, combined with a verb in the third person singular (he/she), is used with people older than you or those you don't know very well. In this book we've used the form that best suits the context – generally this means the polite form unless the phrase is marked otherwise.

~ SUBJECT PRONOUNS ~

I	eu	*e·oo*	**we**	nós	*nosh*
you sg inf	tu	*too*	**you** pl inf	vocês	*vo·sesh*
you sg pol	você	*vo·se*	**you** pl pol	vós	*vosh*
he	ele	*e·le*	**they** m	eles	*e·lesh*
she	ela	*e·la*	**they** f	elas	*e·lash*

The direct object pronouns corresponding to 'me', 'you' and so on are listed below.

~ DIRECT OBJECT PRONOUNS ~

me	me	*me*	**us**	nos	*noosh*
you sg inf	te	*te*	**you** pl inf	vos	*voosh*
you sg pol m/f	o/a	*oo/a*	**you** pl pol m/f	os/as	*oosh/ash*
him	o	*oo*	**them** m	os	*oosh*
her	a	*a*	**them** f	as	*ash*

Plurals

Naming People/Things

If a noun ends in a vowel, you can make it plural by simply adding *-s* sh.

~ SINGULAR ~		~ PLURAL ~	
book	livro m *lee·vroo*	**books**	livros m *lee·vroosh*
bed	cama f *ka·ma*	**beds**	camas f *ka·mash*

If a noun ends in *-s*, *-z* or *-r* and the final syllable is stressed, the plural is formed by adding *-es* esh.

~ SINGULAR ~		~ PLURAL ~	
Portuguese	português poor·too·*gesh*	**Portuguese**	portugueses poor·too·*ge*·zesh
nose	nariz na·*reesh*	**noses**	narizes na·*ree*·zesh
flower	flor flor	**flowers**	flores *flo*·resh

Don't forget, you have to change any articles and adjectives you use with a plural noun to their plural forms too.

See also **articles**, **adjectives & adverbs** and **gender**.

Possessives

Naming People/Things • Possessing

There are various ways to indicate possession in Portuguese, for example by using the verb *ter* (see **have**). Simplest of all is to use the preposition *de* de (of), followed by the name of the person who owns the object.

It's Carla's backpack.	É a mochila da Carla. (lit: it-is the-**f-sg** backpack of-**f-sg** Carla) e a moo·*shee*·la da *kaar*·la

Also, as you do in English, you can indicate possession using pronouns. The table opposite lists the equivalents for the English possessive adjectives 'my', 'your' and 'our'. They are placed between the article and the noun they describe, and agree in number (singular or plural) and gender (masculine or feminine) with the noun.

It's my ticket.	É o meu bilhete. (lit: it-is the-**m-sg** my-**m-sg** ticket) e oo *me*·oo bee·*lye*·te

	~ SINGULAR NOUN ~		~ PLURAL NOUN ~	
	m	f	m	f
my	meu *me*·oo	minha *mee*·nya	meus *me*·oosh	minhas *mee*·nyash
your sg inf	teu *te*·oo	tua *too*·a	teus *te*·oosh	tuas *too*·ash
your sg pol	seu *se*·oo	sua *soo*·a	seus *se*·oosh	suas *soo*·ash
our	nosso *no*·soo	nossa *no*·sa	nossos *no*·soosh	nossas *no*·sash
your pl	vosso *vo*·soo	vossa *vo*·sa	vossos *vo*·soos	vossas *vo*·sash

For the equivalents of 'his', 'her' and 'their', it's a bit different. The adjective goes after the noun, and the gender and number match the owner rather than the noun they describe – eg 'her book' is *o livro dela* oo *lee*·vroo *de*·la (lit: the-**m-sg** book her).

his	dele	*de*·le	**their** m	deles	*de*·lesh
her	dela	*de*·la	**their** f	delas	*de*·lash

See also **gender** and **articles**.

Prepositions

Giving Instructions • Indicating Location • Pointing Things Out

Prepositions in Portuguese can be placed before the noun – eg *com leite* kong *lay*·te (with milk) – or after verbs. Here are some common prepositions:

~ PREPOSITIONS ~					
between	entre	*eng*·tre	**over**	por cima de	poor *see*·ma de
to/for	para	*pa*·ra	**under**	debaixo de	de·*bai*·shoo de
until	até	a·*te*	**with**	com	kong

Some other prepositions have a standard form, but when they come before an article they combine with the article (which agrees in gender and number with the noun it goes with). 'In the rooms', for example, is *nos quartos* noosh *kwaar*·toosh – *nos* is a combination of *em* eng (in) and *os* oosh (the-m-pl).

	STANDARD FORM	COMBINED WITH AN ARTICLE			
		m sg	f sg	m pl	f pl
by/for	por por	pelo *pe*·loo	pela *pe*·la	pelos *pe*·loosh	pelas *pe*·lash
in/on	*em* eng	no noo	na na	nos noosh	nas nash
of/from	*de* de	do doo	da da	dos doosh	das dash
to	*a* a	ao ow	à aa	aos owsh	às aash

See also **articles** and **gender**.

Questions

Asking Questions

To ask a question, simply make a statement but raise your voice inquisitively at the end of the sentence, as you would in English.

Do you speak Portuguese?	Fala português? (lit: you-speak-sg-inf Portuguese) *faa*·la poor·too·*gesh*

You can also use one of the question words from the table opposite. They go at the beginning of the sentence, just like in English.

~ QUESTION WORDS ~

How?	Como?	*ko*·moo
How much?	Quanto?	*kwang*·too
How many?	Quantos? **m pl** Quantas? **f pl**	*kwang*·toosh *kwang*·tash
What?	Quê?	ke
What/Which?	Qual?	kwaal
Where?	Onde?	*ong*·de
Who?	Quem?	keng
Why?	Porquê?	poor·*ke*

There Is/Are

Indicating Location • Negating • Pointing Things Out

To say 'there is' or 'there are' in Portuguese, use *há* aa (lit: it-has). Add *não* nowng (no) before *há* to make a negative sentence.

There's a seat available.	Há um lugar vago. (lit: it-has a-**m-sg** seat free-**m-sg**) aa oong loo·*gaar vaa*·goo
There aren't any seats available.	Não há lugares vagos. (lit: no it-has seats free-**m-pl**) nowng aa loo·*gaa*·resh *vaa*·goosh

See also **be**.

Verbs

Asking Questions • Doing Things • Giving Instructions • Making Requests

Portuguese has three types of verbs: those ending in *-ar* aar (*morar* mor·*aar*, 'live'), those ending in *-er* er (*comer* koo·*mer*, 'eat') and those ending in *-ir* eer (*partir* par·*teer*, 'leave'). The present tense verb endings for each person ('I', 'you', 'we' etc) are very similar for all three, so you can recognise them easily.

	~ -AR ~	~ -ER ~	~ -IR ~
I	-o ·oo	-o ·oo	-o ·oo
you sg inf	-a ·ash	-es ·esh	-es ·esh
you sg pol	-a ·a	-e ·e	-e ·e
he/she	-a ·a	-e ·e	-e ·e
we	-amos ·*a*·moosh	-emos ·*e*·moosh	-imos ·*ee*·moosh
you pl pol	-ais ·aish	-eis ·aysh	-is ·eesh
you pl inf	-am ·owng	-em ·eng	-em ·eng
they	-am ·owng	-em ·eng	-em ·eng

As in any language, some Portuguese verbs are irregular. The most important ones are *ser* ser (be), *estar* shtaar (be) and *ter* ter (have). For more details see **be** and **have**.

Word Order

Doing Things • Giving Instructions • Making Requests

Generally, the order of words in a sentence is the same as in English (subject–verb–object).

I'd like a room.	Eu queria um quarto. (lit: I would-like a-m-sg room) *e·oo ke·ree·a oong kwaar·too*

A
B
C
Basics

Understanding

KEY PHRASES

Do you speak English?	Fala inglês?	*faa*·la eeng·*glesh*
I don't understand.	Não entendo.	nowng eng·*teng*·doo
What does ... mean?	O que quer dizer ...?	oo ke ker dee·*zer* ...

Q **Do you speak (English)?**	Fala (inglês)? *faa*·la (eeng·*glesh*)
Q **Does anyone speak (English)?**	Alguém aqui fala (inglês)? aal·*geng* a·*kee* *faa*·la (eeng·*glesh*)
A **I speak (English).**	Falo (inglês). *faa*·loo (eeng·*glesh*)
A **I don't speak (Portuguese).**	Não falo (português). nowng *faa*·loo (poor·too·*gesh*)
A **I speak a little.**	Falo um pouco. *faa*·loo oong *poh*·koo
Q **Do you understand (me)?**	Entende(-me)? eng·*teng*·de(·me)
A **Yes, I understand.**	Sim, entendo. seeng eng·*teng*·doo
A **No, I don't understand.**	Não, não entendo. nowng nowng eng·*teng*·doo
Pardon?	Desculpe? desh·*kool*·pe

UNDERSTANDING

LANGUAGE TIP

False Friends

You can often guess the meaning of Portuguese words, as many are similar to English. But things aren't always what they seem:

constipação	*kong·shtee·pa·sowng*	headcold (not 'constipation')
depressa	*de·pre·sa*	fast (not 'depressed')
massa	*maa·sa*	noodles (not 'Catholic Mass')

What does ... mean?	O que quer dizer ...? *oo ke ker dee·zer ...*
How do you pronounce this?	Como é que se pronuncia isto? *ko·moo e ke se proo·noong·see·a eesh·too*
How do you write ...?	Como é que se escreve ...? *ko·moo e ke se shkre·ve ...*
Could you please repeat that?	Podia repetir isto, por favor? *poo·dee·a rre·pe·teer eesh·too poor fa·vor*
Could you please write it down?	Podia escrever isso, por favor? *poo·dee·a shkre·ver ee·soo poor fa·vor*
Could you please speak more slowly?	Podia falar mais devagar, por favor? *poo·dee·a fa·laar maish de·va·gaar poor fa·vor*

Slowly, please!	Devagar, por favor!	*de·va·gaar poor fa·vor*

Numbers & Amounts

KEY PHRASES

How much?	Quanto?	*kwang*·too
a little	um bocadinho	oong boo·ka·*dee*·nyoo
a lot	muito	*mweeng*·too

Cardinal Numbers

0	zero	*ze*·roo
1	um	oong
2	dois	doysh
3	três	tresh
4	quatro	*kwaa*·troo
5	cinco	*seeng*·koo
6	seis	saysh
7	sete	*se*·te
8	oito	*oy*·too
9	nove	*no*·ve
10	dez	desh
11	onze	*ong*·ze
12	doze	*do*·ze
13	treze	*tre*·ze
14	catorze	ka·*tor*·ze
15	quinze	*keeng*·ze
16	dezasseis	de·za·*saysh*
17	dezassete	de·za·*se*·te

18	dezoito	de·*zoy*·too
19	dezanove	de·za·*no*·ve
20	vinte	*veeng*·te
21	vinte e um	*veeng*·te e oong
22	vinte e dois	*veeng*·te e doysh
30	trinta	*treeng*·ta
40	quarenta	kwa·*reng*·ta
50	cinquenta	seeng·*kweng*·ta
60	sessenta	se·*seng*·ta
70	setenta	se·*teng*·ta
80	oitenta	oy·*teng*·ta
90	noventa	no·*veng*·ta
100	cem	seng
200	duzentos	doo·*zeng*·toosh
300	trezentos	tre·*zeng*·toosh
1000	mil	meel
1,000,000	um milhão	oong mee·*lyowng*

Ordinal Numbers

Ordinal numbers are written with a degree sign in Portuguese – 1st is written *1º*, 10th is *10º*, and so on.

1st	primeiro **m** primeira **f**	pree·*may*·roo pree·*may*·ra
2nd	segundo **m** segunda **f**	se·*goong*·doo se·*goong*·da
3rd	terceiro **m** terceira **f**	ter·*say*·roo ter·*say*·ra
4th	quarto **m** quarta **f**	*kwaar*·too *kwaar*·ta
5th	quinto **m** quinta **f**	*keeng*·too *keeng*·ta

Fractions & Decimals

a quarter	um quarto	oong *kwaar*·too
a third	um terço	oong *ter*·soo
a half	a metade	a me·*taa*·de
three-quarters	três quartos	tresh *kwaar*·toosh

In Portugal, decimals are written – and pronounced – as in English, except that the period is replaced by a comma (*vírgula veer*·goo·la).

3.14	três vírgula catorze (3,14)	tresh *veer*·goo·la ka·*tor*·ze

Amounts

How much?	Quanto? *kwang*·too
How many?	Quantos? **m pl** *kwang*·toosh Quantas? **f pl** *kwang*·tash
Please give me ...	Por favor dê-me ... poor fa·*vor de*·me ...

a few	uns poucos **m pl** umas poucas **f pl**	oongsh *poh*·koosh *oo*·mash *poh*·kash
(just) a little	(só) um bocadinho	(so) oong boo·ka·*dee*·nyoo
a lot	muito	*mweeng*·too
less	menos	*me*·noosh
many	muitos **m pl** muitas **f pl**	*mweeng*·toosh *mweeng*·tash
more	mais	maish
some	uns **m pl** umas **f pl**	oongsh *oo*·mash

Time & Dates

KEY PHRASES

What time is it?	Que horas são?	kee *o*·rash sowng
At what time ...?	A que horas ...?	a ke *o*·rash ...
What date?	Qual data?	kwaal *daa*·ta

Telling the Time

Generally, the 12-hour clock is used for telling the time in Portuguese, though the 24-hour clock is often what you'll see written down.

Q **What time is it?**	Que horas são?	kee *o*·rash sowng
A **It's (one) o'clock.**	É (uma) hora.	e (*oo*·ma) *o*·ra
A **It's (10) o'clock.**	São (dez) horas.	sowng (desh) *o*·rash
A **Five past (10).**	(Dez) e cinco.	(desh) e *seeng*·koo
A **Quarter past (10).**	(Dez) e quinze.	(desh) e *keeng*·ze
A **Half past (10).**	(Dez) e meia.	(desh) e *may*·a
A **Quarter to (11).**	Quinze para as (onze).	*keeng*·ze *pa*·ra ash (*ong*·ze)
am	da manhã	da ma·*nyang*
pm (afternoon)	da tarde	da *taar*·de
pm (evening)	da noite	da *noy*·te

At what time...?	A que horas ...?	a ke *o*·rash ...
At (one).	À (uma).	aa (*oo*·ma)
At (five).	Às (cinco).	aash (*seeng*·koo)
At (7.57pm).	Às (sete e cinquenta e sete da noite).	aash (*se*·te e seeng·*kweng*·ta e *se*·te da *noy*·te)
afternoon	tarde **f**	*taar*·de
dawn	madrugada **f**	ma·droo·*gaa*·da
day	dia **m**	*dee*·a
evening	noite **f**	*noy*·te
midday	meio dia **m**	*may*·oo *dee*·a
midnight	meia noite **f**	*may*·a *noy*·te
morning	manhã **f**	ma·*nyang*
night	noite **f**	*noy*·te
sunrise	nascer do sol **m**	nash·*ser* doo sol
sunset	pôr do sol **m**	por doo sol

The Calendar

Monday	segunda-feira **f**	se·*goong*·da·*fay*·ra
Tuesday	terça-feira **f**	*ter*·sa·*fay*·ra
Wednesday	quarta-feira **f**	*kwaar*·ta·*fay*·ra
Thursday	quinta-feira **f**	*keeng*·ta·*fay*·ra
Friday	sexta-feira **f**	*saysh*·ta·*fay*·ra
Saturday	sábado **m**	*saa*·ba·doo
Sunday	domingo **m**	doo·*meeng*·goo

January	Janeiro **m**	zha·*nay*·roo
February	Fevereiro **m**	fe·*vray*·roo
March	Março **m**	*maar*·soo
April	Abril **m**	a·*breel*
May	Maio **m**	*maa*·yoo
June	Junho **m**	*zhoo*·nyoo
July	Julho **m**	*zhoo*·lyoo
August	Agosto **m**	a·*gosh*·too
September	Setembro **m**	se·*teng*·broo
October	Outubro **m**	oh·*too*·broo
November	Novembro **m**	no·*veng*·broo
December	Dezembro **m**	de·*zeng*·broo

What date?	Qual data?	kwaal *daa*·ta
Q **What date is it today?**	Qual é a data de hoje?	kwaal e a *daa*·ta de *o*·zhe
A **It's (18 October).**	Hoje é dia (dezoito de Outubro).	*o*·zhe e *dee*·a (de·*zoy*·too de oh·*too*·broo)

spring	primavera **f**	pree·ma·*ve*·ra
summer	verão **m**	ve·*rowng*
autumn/fall	outono **m**	oh·*to*·noo
winter	inverno **m**	eeng·*ver*·noo

Present

now	agora	a·*go*·ra
today	hoje	*o*·zhe
tonight	hoje à noite	*o*·zhe aa *noy*·te
this morning	esta manhã	*esh*·ta ma·*nyang*

this afternoon	esta tarde	*esh*·ta *taar*·de
this week	esta semana	*esh*·ta se·*ma*·na
this month	este mês	*esh*·te mesh
this year	este ano	*esh*·te *a*·noo

Past

day before yesterday	anteontem	ang·tee·*ong*·teng
(three days) ago	há (três dias)	aa (tresh *dee*·ash)
since (May)	desde (Maio)	*desh*·de (*maa*·yoo)
last night	a noite passada	a *noy*·te pa·*saa*·da
last week	a semana passada	a se·*ma*·na pa·*saa*·da
last month	o mês passado	oo mesh pa·*saa*·doo
last year	o ano passado	oo *a*·noo pa·*saa*·doo
yesterday morning	ontem de manhã	*ong*·teng de ma·*nyang*
yesterday afternoon	ontem à tarde	*ong*·teng aa *taar*·de
yesterday evening	ontem à noite	*ong*·teng aa *noy*·te

Future

day after tomorrow	depois de amanhã	de·*poysh* de aa·ma·*nyang*
in (six days)	daqui à (seis dias)	da·*kee* a (saysh *dee*·ash)
until (June)	até (Junho)	a·*te* (*zhoo*·nyoo)

next week	na próxima semana	na *pro*·see·ma se·*ma*·na
next month	no próximo mês	noo *pro*·see·moo mesh
next year	no próximo ano	noo *pro*·see·moo *a*·noo
tomorrow morning	amanhã de manhã	aa·ma·*nyang* de ma·*nyang*
tomorrow afternoon	amanhã à tarde	aa·ma·*nyang* aa *taar*·de
tomorrow evening	amanhã à noite	aa·ma·*nyang* aa *noy*·te

LOOK FOR

Aberto	a·*ber*·too	Open
Casa de Banho	*kaa*·za de *ba*·nyoo	Toilets/WC
Entrada	eng·*traa*·da	Entrance
Fechado	fe·*shaa*·doo	Closed
Homens	*o*·mengsh	Men
Informação	eeng·for·ma·*sowng*	Information
Mulheres	moo·*lye*·resh	Women
Não Fotografar	nowng foo·too·gra·*faar*	No Photography
Não Fumar	nowng foo·*maar*	No Smoking
Proibido	pro·ee·*bee*·doo	Prohibited
Saída	sa·ee·da	Exit

CULTURE TIP

Public Holidays

New Year's Day	Dia de Ano Novo	*dee*·a de *a*·noo *no*·voo
Mardi Gras	Carnaval	kar·na·*vaal*
Good Friday	Sexta-feira Santa	*sesh*·ta·*fay*·ra *sang*·ta
Liberation Day (25 April)	Dia da Liberdade	*dee*·a da lee·ber·*daa*·de
Labour Day (1 May)	Dia do Trabalhador	*dee*·a doo tra·ba·lya·*dor*
Corpus Christi	Corpo de Deus	*kor*·poo de *de*·oosh
Portugal Day (10 June)	Dia de Portugal	*dee*·a de poor·too·*gaal*
Assumption (15 August)	Assunção de Nossa Senhora	aa·soong·*sowng* de *no*·sa se·*nyo*·ra
Republic Day (5 October)	Implantação da República	eeng·plang·ta·*sowng* da rre·*poo*·blee·ka
All Saints' Day (1 November)	Dia de Todos-os-Santos	*dee*·a de *to*·doosh·oosh·*sang*·toosh
Independence Restoration Day (1 December)	Restauração da Independência	resh·tow·ra·*sowng* da eeng·de·peng·*deng*·sya
Immaculate Conception (8 December)	Imaculada Conceição	ee·ma·koo·*laa*·da kong·say·*sowng*
Christmas Day (25 December)	Natal	na·*taal*

For some holiday greetings in Portuguese, see **well-wishing** (p119).

Practical

Transport

KEY PHRASES

When's the next bus?	Quando é que sai o próximo autocarro?	*kwang*·doo e ke sai oo *pro*·see·moo ow·to·*kaa*·rroo
A ticket to ...	Um bilhete para ...	oong bee·*lye*·te *pa*·ra ...
Please tell me when we get to ...	Por favor avise-me quando chegamos a ...	poor fa·*vor* a·*vee*·ze·me *kwang*·doo she·*ga*·moosh a ...
Please take me to this address.	Leve-me para este endereço, por favor.	*le*·ve·me *pa*·ra *esh*·te eng·de·*re*·soo poor fa·*vor*
I'd like to hire a car.	Queria alugar um carro.	ke·*ree*·a a·loo·*gaar* oong *kaa*·rroo

Getting Around

Which ... goes to (Lisbon)?	Qual é o ... que vai para (Lisboa)? kwaal e oo ... ke vai pra (leezh·*bo*·a)
Is this the ... to (Peniche)?	Este é o ... para (Peniche)? *esh*·te e oo ... pra (pe·*neesh*)

boat	barco	*baar*·koo
bus	autocarro	ow·to·*kaa*·rroo
train	comboio	kong·*boy*·oo
tram	eléctrico	e·*le*·tree·koo

When's the first (bus)?	Quando é que sai o primeiro (autocarro)? *kwang*·doo e ke sai oo pree·*may*·roo (ow·to·*kaa*·rroo)
When's the last (bus)?	Quando é que sai o último (autocarro)? *kwang*·doo e ke sai oo *ool*·tee·moo (ow·to·*kaa*·rroo)
When's the next (bus)?	Quando é que sai o próximo (autocarro)? *kwang*·doo e ke sai oo *pro*·see·moo (ow·to·*kaa*·rroo)
Where's the station?	Onde é a estação? *ong*·de e a shta·*sowng*
How long does the trip take?	Quanto tempo é que leva a viagem? *kwang*·too *teng*·poo e ke *le*·va a vee·*aa*·zheng
Is it a direct route?	É uma rota directa? e *oo*·ma *rro*·ta dee·*re*·ta
Does it stop at (Amarante)?	Pára em (Amarante)? *paa*·ra eng (a·ma·*rang*·te)
What time does it get to (Porto)?	A que horas chega ao (Porto)? a ke *o*·rash *she*·ga ow (*por*·too)
How long will it be delayed?	Quanto tempo é que vai chegar atrasado? *kwang*·too *teng*·poo e ke vai she·*gaar* a·tra·*zaa*·doo
Is this seat available?	Este lugar está vago? *esh*·te loo·*gaar* shtaa *va*·goo

✂ **Is it free?** Está vago? shtaa *va*·goo

That's my seat.	Este é o meu lugar. *esh*·te e oo *me*·oo loo·*gaar*
Please tell me when we get to (Évora).	Por favor avise-me quando chegamos a (Évora). poor fa·*vor* a·*vee*·ze·me *kwang*·doo she·*ga*·moosh a (e·voo·ra)
I'd like to get off at (Cascais).	Queria sair em (Cascais). ke·*ree*·a sa·*eer* eng (kash·*kaa*·eesh)
How long do we stop here?	Quanto tempo vamos ficar parados aqui? *kwang*·too *teng*·poo *va*·moosh fee·*kaar* pa·*raa*·doosh a·*kee*

Buying Tickets

Where do I buy a ticket?	Onde é que eu compro o bilhete? *ong*·de e ke *e*·oo *kong*·proo oo bee·*lye*·te
Where's the ticket machine?	Onde está a bilheteira automática? *ong*·de shtaa a bee·lye·*tay*·ra ow·too·*maa*·tee·ka
Do I need to book (very far in advance)?	Preciso de fazer reserva (muito antecipada)? pre·*see*·zoo de fa·*zer* rre·*zer*·va (*mweeng*·too ang·te·see·*paa*·da)
Can I get a stand-by ticket?	Posso comprar um bilhete de última hora? *po*·soo kong·*praar* oong bee·*lye*·te de *ool*·tee·ma *o*·ra

Buying a Ticket

What time is the next ...?

Quando é que sai o próximo ...?

kwang·doo e ke sai oo *pro*·see·moo ...

boat
barco
baar·koo

bus
autocarro
ow·to·*kaa*·rroo

train
comboio
kong·*boy*·oo

One ... ticket, please.

Um bilhete ..., por favor.

oong bee·*lye*·te ... poor fa·*vor*

one-way
de ida
de *ee*·da

return
de ida e volta
de *ee*·da ee *vol*·ta

I'd like a/an ... seat.

Queria um lugar ...

ke·*ree*·a oong loo·*gaar* ...

aisle
na coxia
na koo·*shee*·a

window
à janela
aa zha·*ne*·la

Which platform does it depart from?

Em qual plataforma parte?

eng kwaal pla·ta·*for*·ma *paar*·te

A ... ticket (to Braga).	Um bilhete de ... (para Braga).	oong bee·*lye*·te de ... (pra *braa*·ga)

1st-class	primeira classe	pree·*may*·ra *klaa*·se
2nd-class	segunda classe	se·*goong*·da *klaa*·se
child's	criança	kree·*ang*·sa
one-way	ida	ee·da
return	ida e volta	ee·da ee *vol*·ta
student	estudante	shtoo·*dang*·te

I'd like a/an ... seat.	Queria um lugar ...	ke·*ree*·a oong loo·*gaar* ...

aisle	na coxia	na koo·*shee*·a
nonsmoking	de não fumadores	de nowng foo·ma·*do*·resh
smoking	para fumadores	pra foo·ma·*do*·resh
window	à janela	aa zha·*ne*·la

Is there (a) ...?	Tem ...?	teng ...

air-conditioning	ar condicionado	aar kong·dee·syoo·*naa*·doo
blanket	cobertor	koo·ber·*tor*
sick bag	saco para vomitar	*saa*·koo pra voo·mee·*taar*
toilet	casa de banho	*kaa*·za de *ba*·nyoo

LISTEN FOR

agente de viagens m&f	a·*zheng*·te de vee·*aa*·zhengsh	travel agent
atrasado/atrasada m/f	a·tra·*zaa*·doo/a·tra·*zaa*·da	delayed
bilheteira f	bee·lye·*tay*·ra	ticket window
cancelado/cancelada m/f	kang·se·*laa*·doo/kang·se·*laa*·da	cancelled
cheio/cheia m/f	*shay*·oo/*shay*·a	full
horário m	o·*raa*·ryoo	timetable
plataforma f	pla·ta·*for*·ma	platform

I'd like to cancel my ticket, please.	Queria cancelar o bilhete, por favor. ke·*ree*·a kang·se·*laar* oo bee·*lye*·te poor fa·*vor*
I'd like to change my ticket, please.	Queria trocar o bilhete, por favor. ke·*ree*·a troo·*kaar* oo bee·*lye*·te poor fa·*vor*
I'd like to confirm my ticket, please.	Queria confirmar o bilhete, por favor. ke·*ree*·a kong·feer·*maar* oo bee·*lye*·te poor fa·*vor*
Can I get a sleeping berth?	Tem carruagem cama? teng ka·rroo·*aa*·zheng *ka*·ma
What time should I check in?	A que horas devo fazer o check-in? a ke *o*·rash *de*·voo fa·*zer* oo *shek*·eeng

Luggage

Where can I find a/the ...?	Onde fica ...? *ong*·de *fee*·ka ...

baggage claim	o balcão de bagagens	oo bal·*kowng* de ba·*gaa*·zhengsh
lost and found office	o balcão de perdidos e achados	oo bal·*kowng* de per·*dee*·doosh e a·*shaa*·doosh
luggage locker	o depósito de bagagens	oo de·*po*·zee·too de ba·*gaa*·zhengsh
trolley	um carrinho	oong ka·*rree*·nyoo

Can I have some coins/tokens?	Pode-me dar umas moedas/fichas? *po*·de·me daar *oo*·mash mo·e·dash/*fee*·shash
My luggage has been damaged.	A minha bagagem foi danificada. a *mee*·nya ba·*gaa*·zheng foy da·nee·fee·*kaa*·da
My luggage has been lost.	A minha bagagem perdeu-se. a *mee*·nya ba·*gaa*·zheng per·*de*·oo·se
My luggage has been stolen.	A minha bagagem foi roubada. a *mee*·nya ba·*gaa*·zheng foy rroh·*baa*·da
That's (not) mine.	Isto (não) é meu. *eesh*·too (nowng) e *me*·oo

Bus, Coach & Tram

Is this a bus/tram stop?	Isto é uma paragem de autocarro/eléctrico? *eesh*·too e *oo*·ma pa·*raa*·zheng de ow·to·*kaa*·rroo/e·*le*·tree·koo
How do I get to the bus terminal?	Como posso chegar á rodoviária? *ko*·moo *po*·soo she·*gaar* aa rroo·doo·vee·*aa*·ree·a
How often do buses/ trams come?	Qual é a frequência dos autocarros/eléctricos? kwaal e a fre·*kweng*·sya doosh ow·to·*kaa*·rroosh/ e·*le*·tree·koosh
What's the next stop?	Qual é a próxima paragem? kwaal e a *pro*·see·ma pa·*raa*·zheng
city bus	autocarro da cidade m ow·to·*kaa*·rroo da see·*daa*·de
departure bay	portão de embarque m poor·*towng* de eng·*baar*·ke

LOOK FOR

Bilheteira	bee·lye·*tay*·ra	Ticket Booth
Chegadas	she·*gaa*·dash	Arrivals
Depósito de Bagagens	de·*po*·zee·too de ba·*gaa*·zhengsh	Luggage Check-In
Embarque	eng·*baar*·ke	Departure
Gare de Embarque	*gaa*·re de eng·*baar*·ke	Boarding Area
Passageiros	pa·sa·*zhay*·roosh	Passengers
Sala de Espera	*saa*·la de *shpe*·ra	Waiting Room

intercity bus	autocarro inter-cidades **m** ow·to·*kaa*·rroo eeng·ter·see·*daa*·desh
local bus	autocarro local **m** ow·to·*kaa*·rroo loo·*kaal*
(hotel) shuttle bus	carrinha do hotel **f** ka·*rree*·nya doo o·*tel*
timetable display	horário de partidas e chegadas **m** o·*raa*·ryoo de par·*tee*·dash e she·*gaa*·dash

For bus numbers, see **numbers & amounts** (p30).

Train

What station is this?	Qual estação é este? kwaal shta·*sowng* e *esh*·te
What's the next station?	Qual é a próxima estação? kwaal e a *pro*·see·ma shta·*sowng*
Do I need to change?	Preciso de mudar de comboio? pre·*see*·soo de moo·*daar* de kong·*boy*·oo
Which carriage is (for) ...?	Qual é a carruagem ...? kwaal e a ka·rroo·*aa*·zheng ...

1st class	de primeira classe	de pree·*may*·ra *klaa*·se
2nd class	de segunda classe	de se·*goong*·da *klaa*·se
dining	restaurante	rresh·tow·*rang*·te
(Faro)	para o (Faro)	pra oo (*fa*·roo)

Taxi

I'd like a taxi at (9am).	Queria chamar um táxi para as (nove da manhã). ke·*ree*·a sha·*maar* oong *taak*·see pra ash (*no*·ve da ma·*nyang*)
I'd like a taxi tomorrow.	Queria chamar um táxi amanhã. ke·*ree*·a sha·*maar* oong *taak*·see aa·ma·*nyang*
Where's the taxi rank?	Onde é a praça de táxis? *ong*·de e a *praa*·sa de *taak*·seesh

Qual é a próxima paragem?
kwaal e a *pro*·see·ma pa·*raa*·zheng
What's the next stop?

Is this taxi available?	Este táxi está livre? *esh*·te *taak*·see shtaa *lee*·vre	
Is it free?	Está livre?	shtaa *lee*·vre
How much is it (to Silves)?	Quanto custa (até ao Silves)? *kwang*·too *koosh*·ta (a·*te* ow *seel*·vesh)	
How much is the flag fall/ hiring charge?	Quanto custa a bandeirada base? *kwang*·too *koosh*·ta a bang·day·*raa*·da *baa*·ze	
Please take me to (this address).	Leve-me para (este endereço), por favor. *le*·ve·me *pa*·ra (*esh*·te eng·de·*re*·soo) poor fa·*vor*	
To ...	Para ...	*pa*·ra ...
I don't want to pay a flat fare.	Eu não quero pagar uma tarifa estipulada. *e*·oo nowng *ke*·roo pa·*gaar* *oo*·ma ta·*ree*·fa shtee·poo·*laa*·da	
Please ...	Por favor ... poor fa·*vor* ...	

come back at (10am)	volte (às dez da manhã)	*vol*·te (aash desh da ma·*nyang*)
slow down	vá mais devagar	vaa maish de·va·*gaar*
stop here	pare aqui	*paa*·re a·*kee*
wait here	espere aqui	*shpe*·re a·*kee*

For other useful phrases, see **directions** (p58), and **money & banking** (p92).

Car & Motorbike

I'd like to hire a/an ... car.	Queria alugar um carro ... ke·*ree*·a a·loo·*gaar* oong *kaa*·rroo ...

4WD	com tracção às quatro rodas	kong traa·*sowng* aash *kwaa*·troo *rro*·dash
automatic	de mudanças automáticas	de moo·*dang*·sash ow·too·maa·*tee*·kash
manual	de mudanças manuais	de moo·*dang*·sash ma·noo·*aish*

I'd like to hire a motorbike.	Queria alugar uma mota. ke·*ree*·a a·loo·*gaar* *oo*·ma *mo*·ta
How much for daily hire?	Quanto custa para alugar por dia? *kwang*·too *koosh*·ta *pa*·ra a·loo·*gaar* poor *dee*·a

LISTEN FOR

carta de condução f	*kaar*·ta de kong·doo·*sowng*	drivers licence
com ar condicionado	kong aar kong·dee·syoo·*naa*·doo	with air-conditioning
com motorista	kong moo·too·*reesh*·ta	with a driver
multa f	*mool*·ta	fine
parquímetro m	par·*kee*·me·troo	parking meter
portagem f	por·*taa*·zheng	motorway pass

How much for weekly hire?	Quanto custa para alugar por semana? *kwang*·too *koosh*·ta *pa*·ra a·loo·*gaar* poor se·*ma*·na
Does that include insurance/mileage?	Inclui seguro/ kilometragem? eeng·*kloo*·ee se·*goo*·roo/ kee·lo·me·*traa*·zheng
Do you have a road map?	Tem um mapa de estradas? teng oong *maa*·pa de *shtraa*·dash
What's the speed limit?	Qual é o limite de velocidade? kwaal e oo lee·*mee*·te de ve·loo·see·*daa*·de
Is this the road to ...?	Esta é a estrada para ...? *esh*·ta e a *shtraa*·da *pa*·ra ...

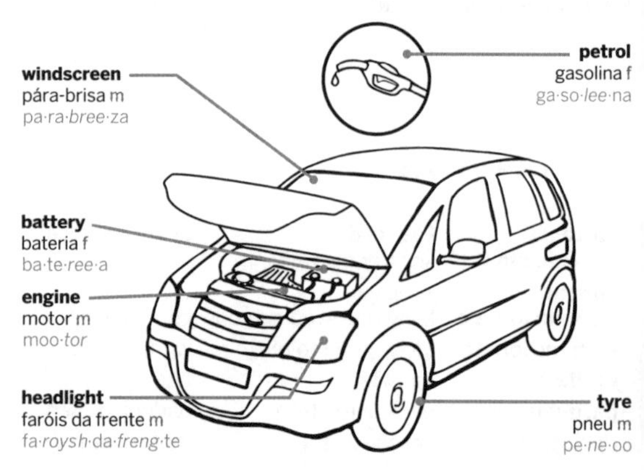

LOOK FOR

diesel m	*dee*·zel	diesel
gás m	gash	LPG
gasolina f **sem chumbo**	ga·zoo·*lee*·na seng *shoong*·boo	unleaded petrol/gas

Where's a petrol/gas station?	Onde fica um posto de gasolina? *ong*·de *fee*·ka oong *posh*·too de ga·zoo·*lee*·na
Please fill it up.	Encha o tanque, por favor. *eng*·sha oo *tang*·ke poor fa·*vor*
(How long) Can I park here?	(Quanto tempo) Posso estacionar aqui? (*kwang*·too *teng*·poo) *po*·soo shta·see·oo·*naar* a·*kee*
Can you check the oil?	Pode verificar o óleo? *po*·de ve·ree·fee·*kaar* oo *o*·le·oo
Can you check the tyre pressure?	Pode verificar os pneus? *po*·de ve·ree·fee·*kaar* oosh pe·*ne*·oosh
Can you check the water?	Pode verificar a água? *po*·de ve·ree·fee·*kaar* a *aa*·gwa
Do I have to pay?	Tenho que pagar? *ta*·nyoo ke pa·*gaar*
I need a mechanic.	Preciso de um mecânico. pre·*see*·zoo de oong me·*kaa*·nee·koo
I've had an accident.	Tive um acidente. *tee*·ve oong a·see·*deng*·te

 LOOK FOR

Dar Prioridade	daar pree·oo·ree·*daa*·de	Give Way
Entrada	eng·*traa*·da	Entrance
Pare	*paa*·re	Stop
Portagem	por·*taa*·zheng	Toll
Proibido Entrar	pro·ee·*bee*·doo eng·*traar*	No Entry
Sair da Autoestrada	sa·*eer* da ow·to·*shtraa*·da	Freeway Exit
Sentido Único	seng·*tee*·doo *oo*·nee·koo	One-Way

The car has broken down (at Setúbal).	O carro avariou-se (em Setúbal). oo *kaa*·rroo a·va·ree·*oh*·se (eng se·*too*·baal)
I've run out of petrol.	Estou sem gasolina. shtoh seng ga·zoo·*lee*·na
Can you fix it (today)?	Pode-se arranjar (hoje)? *po*·de·se a·rrang·*zhaar* (*o*·zhe)
How long will it take?	Quanto tempo vai levar? *kwang*·too *teng*·poo vai le·*vaar*

Bicycle

I'd like my bicycle repaired.	Queria consertar a minha bicicleta. ke·*ree*·aa kong·ser·*taar* a *mee*·nya bee·see·*kle*·ta

I'd like to buy a bicycle.	Queria comprar uma bicicleta. ke·*ree*·aa kong·*praar oo*·ma bee·see·*kle*·ta
I'd like to hire a bicycle.	Queria alugar uma bicicleta. ke·*ree*·aa a·loo·*gaar oo*·ma bee·see·*kle*·ta
I'd like a mountain bike.	Queria uma bicicleta de montanha. ke·*ree*·a *oo*·ma bee·see·*kle*·ta de mong·*taa*·nya
I'd like a racing bike.	Queria uma bicicleta de corrida. ke·*ree*·a *oo*·ma bee·see·*kle*·ta de koo·*rree*·da
I'd like a second-hand bike.	Queria uma bicicleta em segunda mão. ke·*ree*·a *oo*·ma bee·see·*kle*·ta eng se·*goong*·da mowng
How much is it per day/hour?	Quanto custa por dia/hora? *kwang*·too *koosh*·ta poor *dee*·a/*o*·ra
Do I need a helmet?	Preciso de usar capacete? pre·*see*·soo de oo·*zaar* ka·pa·*se*·te
Are there bicycle paths?	Há trilhos para bicicletas? aa *tree*·lyoosh *pa*·ra bee·see·*kle*·tash
I have a puncture.	Tenho um furo no pneu. *ta*·nyoo oong *foo*·roo noo pe·*ne*·oo

Border Crossing

KEY PHRASES

I'm here for ... days.	Vou ficar por ... dias.	voh fee·*kaar* poor ... *dee*·ash
I'm staying at ...	Estou no ...	shtoh noo ...
I have nothing to declare.	Não tenho nada a declarar.	nowng *ta*·nyoo *naa*·da a de·kla·*raar*

Passport Control

I'm in transit.	Estou em trânsito. shtoh eng *trang*·zee·too
I'm on business.	Estou em negócios. shtoh eng ne·*go*·syoosh
I'm on holiday.	Estou de férias. shtoh de *fe*·ree·ash
I'm here for (10) days.	Vou ficar por (dez) dias. voh fee·*kaar* poor (desh) *dee*·ash
I'm here for (three) weeks.	Vou ficar por (três) semanas. voh fee·*kaar* poor (tresh) se·*ma*·nash

LISTEN FOR

família f	fa·*mee*·lya	family
grupo m	*groo*·poo	group
passaporte m	paa·sa·*por*·te	passport
visto m	*veesh*·too	visa

LOOK FOR

Alfândega	aal·*fang*·de·ga	Customs
Controlo de Passaportes	kong·*tro*·loo de paa·sa·*por*·tesh	Passport Control
Imigração	ee·mee·gra·*sowng*	Immigration
Quarentena	kwa·reng·*te*·na	Quarantine

I'm here for (two) months.	Vou ficar por (dois) meses. voh fee·*kaar* poor (doysh) *me*·zesh
I'm going to (Elvas).	Vou para (Elvas). voh *pa*·ra (*el*·vash)
I'm staying at ...	Estou no ... shtoh noo ...

At Customs

I have nothing to declare.	Não tenho nada a declarar. nowng *ta*·nyoo *naa*·da a de·kla·*raar*
I have something to declare.	Tenho algo a declarar. *ta*·nyoo *al*·goo a de·kla·*raar*
That's (not) mine.	Isto (não) é meu. *eesh*·too (nowng) e *me*·oo
Do you have this form in (English)?	Tem este formulário em (inglês)? teng *esh*·te foor·moo·*laa*·ree·oo eng (eeng·*glesh*)
Could I please have an (English) interpreter?	Pode-me arranjar um intérprete de (inglês), por favor? *po*·de·me a·rrang·*zhaar* oong eeng·*ter*·pre·te de (eeng·*glesh*) poor fa·*vor*

Directions

KEY PHRASES

Where's ...?	Onde é ...?	*ong*·de e ...
What's the address?	Qual é o endereço?	kwaal e oo eng·de·*re*·soo
How far is it?	A que distância fica?	a ke deesh·*tang*·sya *fee*·ka

Q Where's (the market)?	Onde é (o mercado)? *ong*·de e oo (mer·*kaa*·doo)
A It's ...	É ... e ...
What's the address?	Qual é o endereço? kwaal e oo eng·de·*re*·soo
What (street) is this?	Que (rua) é isto? ke (*rroo*·a) e *eesh*·too
How far is it?	A que distância fica? a ke deesh·*tang*·sya *fee*·ka
Can you show me (on the map)?	Pode-me mostrar (no mapa)? *po*·de·me moosh·*traar* (noo *maa*·pa)
north	norte *nor*·te
south	sul sool
east	leste *lesh*·te
west	oeste o·*esh*·te

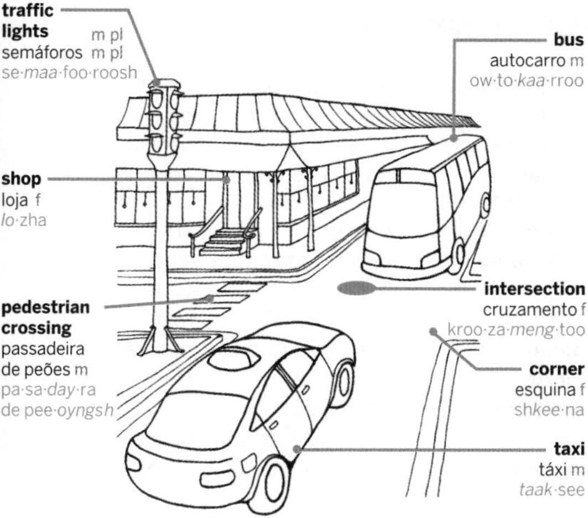

traffic lights m pl
semáforos m pl
se·*maa*·foo·roosh

bus
autocarro m
ow·to·*kaa*·rroo

shop
loja f
lo·zha

intersection
cruzamento f
kroo·za·*meng*·too

pedestrian crossing
passadeira de peões m
pa·sa·*day*·ra de pee·*oyngsh*

corner
esquina f
sh*kee*·na

taxi
táxi m
taak·see

How do I get there?	Como é que eu chego lá? *ko*·moo e ke *e*·oo *she*·goo laa
by bus	de autocarro de ow·to·*kaa*·rroo
by taxi	de táxi de *taak*·see
by train	de comboio de kong·*boy*·oo
by tram	de tram de trang
on foot	a pé a pe

LISTEN FOR

ao lado de ...	ow *laa*·doo de ...	next to ...
aqui	a·*kee*	here
atrás de ...	a·*traash* de ...	behind ...
do lado oposto ...	doo *laa*·doo oo·*posh*·too ...	opposite ...
em frente	eng *freng*·te	straight ahead
em frente de ...	eng *freng*·te de ...	in front of ...
lá	laa	there
metros	*me*·troosh	metres
minutos	mee·*noo*·toosh	minutes
perto	*per*·too	close
perto de ...	*per*·too de ...	near ...
quarteirões	kwar·tay·*royngsh*	blocks
quilómetros	kee·*lo*·me·troosh	kilometres

Turn ... Vire ...
vee·re ...

at the corner	na esquina	na *shkee*·na
at the traffic lights	nos semáforos	noosh se·*maa*·foo·roosh
left	à esquerda	aa *shker*·da
right	à direita	aa dee·*ray*·ta

For information on reading Portuguese addresses, see the box on page 132.

Accommodation

KEY PHRASES

Where's a hotel?	Onde é que há um hotel?	*ong*·de e ke aa oong o·*tel*
Do you have a double room?	Tem um quarto de casal?	teng oong *kwaar*·too de ka·*zaal*
How much is it per night?	Quanto custa por noite?	*kwang*·too *koosh*·ta poor *noy*·te
Is breakfast included?	Inclui o pequeno almoço?	eeng·*kloo*·ee oo pe·*ke*·noo aal·*mo*·soo
What time is checkout?	A que horas é a partida?	a ke *o*·rash e a par·*tee*·da

Finding Accommodation

Where's a ...? Onde é que há ...? *ong*·de e ke aa ...

bed and breakfast	um turismo de habitação	oong too·*reezh*·moo de a·bee·ta·*sowng*
guesthouse	uma casa de hóspedes	*oo*·ma *kaa*·za de *osh*·pe·desh
hotel	um hotel	oong o·*tel*
inn	uma pousada	*oo*·ma poh·*zaa*·da
youth hostel	uma pousada de juventude	*oo*·ma poh·*zaa*·da de zhoo·veng·*too*·de

Can you recommend somewhere ...?

Pode recomendar algum lugar ...?
po·de rre·koo·meng·*daar* aal·*goong* loo·*gaar* ...

cheap	barato	ba·*raa*·too
clean	limpo	*leeng*·poo
nearby	perto daqui	*per*·too da·*kee*
safe for women travellers	seguro para viajantes do sexo feminino	se·*goo*·ro *pa*·ra vee·a·*zhang*·tesh doo *sek*·soo fe·me·*nee*·noo

I want something near the ...

Eu quero algo perto ...
e·oo *ke*·roo *aal*·goo *per*·too ...

beach	da praia	da *prai*·a
city centre	do centro da cidade	doo *sen*·troo da see·*daa*·de
shops	de lojas	de *lo*·zhash
train station	da estação do comboio	da shta·*sowng* doo kong·*boy*·oo

Booking Ahead & Checking In

I'd like to book a room, please.

Eu queria fazer uma reserva, por favor.
e·oo ke·*ree*·a fa·*zer* *oo*·ma rre·*zer*·va poor fa·*vor*

Are there rooms? Tem vaga? teng *va*·ga

Finding a Room

Do you have a ... room?

Tem um quarto ...?
teng oong *kwaar*·too ...

double
de casal
de ka·*zaal*

single
de solteiro
de sol·*tay*·roo

How much is it per ...?

Quanto custa por ...?
kwang·too *koosh*·ta poor ...

night
noite
noy·te

person
pessoa
pe·*so*·a

Is breakfast included?

Inclui o pequeno almoço?
eeng·*kloo*·ee oo pe·*ke*·noo aal·*mo*·soo

Can I see it?

Posso ver?
po·soo ver

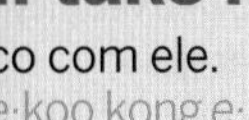

ll take it.

co com ele.
e·koo kong e·le

No, thanks.

Não, obrigado/a. m/f
nowng o·bree·*gaa*·doo/da

I have a reservation.	Eu tenho uma reserva. *e*·oo *ta*·nyoo *oo*·ma rre·*zer*·va
For (three) nights/weeks.	Para (três) noites/ semanas. *pa*·ra (tresh) *noy*·tesh/ se·*ma*·nash
From (2 July) to (6 July).	De (dois de julho) até (seis de julho). de (doysh de *zhoo*·lyoo) a·*te* (saysh de zhoo·*lyoo*)
Do you have a double room?	Tem um quarto de casal? teng oong *kwaar*·too de ka·*zaal*
Do you have a single room?	Tem um quarto de solteiro? teng oong *kwaar*·too de sol·*tay*·roo
Do you have a twin room?	Tem um quarto duplo? teng oong *kwaar*·too *doo*·ploo
How much is it per night?	Quanto custa por noite? *kwang*·too *koosh*·ta poor *noy*·te
How much is it per person?	Quanto custa por pessoa? *kwang*·too *koosh*·ta poor pe·*so*·a

LISTEN FOR

Quantas noites?	*kwang*·tash *noy*·tesh	How many nights?
chave f	*shaa*·ve	key
identificação f	ee·deng·tee·fee·ka·*sowng*	identification
não há vaga	nowng aa *vaa*·ga	full/no vacancy
recepção f	rre·se·*sowng*	reception

How much is it per week?	Quanto custa por semana? *kwang*·too *koosh*·ta poor se·*ma*·na
Do I need to pay upfront?	Tenho que pagar adiantado? *ta*·nyoo ke pa·*gaar* aa·dee·ang·*taa*·doo
Can I see it?	Posso ver? *po*·soo ver
I'll take it.	Fico com ele. *fee*·koo kong *e*·le

Requests & Queries

Is breakfast included?	Inclui o pequeno almoço? eeng·*kloo*·ee oo pe·*ke*·noo aal·*mo*·soo
When/Where is breakfast served?	Quando/Onde é que servem o pequeno almoço? *kwang*·doo/*ong*·de e ke *ser*·veng oo pe·*ke*·noo aal·*mo*·soo
Is there hot water all day?	Há água quente todo o dia? aa *aa*·gwa *keng*·te *to*·doo oo *dee*·a
Please wake me at (seven).	Por favor acorde-me às (sete). poor fa·*vor* aa·*kor*·de·me aash (*se*·te)
Can I use the kitchen?	Posso usar a cozinha? *po*·soo oo·*zaar* a koo·*zee*·nya
Can I use the laundry?	Posso usar a lavandaria? *po*·soo oo·*zaar* a la·vang·da·*ree*·a
Can I use the telephone?	Posso usar o telefone? *po*·soo oo·*zaar* oo te·le·*fo*·ne

Do you have a/an ...?	Tem ...? teng ...

elevator	elevador	e·le·va·*dor*
laundry service	tratamento de roupas	tra·ta·*meng*·too de *rroh*·pash
message board	quadro de recados	*kwaa*·droo de rre·*kaa*·doosh
safe	cofre	*ko*·fre
swimming pool	piscina	pesh·*see*·na

Do you arrange tours here?	Organizam passeios aqui? or·ga·*nee*·zowng pa·*say*·oosh aa·*kee*
Do you change money here?	Trocam dinheiro aqui? *tro*·kowng dee·*nyay*·roo aa·*kee*
Could I have my key, please?	Pode-me dar a minha chave, por favor? *po*·de·me daar a *mee*·nya *shaa*·ve poor fa·*vor*
I'm locked out of my room.	Fiquei fechado/fechada fora do quarto. **m/f** fee·*kay* fe·*shaa*·doo/fe·*shaa*·da *fo*·ra doo *kwaar*·too
Is there a message for me?	Há algum recado para mim? aa aal·*goong* rre·*kaa*·doo *pa*·ra meeng
Can I leave a message for someone?	Posso deixar um recado para alguém? *po*·soo day·*shaar* oong rre·*kaa*·doo *pa*·ra aal·*geng*

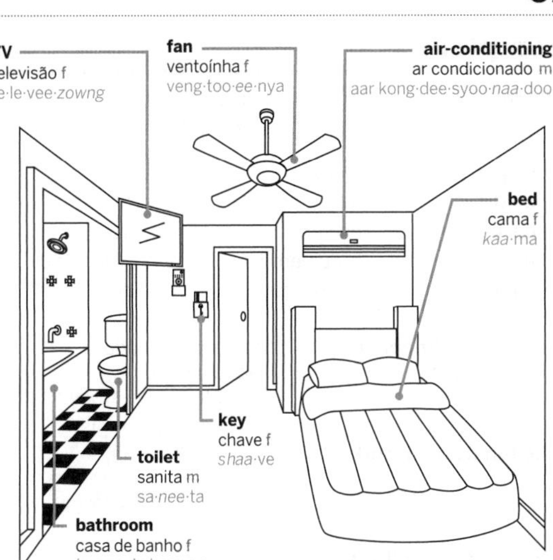

Answering the Door

Who is it?	Quem é? keng e
Just a moment.	Um minuto. oong mee·*noo*·too
Come in.	Pode entrar. *po*·de eng·*traar*
Come back later, please.	Volte mais tarde, por favor. *vol*·te maish *taar*·de poor fa·*vor*

Complaints

It's too ...	É demasiado ... e de·ma·zee·*aa*·doo ...

bright	claro	*klaa*·roo
cold	frio	*free*·oo
dark	escuro	*shkoo*·roo
noisy	barulhento	ba·roo·*lyeng*·too
small	pequeno	pe·*ke*·noo

The air-conditioning doesn't work.	O ar condicionado não funciona. oo aar kong·dee·syoo·*naa*·doo nowng foong·see·*o*·na
The fan doesn't work.	A ventoínha não funciona. a veng·too·*ee*·na nowng foong·see·*o*·na
The toilet doesn't work.	A sanita não funciona. a sa·*nee*·ta nowng foong·see·*o*·na
Can I get another (blanket)?	Pode-me dar mais um (cobertor)? *po*·de·me daar maish oong (koo·ber·*tor*)
This (pillow) isn't clean.	Esta (almofada) está suja. *esh*·ta (aal·moo·*faa*·da) shtaa *soo*·zha
There's no hot water.	Não há água quente. nowng aa *aa*·gwa *keng*·te

Checking Out

What time is checkout?	A que horas é a partida? a ke *o*·rash e a par·*tee*·da
Can I have a late checkout?	Posso deixar o quarto mais tarde? *po*·soo day·*shaar* oo *kwaar*·too maish *taar*·de
Can you call a taxi for me (for 11am)?	Pode-me chamar um taxi (para as onze da manhã)? *po*·de·me sha·*maar* oong *taak*·see (*pa*·ra ash *ong*·ze da ma·*nyang*)
Can I leave my bags here?	Posso deixar as minhas malas aqui? *po*·soo day·*shaar* ash *mee*·nyash *maa*·lash a·*kee*

Posso ficar na sua casa?
po·soo fee·*kaar* na *soo*·a *kaa*·*za*
Can I stay at your place?

I'm leaving now.	Vou sair agora. voh sa·*eer* a·*go*·ra
I had a great stay, thanks.	A estadia foi óptima, obrigado/obrigada. m/f a shta·*dee*·a foy *o*·tee·ma o·bree·*gaa*·doo/o·bree·*gaa*·da
Could I have my deposit, please?	Pode-me devolver o depósito, por favor? *po*·de·me de·vol·*ver* oo de·*po*·zee·too poor fa·*vor*
Could I have my passport, please?	Pode-me devolver o passaporte, por favor? *po*·de·me de·vol·*ver* oo paa·sa·*por*·te poor fa·*vor*
Could I have my valuables, please?	Pode-me devolver os objectos de valor, por favor? *po*·de·me de·vol·*ver* oosh o·be·*zhe*·toosh de va·*lor* poor fa·*vor*
I'll be back in (three) days.	Vou regressar em (três) dias. voh rre·gre·*saar* eng (tresh) *dee*·ash
I'll be back on (Tuesday).	Vou regressar na (terça-feira). voh rre·gre·*saar* na (*ter*·sa *fay*·ra)

Camping

Can I camp here?	Posso acampar aqui? *po*·soo a·kang·*paar* a·*kee*
Who do I ask to stay here?	A quem é que peço para ficar aqui? a keng e ke *pe*·soo *pa*·ra fee·*kaar* a·*kee*

Can I park next to my tent?	Posso estacionar ao lado da minha tenda? *po*·soo shta·syoo·*naar* ow *laa*·doo da *mee*·nya *teng*·da
Do you have (a) ...?	Tem ...? teng ...

campsite	um lugar para acampar	oong loo·*gaar pa*·ra a·kang·*paar*
electricity	eletricidade	ee·le·tree·see·*daa*·de
laundry	uma lavandaria	*oo*·ma la·vang·da·*ree*·a
shower facilities	chuveiro	shoo·*vay*·roo
tents for hire	tendas para alugar	*teng*·dash *pa*·ra a·loo·*gaar*

How much is it per ...?	Quanto custa por ...? *kwang*·too *koosh*·ta poor ...

caravan	caravana	ka·ra·*va*·na
person	pessoa	pe·*so*·a
tent	tenda	*teng*·da
vehicle	veículo	ve·*ee*·koo·loo

Is the water drinkable?	A água é potável? a *aa*·gwa e poo·*taa*·vel
Could I borrow (a lighter)?	Empresta-me (um isqueiro)? eng·*presh*·ta·me (oong eesh·*kay*·roo)

Renting

Do you have a/an ... for rent?	Tem ... para alugar?	teng ... *pa*·ra a·loo·*gaar*
apartment	um apartamento	oong a·par·ta·*meng*·too
cabin	uma cabana	*oo*·ma ka·*ba*·na
house	uma casa	*oo*·ma *kaa*·za
room	um quarto	oong *kwaar*·too
I'm here about the ... for rent.	Estou aqui por causa de ... para alugar.	shtoh a·*kee* poor *kow*·za de ... *pa*·ra a·loo·*gaar*
furnished	mobilado/mobilada m/f	moo·bee·*laa*·doo/moo·bee·*laa*·da
unfurnished	sem mobília	seng moo·*bee*·lya
Is there a deposit?	Há depósito?	aa de·*po*·zee·too
Are bills extra?	As contas são à parte?	ash *kong*·tash sowng aa *par*·te

Staying with Locals

Can I stay at your place?	Posso ficar na sua casa?	*po*·soo fee·*kaar* na *soo*·a *kaa*·za
Is there anything I can do to help?	Posso ajudar nalguma coisa?	*po*·soo a·zhoo·*daar* naal·*goo*·ma *koy*·za

LOOK FOR

Casa de Banho	*kaa*·za de *ba*·nyoo	Bathroom
Há Vaga	aa *vaa*·ga	Vacancy
Lavandaria	la·vang·da·*ree*·a	Laundry
Não Há Vaga	nowng aa *vaa*·ga	No Vacancy

I have my own mattress.	Tenho o meu próprio colchão. *ta*·nyoo o *me*·oo *pro*·pree·oo kol·*showng*
I have my own sleeping bag.	Tenho o meu próprio saco cama. *ta*·nyoo o *me*·oo *pro*·pree·oo *saa*·koo *kaa*·ma
Can I ...?	Posso ...? *po*·soo ...

bring anything for the meal	trazer alguma coisa para a refeição	tra·*zer* aal·*goo*·ma *koy*·za *pa*·ra a rre·fay·*sowng*
do the dishes	lavar a loiça	la·*vaar* a *loy*·sa
set/clear the table	por/tirar a mesa	poor/tee·*raar* a *me*·za
take out the rubbish	deitar o lixo fora	day·*taar* oo *lee*·shoo *fo*·ra

Thanks for your hospitality.	Obrigado/ Obrigada pela hospitalidade. **m/f** o·bree·*gaa*·doo/ o·bree·*gaa*·da *pe*·la osh·pee·ta·lee·*daa*·de

To compliment your hosts' cooking, see **eating out** (p180).

Shopping

KEY PHRASES

I'd like to buy ...	Queria comprar ...	ke·*ree*·a kong·*praar* ...
Can I look at it?	Posso ver?	*po*·soo ver
Can I try it on?	Posso experimentar?	*po*·soo shpree·meng·*taar*
How much is this?	Quanto custa isto?	*kwang*·too *koosh*·ta *eesh* too
That's too expensive.	Está muito caro.	shtaa *mweeng*·too *kaa*·roo

Looking For ...

What hours are the shops open?	Qual é o horário de abertura das lojas? kwaal e oo o·*raa*·ryoo de a·ber·*too*·ra dash *lo*·zhash
Where's (a convenience store)?	Onde fica (um mini-mercado)? *ong*·de *fee*·ka (oong *mee*·nee·mer·*kaa*·doo)
Where can I buy (a padlock)?	Onde é que posso comprar (um cadeado)? *ong*·de e ke *po*·soo kong·*praar* (oong ka·de·*aa*·doo)

For more items and shopping locations, see the **dictionary**.

Making a Purchase

I'm just looking.	Estou só a ver. shtoh so a ver
I'd like to buy (an adaptor plug).	Queria comprar (um adaptador). ke·*ree*·a kong·*praar* (oong a·da·pe·ta·*dor*)
How much is this?	Quanto custa isto? *kwang*·too *koosh*·ta *eesh*·too

How much?	Quanto custa?	*kwang*·too *koosh*·ta

Can you write down the price?	Pode escrever o preço? *po*·de shkre·*ver* oo *pre*·soo
Do you have any others?	Tem outros? teng *oh*·troosh
Can I look at it?	Posso ver? *po*·soo ver
Do you accept credit cards?	Aceitam cartão de crédito? a·*say*·tang kar·*towng* de *kre*·dee·too
Do you accept debit cards?	Aceitam multi-banco? a·*say*·tang mool·tee·*bang*·koo
Do you accept travellers cheques?	Aceitam traveller cheques? a·*say*·tang *tra*·ve·ler *she*·kesh
Could I have a bag, please?	Pode-me dar um saco, por favor? *po*·de·me daar oong *saa*·koo poor fa·*vor*

I don't need a bag, thanks.	Não preciso de saco, obrigado/obrigada. **m/f** nowng pre·*see*·zoo de *saa*·koo o·bree·*gaa*·doo/o·bree·*gaa*·da
Could I have a receipt, please?	Pode-me dar um recibo, por favor? *po*·de·me daar oong rre·*see*·boo poor fa·*vor*

Receipt, please.	O recibo, por favor.	oo rre·*see*·boo poor fa·*vor*

Could I have it wrapped?	Pode embrulhar? *po*·de eng·broo·*lyaar*
Does it have a guarantee?	Tem garantia? teng ga·rang·*tee*·a
It's faulty.	Tem defeito. teng de·*fay*·too
I'd like (a) ..., please.	Queria ..., por favor. ke·*ree*·a ... poor fa·*vor*

my change	o troco	oo *tro*·koo
receipt	um recibo	oong rre·*see*·boo
refund	ser reembolsado/ reembolsada **m/f**	ser rre·eng·bol·*saa*·doo/ rre·eng·bol·*saa*·da
to return this	devolver isto	de·vol·*ver eesh*·too

Bargaining

That's too expensive.	Está muito caro. shtaa *mweeng*·too *kaa*·roo
Can you lower the price?	Pode baixar o preço? *po*·de bai·*shaar* oo *pre*·soo

Making a Purchase

I'd like to buy ...

Queria comprar ...
ke·ree·a kong·praar ...

How much is it?

Quanto custa?
kwang·too koosh·ta

Can you write down the price?

Pode escrever o preço?
po·de shkre·ver oo pre·soo

Do you accept credit cards?

Aceitam cartão de crédito?
a·say·tang kar·towng de kre·dee·too

Could I have a ..., please?

Pode-me dar um ..., por favor?
po·de·me daar oong ... poor fa·vor

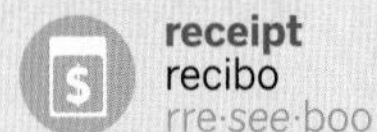

receipt
recibo
rre·see·boo

bag
saco
saa·koo

LISTEN FOR

Posso ajudar?	*po*·soo a·zhoo·*daar*	Can I help you?
O que deseja?	oo ke de·*ze*·zha	What would you like?
Não, não temos.	nowng nowng *te*·moosh	No, we don't have any.
Mais alguma coisa?	maish al·*goo*·ma *koy*·za	Anything else?

Do you have something cheaper?	Tem algo mais barato? teng *aal*·goo maish ba·*raa*·too
I'll give you (five euros).	Dou-lhe (cinco euros). *doh*·lye (*seeng*·koo e·*oo*·roosh)

Books & Reading

Is there an English-language bookshop?	Há uma livraria de língua inglesa? aa *oo*·ma lee·vra·*ree*·a de *leeng*·gwa eeng·*gle*·za
Is there an English-language section?	Há uma secção de língua inglesa? aa *oo*·ma sek·*sowng* de *leeng*·gwa eeng·*gle*·za
Do you have a book (by Fernando Pessoa)?	Tem algum livro (do Fernando Pessoa)? teng aal·*goong lee*·vroo (doo fer·*nang*·doo pe·*so*·a)
Can you recommend a book for me?	Recomenda-me algum livro? rre·koo·*meng*·da·me aal·*goong lee*·vroo

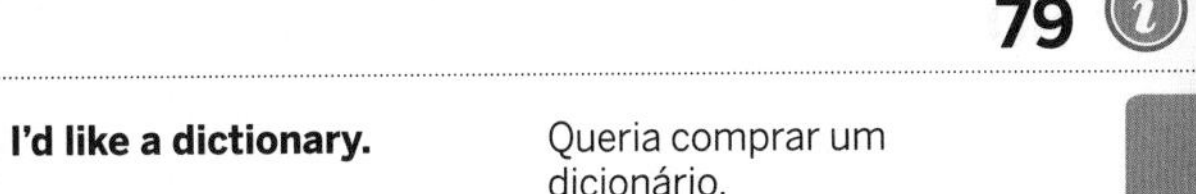

I'd like a dictionary.	Queria comprar um dicionário. ke·*ree*·a kong·*praar* oong dee·see·oo·*naa*·ryoo
I'd like a newspaper (in English).	Queria comprar um jornal (em inglês). ke·*ree*·a kong·*praar* oong zhor·*naal* (eng eeng·*glesh*)

Clothes

My size is ...	O meu número é ... oo *me*·oo *noo*·me·roo e ...

(40)	(quarenta)	(kwa·*reng*·ta)
small	pequeno	pe·*ke*·noo
medium	médio	*me*·dyoo
large	grande	*grang*·de

Can I try it on?	Posso experimentar? *po*·soo shpree·meng·*taar*
It doesn't fit.	Não serve. nowng *ser*·ve

For different types of clothing and colours see the **dictionary**, and for sizes see **numbers & amounts** (p30).

Music & DVD

I'd like a CD/DVD.	Queria comprar um CD/DVD. ke·*ree*·a kong·*praar* oong se·*de*/de·ve·*de*
I'd like a video.	Queria comprar um vídeo. ke·*ree*·a kong·*praar* oong *vee*·dee·oo

Estou só a ver.
shtoh so a ver
I'm just looking.

I'm looking for something by (Amália Rodrigues).	Estou à procura de qualquer coisa (da Amália Rodrigues). shtoh aa proo·*koo*·ra de kwaal·*ker koy*·za (da a·*maa*·lya rroo·*dree*·gesh)
What's his/her best recording?	Qual é o melhor disco dele/dela? **m/f** kwaal e oo me·*lyor deesh*·koo *de*·le/*de*·la
What region is this DVD for?	Qual é região deste DVD? kwaal e rre·zhee·*owng desh*·te de·ve·*de*
Is this for a PAL or NTSC system?	Que sistema é este, PAL ou NTSC? ke seesh·*te*·ma e *esh*·te paal oh e·ne te e·se se

Video & Photography

I need a cable to recharge this battery.	Preciso de um cabo para carregar esta pilha. pre·*see*·zoo de oong *kaa*·boo *pa*·ra ka·rre·*gaar esh*·ta *pee*·lya
I need a cable to connect my camera to a computer.	Preciso de um cabo para ligar a minha máquina a um computador. pre·*see*·zoo de oong *kaa*·boo *pa*·ra lee·*gaar* a *mee*·nya *maa*·kee·na a oong kong·poo·ta·*dor*
Do you have (a) ... for this camera?	Tem ... para esta máquina? teng ... *pa*·ra *esh*·ta *maa*·kee·na

batteries	pilhas	*pee*·lyash
(zoom) lens	lente (zoom)	*leng*·te (zoom)
memory cards	cartão de memória	kar·*towng* de me·*mo*·ree·a
video cassette	uma cassete de vídeo	*oo*·ma ka·*se*·te de *vee*·dee·oo

CULTURE TIP

Souvenirs

Portugal's most famous export is *porto por*·too (port wine). If you want to support the Portuguese cork (*cortiça* koor·*tee*·sa) industry further, you can pick up cork handicrafts in most towns. The famous hand-painted tiles (*azulejos* a·zoo·*le*·zhoosh) are another distinctive option. For something a bit more utilitarian, consider a leather belt (*cinto de couro seeng*·too de *koh*·roo) or bag (*saco de couro sa*·koo de *koh*·roo), as leather products are of good quality in Portugal.

I need a/an ... film for this camera.	Preciso de filme ... para esta máquina. *pre·see·zoo de feel·me ... pa·ra esh·ta maa·kee·na*

(200) ASA	de (duzentos) ASA	de (doo·*zeng*·toosh) *aa*·za
B&W	a preto e branco	a *pre*·too e *brang*·koo
colour	a cores	a *ko*·resh
slide	de diapositivos	de dee·a·po·zee·*tee*·voosh

Can you ...?	Pode ...? *po·de ...*

develop digital photos	revelar fotos digitais	rre·ve·*laar* *fo*·toosh dee·zhee·*taysh*
develop this film	revelar este filme	rre·ve·*laar* *esh*·te *feel*·me
recharge the battery for my digital camera	carregar a pilha da minha máquina fotográfica digital	ka·rre·*gaar* a *pee*·lya da *mee*·nya *maa*·kee·na foo·too·*graa*·fee·ka dee·zhee·*tal*
transfer photos from my camera to CD	transferir as fotografias da minha máquina para um CD	trangsh·fe·*reer* ash foo·too·gra·*fee*·ash da *mee*·nya *maa*·kee·na *pa*·ra oong se·*de*

I need a passport photo taken.	Preciso de tirar fotos para o passaporte. *pre·see·zoo de tee·raar fo·toosh pa·ra oo paa·sa·por·te*

LISTEN FOR

pechincha f	pe·*sheeng*·sha	bargain
preço especial m	*pre*·soo es·pe·see·*al*	specials
roubo m	*rroh*·boo	rip-off
saldos m pl	*saal*·doosh	sale

I'm not happy with these photos.	Não gostei destas fotos. nowng gosh·*tay desh*·tash *fo*·toosh

Repairs

Can I have my ... repaired here?	Vocês consertam ...? vo·*sesh* kong·*ser*·tang ...
When will my ... be ready?	Quando é que ...? *kwang*·doo e ke ...

bag	o saco está pronto	oo *saa*·koo shtaa *prong*·too
camera	a câmera está pronta	*kaa*·me·ra shtaa *prong*·ta
(sun)glasses	os óculos (de sol) estão prontos	oosh o·koo·loosh (de sol) shtowng *prong*·toosh
shoes	os sapatos estão prontos	oosh sa·*paa*·toosh shtowng *prong*·toosh

Communications

KEY PHRASES

Where's the local internet cafe?	Onde fica um café da internet nas redondezas?	*ong*·de *fee*·ka oong ka·*fe* da eeng·ter·*net* nash rre·dong·*de*·zash
I'd like to check my email.	Queria ler o meu email.	ke·*ree*·a ler oo *me*·oo ee·*mayl*
I want to send a parcel.	Quero enviar uma encomenda.	*ke*·roo eng·vee·*aar oo*·ma eng·koo·*meng*·da
I want to make a call to ...	Quero fazer uma chamada para ...	*ke*·roo fa·*zer oo*·ma sha·*maa*·da *pa*·ra ...
I'd like a SIM card.	Queria um cartão SIM.	ke·*ree*·a oong kar·*towng* seeng

The Internet

Where's the local internet cafe?	Onde fica um café da internet nas redondezas? *ong*·de *fee*·ka oong ka·*fe* da eeng·ter·*net* nash rre·dong·*de*·zash
Do you have internet access here?	Você tem acesso à internet? vo·*se* teng a·*se*·soo a eeng·ter·*net*
Is there wireless internet access here?	Você tem conexão sem fio a internet? vo·*se* teng kon·nayk·*sowng* seng *fee*·o a eeng·ter·*net*

I'd like to ...	Queria ... ke·*ree*·a ...

burn a CD	gravar um CD	gra·*vaar* oong se·*de*
check my email	ler o meu email	ler oo *me*·oo ee·*mayl*
download my photos	fazer o download das minhas fotos	fa·*zer* oo down·*lohd* dash *mee*·nyash *fo*·toosh
get internet access	ter acesso à internet	ter a·*se*·soo aa eeng·ter·*net*
use a printer	usar uma impressora	oo·*zaar oo*·ma eeng·pre·*so*·ra
use a scanner	usar um digitalizador	oo·*zaar* oong dee·zhee·ta·lee·za·*dor*
use Skype	usar o Skype	oo·*zaar* oo skaip

Can I connect my laptop here?	Posso conectar meu computador portátil? *po*·soo ko·nek·*taar me*·oo kong·poo·ta·*dor* por·*taa*·teel
Do you have headphones (with a microphone)?	Você tem fone de ouvidos (com microfone)? vo·*se* teng *fo*·ne de oo·*vee*·doosh (kong mee·kro·*fo*·ne)
Do you have PCs/Macs?	Tem PCs/Macs? teng pe·*sesh*/maksh
Do you have a Zip drive?	Tem um zip drive? teng oong zeep draiv
How much is it per hour/page?	Quanto custa por hora/página? *kwang*·too *koosh*·ta poor o·ra/*paa*·zhee·na

Can I connect my ... to this computer?	Posso ligar a minha ... a este computador? *po*·soo *lee*·gar a *mee*·nya ... a *esh*·te kong·poo·ta·*dor*

camera	máquina	*maa*·kee·na
media player	mp3	e·me·pe·*tresh*
portable hard drive	impulsor rígido portátil	eeng·pool·*sor* rree·zhee·doo por·*taa*·tel
USB flash drive	flash drive USB	flash draiv oo·e·se·*be*

How do I log on?	Como é que eu entro? *ko*·moo e ke e·oo *eng*·troo
Please change it to the English-language setting.	Mude o programa para inglês, por favor. *moo*·de oo proo·*gra*·ma *pa*·ra eeng·*glesh* poor fa·*vor*
It's crashed.	Desligou-se. desh·lee·*goh*·se
I've finished.	Acabei. a·ka·*bay*

Mobile/Cell Phone

What are the call rates?	Qual é o valor cobrado? kwaal e oo va·*lor* koo·*braa*·doo

LISTEN FOR

(Trinta cêntimos) por (trinta) segundos.	(*treeng*·ta *seng*·tee·moosh) poor (*treeng*·ta) se·*goong*·doosh (30c) per (30) seconds.

I'd like a ... Queria ...
ke·ree·a ...

battery for my phone	uma pilha para o meu telefone	*oo·ma pee·lya pa·ra oo me·oo te·le·fo·ne*
mobile/cell phone for hire	alugar um telemóvel	*a·loo·gaar oong te·le·mo·vel*
prepaid mobile/cell phone	um telemóvel pré-pago	*oong te·le·mo·vel pre·paa·goo*
SIM card for your network	um cartão SIM para a sua rede	*oong kar·towng seeng pa·ra a soo·a rre·de*

Phone

Q What's your phone number? Qual é o seu número de telefone?
kwaal e oo se·oo noo·me·roo de te·le·fo·ne

A The number is ... O número é ...
oo noo·me·roo e ...

Where's the nearest public phone? Onde fica o telefone público mais perto?
ong·de fee·ka o te·le·fo·ne poo·blee·koo maish per·too

Can I have some coins/tokens? Pode-me dar algumas moedas/fichas?
po·de·me daar aal·goo·mash moo·e·dash/fee·shash

What's the code for (New Zealand)? Qual é o indicativo para (a Nova Zelândia)?
kwaal e o eeng·dee·ka·tee·voo pa·ra (a no·va ze·lang·dee·a)

I want to ... — Quero ...
ke·roo ...

buy a phonecard	comprar um cartão telefónico	kong·*praar* oong kar·*towng* te·le·*fo*·nee·koo
call (Singapore)	telefonar (para Singapura)	te·le·foo·*naar* (*pa*·ra seeng·ga·*poo*·ra)
make a (local) call	fazer uma chamada (local)	fa·*zer oo*·ma sha·*maa*·da (loo·*kaal*)
reverse the charges	fazer uma chamada a cobrar	fa·*zer oo*·ma sha·*maa*·da a koo·*braar*
speak for (three) minutes	falar por (três) minutos	fa·*laar* poor (tresh) mee·*noo*·toosh

How much does a (three)-minute call cost?	Quanto custa uma ligação de (três) minutos? *kwang*·too *koosh*·ta *oo*·ma lee·ga·*sowng* de (tresh) mee·*noo*·toosh
How much does each extra minute cost?	Quanto custa cada minuto extra? *kwang*·too *koosh*·ta *kaa*·da mee·*noo*·too *aysh*·tra
It's engaged.	Está ocupado. shtaa o·koo·*paa*·doo
I've been cut off.	Desligaram. desh·lee·*gaa*·rowng
The connection's bad.	A ligação está má. a lee·ga·*sowng* shtaa maa

LANGUAGE TIP

Text-Message Shortcuts

Indulging in a little SMS or online flirting in Portugal can be difficult. Some letters tend to get dropped from Portuguese words in text messages – just like in English – so that a simple phrase such as 'Where do you want to meet?' (*Onde é que te queres encontrar comigo?* *ong*·de e ke te *ke*·resh eng·kong·*trar* koo·*mee*·goo) becomes the novice learner's nightmare: *Od é k t keres enctr cmg?*

Hello.	Está? shtaa
It's ...	Daqui fala ... da·*kee faa*·la ...
Can I speak to ...?	Queria falar com ...? ke·*ree*·a fa·*laar* kong ...
Can I leave a message?	Posso deixar um recado? *po*·soo day·*shaar* oong rre·*kaa*·doo
Please tell him/her I called.	Por favor diga-lhe que eu telefonei. poor fa·*vor dee*·ga·lye ke *e*·oo te·le·foo·*nay*
I don't have a contact number.	Eu não tenho um número de contacto. *e*·oo nowng *ta*·nyoo oong *noo*·me·roo de kong·*taak*·too
My number is ...	O meu número é ... oo *me*·oo *noo*·me·roo e ...
I'll call back later.	Volto a telefonar mais tarde. *vol*·too a te·le·foo·*naar* maish *taar*·de

LISTEN FOR

Quem fala?	keng *faa*·la Who's calling?
Com quem quer falar?	kong keng ker fa·*laar* Who do you want to speak to?
Só um minuto.	so oong mee·*noo*·too One moment.
Ele/Ela não está.	*e*·le/*e*·la nowng shtaa He/She isn't here.
Marcou o número errado.	mar·*koh* oo *noo*·me·roo ee·*rraa*·doo Wrong number.

What time should I call?	A que horas devo telefonar? a ke *o*·rash *de*·voo te·le·foo·*naar*

Post Office

I want to buy a postcard/stamp.	Quero comprar um postal/selo. ke·*roo* kong·*praar* oong poosh·*taal*/se·*loo*
I want to send a letter/parcel.	Quero enviar uma carta/encomenda. *ke*·roo eng·vee·*aar oo*·ma *kaar*·ta/eng·koo·*meng*·da
It contains (souvenirs).	Contém (lembranças). kong·*teng* (leng·*brang*·sash)
Where's the poste restante section?	Onde é a secção de posta restante? *ong*·de e a sek·*sowng* de *posh*·ta rresh·*tang*·te

Is there any mail for me?	Há alguma correspondência para mim? aa aal·*goo*·ma koo·rresh·pong·*deng*·sya *pa*·ra meeng

LISTEN FOR

código postal m	*ko*·dee·goo poosh·*taal*	postcode
correio azul m	koo·*rray*·oo a·*zool*	express mail
declaração f **de alfândega**	de·kla·ra·*sowng* de aal·*fang*·de·ga	customs declaration
doméstico	doo·*mesh*·tee·koo	domestic
envelope m **(almofadado)**	eng·ve·*lo*·pe (aal·moo·fa·*daa*·doo)	(padded) envelope
internacional	eeng·ter·na·syoo·*naal*	international
registada f	rre·zheesh·*taa*·da	registered
registado m	rre·zheesh·*taa*·doo	registered
selo m	*se*·loo	stamp
via aérea	*vee*·a a·e·ree·a	by air
via marítima	*vee*·a ma·*ree*·tee·ma	by sea
via terrestre	*vee*·a te·*rresh*·tre	by land

Money & Banking

KEY PHRASES

How much is it?	Quanto custa?	*kwang*·too *koosh*·ta
What's the exchange rate?	Qual é o câmbio do dia?	kwaal e oo *kang*·byoo doo *dee*·a
Where's an ATM?	Onde há um caixa automático?	*ong*·de aa oong *kai*·sha ow·too·*maa*·tee·koo
I'd like to change money.	Queria trocar dinheiro.	ke·*ree*·a troo·*kaar* dee·*nyay*·roo
I'd like to get change for this note.	Queria trocar esta nota.	ke·*ree*·a troo·*kaar* *esh*·ta *no*·ta

Paying the Bill

Do I have to pay?	Tenho de pagar? *ta*·nyoo de pa·*gaar*
Q **How much is it?**	Quanto custa? *kwang*·too *koosh*·ta
A **It's (12) euros.**	É (doze) euros. e (*do*·ze) e·*oo*·roosh
A **It's free.**	É gratuito. e gra·*twee*·too
Can you write down the price?	Pode escrever o preço? *po*·de shkre·*ver* oo *pre*·soo
Do you accept credit cards?	Aceitam cartão de crédito? a·*say*·tang kar·*towng* de *kre*·dee·too

Do you accept debit cards?	Aceitam multibanco? a·*say*·tang mool·tee·*bang*·koo
I'd like my change, please.	Queria o troco, por favor. ke·*ree*·a oo *tro*·koo poor fa·*vor*
I'd like a receipt, please.	Queria um recibo, por favor. ke·*ree*·a oong rre·*see*·boo poor fa·*vor*
I'd like a refund, please.	Queria ser reembolsado/ reembolsada, por favor. **m/f** ke·*ree*·a ser rree·eng·bol·*saa*·doo/ rree·eng·bol·*saa*·da poor fa·*vor*
How much is it per ...?	Quanto é que é por ...? *kwang*·too e ke e poor ...

day	dia	*dee*·a
hour	hora	o·ra
night	noite	*noy*·te
week	semana	se·*ma*·na

Banking

What days is the bank open?	Em que dias é que abre o banco? eng ke *dee*·ash e ke *aa*·bre oo *bang*·koo
What times is the bank open?	A que horas é que abre o banco? a ke *o*·rash e ke *aa*·bre oo *bang*·koo
Where can I ...?	Onde é que posso ...? *ong*·de e ke *po*·soo ...

I'd like to ...	Queria ...	ke·*ree*·a ...
change money	trocar dinheiro	troo·*kaar* dee·*nyay*·roo
get a cash advance	fazer um levantamento adiantado	fa·*zer* oong le·vang·ta·*meng*·too a·dee·ang·*taa*·doo
get change for this note	trocar esta nota	troo·*kaar esh*·ta *no*·ta
withdraw money	levantar dinheiro	le·vang·*taar* dee·*nyay*·roo

Where's an ATM?	Onde há um caixa automático?	*ong*·de aa oong *kai*·sha ow·too·*maa*·tee·koo
Where's a foreign exchange office?	Onde é que há um câmbio?	*ong*·de e ke aa oong *kang*·byoo
What's the charge for that?	Qual é a taxa aplicável?	kwaal e a *taa*·sha a·plee·*kaa*·vel
What's the exchange rate?	Qual é o câmbio do dia?	kwaal e oo *kang*·byoo doo *dee*·a
The ATM took my card.	O caixa automático ficou com o meu cartão.	oo *kai*·sha ow·too·*maa*·tee·koo fee·*koh* kong oo *me*·oo kar·*towng*
I've forgotten my PIN.	Esqueci-me do código.	shke·*see*·me doo *ko*·dee·goo

LISTEN FOR

identificação f — ee·deng·tee·fee·ka·*sowng* — identification

Assine aqui. — a·*see*·ne a·*kee* — Sign here.

Temos um problema. — *te*·moosh oong pro·*ble*·ma — There's a problem.

Não tem mais fundos disponíveis. — nowng teng maish *foong*·doosh deesh·poo·*nee*·vaysh — You have no funds left.

Não podemos fazer isso. — nowng poo·*de*·moosh fa·*zer* *ee*·soo — We can't do that.

Can I use my credit card to withdraw money? — Posso utilizar o cartão de crédito para levantar dinheiro? *po*·soo oo·tee·lee·*zaar* oo kar·*towng* de *kre*·dee·too *pa*·ra le·vang·*taar* dee·*nyay*·roo

Has my money arrived yet? — O meu dinheiro já chegou? oo *me*·oo dee·*nyay*·roo zhaa she·*goh*

How long will it take to arrive? — Quanto tempo vai levar para chegar? *kwang*·too *teng*·poo vai le·*vaar* *pa*·ra she·*gaar*

Business

KEY PHRASES

I'm attending a conference.	Estou a participar numa conferência.	shtoh a par·tee·see·*paar* *noong*·ma kong·fe·*reng*·sya
I have an appointment with ...	Tenho uma reunião marcada com ...	*ta*·nyoo *oo*·ma rree·oo·*nyowng* mar·*kaa*·da kong ...
Can I have your business card?	Pode-me dar o seu cartão de visita?	*po*·de·me daar oo *se*·oo kar·*towng* de vee·*zee*·ta

Where's the business centre?	Onde é o centro de negócios? *ong*·de e oo *seng*·troo de ne·*go*·syoosh
Where's the conference?	Onde é a conferência? *ong*·de e a kong·fe·*reng*·sya
Where's the meeting?	Onde é a reunião? *ong*·de e a rree·oo·*nyowng*
I'm attending a ...	Estou a participar ... shtoh a par·tee·see·*paar* ...

conference	numa conferência	*noong*·ma kong·fe·*reng*·sya
course	num curso	noong *koor*·soo
meeting	numa reunião	*noo*·ma rree·oo·*nyowng*
trade fair	numa feira de comércio	*noo*·ma *fay*·ra de koo·*mer*·syoo

I'm here for (two) days.	Vou ficar aqui por (dois) dias. voh fee·*kaar* a·*kee* poor (doysh) *dee*·ash
I'm here for (three) weeks.	Vou ficar aqui por (três) semanas. voh fee·*kaar* a·*kee* poor (tresh) se·*ma*·nash
I'm with colleagues.	Estou com colegas de trabalho. shtoh kong koo·*le*·gash de tra·*baa*·lyoo
I'm with (two) others.	Estou com outros (dois). shtoh kong *oh*·troosh (doysh)
I'm alone.	Estou sozinho/ sozinha. **m/f** shtoh so·*zee*·nyoo/ so·*zee*·nya
I have an appointment with ...	Tenho uma reunião marcada com ... *ta*·nyoo *oo*·ma rree·oo·*nyowng* mar·*kaa*·da kong ...
I need ...	Preciso de ... pre·*see*·zoo de ...

a computer	um computador	oong kong·poo·ta·*dor*
an internet connection	ligação à internet	lee·ga·*sowng* aa eeng·ter·*net*
an interpreter	um intérprete	oong eeng·*ter*·pre·te
to send a fax	enviar um fax	eng·vee·*aar* oong faks

Q What's your ...?	Qual é o seu ...? kwaal e oo *se*·oo ...
A Here's my ...	Aqui está o meu ... a·*kee* shtaa oo *me*·oo ...

(email) address	endereço (de email)	eng·de·*re*·soo (de ee·*mayl*)
mobile/cell number	número do telemóvel	*noo*·me·roo doo te·le·*mo*·vel
pager number	número do pager	*noo*·me·roo doo *pay*·zher
work number	número de telefone do trabalho	*noo*·me·roo de te·le·*fo*·ne doo tra·*baa*·lyoo

Can I have your business card?	Pode-me dar o seu cartão de visita? *po*·de·me daar oo *se*·oo kar·*towng* de vee·*zee*·ta
Thank you for your time.	Obrigado/Obrigada pela atenção. m/f o·bree·*gaa*·doo/o·bree·*gaa*·da *pe*·la a·teng·*sowng*
Shall we go for a drink?	Vocês gostariam de tomar alguma coisa? vo·*sesh* gosh·ta·*ree*·ang de too·*maar* aal·*goo*·ma *koy*·za
Shall we go for a meal?	Vocês gostariam de jantar? vo·*sesh* gosh·ta·*ree*·ang de zhang·*taar*
It's on me.	Eu pago. e·oo *paa*·goo

Sightseeing

KEY PHRASES

I'd like a guide.	Queria um guia.	ke·*ree*·a oong *gee*·a
Can I take a photo?	Posso tirar uma fotografia?	*po*·soo tee·*raar oo*·ma foo·too·gra·*fee*·a
When's the museum open?	Quando é que o museu está aberto?	*kwaang*·doo e ke oo moo·*ze*·oo shtaa a·*ber*·too
I'm interested in ...	Eu estou interessado/ interessada em ... **m/f**	*e*·oo shtoh eeng·te·re·*saa*·doo/ eeng·te·re·*saa*·da eng ...
When's the next tour?	Quando é a próxima excursão?	*kwang*·doo e a *pro*·see·ma shkoor·*sowng*

I'd like a/an ... Queria ... ke·*ree*·a ...

audio set	um aparelho de áudio	oong a·pa·*re*·lyoo de *ow*·dee·oo
catalogue	um catálogo	oong ka·*taa*·loo·goo
guide (person)	um guia	oong *gee*·a
(local) map	um mapa (local)	oong *maa*·pa (loo·*kaal*)

I'd like to see ... Eu gostava de ver ... *e*·oo goosh·*taa*·va de ver ...

Do you have information on cultural sights?	Tem informações sobre locais culturais? teng eeng·foor·ma·*soyngsh* *so*·bre loo·*kaish* kool·too·*raish*
Do you have information on historical sights?	Tem informações sobre locais históricos? teng eeng·foor·ma·*soyngsh* *so*·bre loo·*kaish* esh·*to*·ree·koosh
Do you have information on religious sights?	Tem informações sobre locais religiosos? teng eeng·foor·ma·*soyngsh* *so*·bre loo·*kaish* rre·lee·zhee·*o*·zoosh
What's that?	O que é aquilo? oo ke e a·*kee*·loo
Could you take a photo of me/us?	Pode-me/Pode-nos tirar uma fotografia? *po*·de·me/*po*·de·noosh tee·*raar oo*·ma foo·too·gra·*fee*·a
Can I take a photo (of you)?	Posso(-lhe) tirar uma fotografia? *po*·soo(·lye) tee·*raar oo*·ma foo·too·gra·*fee*·a
I'll send you the photo.	Eu envio-lhe a fotografia. *e*·oo eng·*vee*·o·lye a foo·too·gra·*fee*·a

Getting In

What time does it open/close?	A que horas abre/fecha? a ke *o*·rash *aa*·bre/*fe*·sha
What's the admission charge?	Qual é o preço de entrada? kwaal e oo *pre*·soo de eng·*traa*·da

ULTURE TIP

Arts & Crafts

A number of regions in Portugal are well-known for specific arts and crafts. Types of ceramics include *porcelana da vista Alegre* poor·se·*la*·na da *veesh*·ta a·*le*·gre from Ílhavo, Barcelos roosters (*galo de Barcelos* *gaa*·loo de bar·*se*·loosh) and black ceramics from Bisalhães. Basketry (*cestaria* ses·ta·*ree*·a), bobbin lace (*renda de bilros* *rreng*·da de *beel*·rroosh) from the Peniche harbour region and embroidery (*bordados* boor·*daa*·doosh) from northern Portugal are also highly regarded.

Is there a discount for ...? — Tem desconto para ...? teng desh·*kong*·too *pa*·ra ...

children	crianças	kree·*ang*·sash
groups	grupos	*groo*·poosh
older people	terceira idade	ter·*say*·ra ee·*daa*·de
students	estudantes	shtoo·*dang*·tesh

Museums & Galleries

When's the museum open? — Quando é que o museu está aberto? *kwaang*·doo e ke oo moo·*ze*·oo shtaa a·*ber*·too

Q **What kind of art are you interested in?** — Qual é o tipo de arte que mais lhe interessa? kwaal e oo *tee*·poo de *aar*·te ke maish lye eeng·te·*re*·sa

A **I'm interested in ...** — Eu estou interessado/interessada em ... **m/f** e·oo shtoh eeng·te·re·*saa*·doo/eeng·te·re·*saa*·da eng ...

LISTEN FOR

arte gráfica f	*aar*·te *graa*·fee·ka	graphic art
arte manuelina f	*aar*·te man·wel·*ee*·na	Manueline art
arte moderna f	*aar*·te moo·*der*·na	modern art
arte mourisca f	*aar*·te moh·*reesh*·ka	Moorish art

Q **What's in the collection?**	Que obras há no museu? ke *o*·brash aa noo moo·*ze*·oo
A **It's an exhibition of ...**	É uma exposição de ... e *oo*·ma shpoo·zee·*sowng* de ...
What do you think of ...?	O que acha de ...? oo ke *aa*·sha de ...

Tours

Can you recommend (a tour)?	Pode recomendar (uma excursão)? *po*·de rre·koo·meng·*daar* (*oo*·ma shkoor·*sowng*)
When's the next boat trip?	Quando é a próxima viagem de barco? *kwang*·doo e a *pro*·see·ma vee·*aa*·zheng de *baar*·koo
When's the next day trip?	Quando é o próximo passeio? *kwang*·doo e oo *pro*·see·moo pa·*say*·oo
Is accommodation included?	Inclui hospedagem? eeng·*kloo*·ee osh·pe·*daa*·zheng

O que é aquilo?
oo ke e a·*kee*·loo
What's that?

Is food included?	Inclui comida? eeng·*kloo*·ee koo·*mee*·da
Is transport included?	Inclui transporte? eeng·*kloo*·ee trangsh·*por*·te
How long is the tour?	Quanto tempo dura a excursão? *kwang*·too *teng*·poo *doo*·ra a shkoor·*sowng*
What time should we be back?	A que hora é que devemos estar de volta? a ke *o*·ra e ke de·*ve*·moosh shtaar de *vol*·ta
I've lost my group.	Perdi o meu grupo. per·*dee* oo *me*·oo *groo*·poo

Senior & Disabled Travellers

KEY PHRASES

I need assistance.	Preciso de ajuda.	pre·*see*·zoo de a·*zhoo*·da
Is there wheelchair access?	Tem acesso para cadeira de rodas?	teng a·*se*·soo *pa*·ra ka·*day*·ra de *rro*·dash
Are there toilets for the disabled?	Tem casa de banho para deficientes físicos?	teng *kaa*·za de *ba*·nyoo *pa*·ra de·fee·see·*eng*·tesh *fee*·zee·koosh

I have a disability.	Eu tenho uma deficiência física. e·oo *ta*·nyoo *oo*·ma de·fee·see·*eng*·sya *fee*·zee·ka
I need assistance.	Preciso de ajuda. pre·*see*·zoo de a·*zhoo*·da
Are there toilets for the disabled?	Tem casa de banho para deficientes físicos? teng *kaa*·za de *ba*·nyoo *pa*·ra de·fee·see·*eng*·tesh *fee*·zee·koosh
Are there parking spaces for the disabled?	Tem estacionamento para deficientes físicos? teng shta·see·oo·na·*meng*·too *pa*·ra de·fee·see·*eng*·tesh *fee*·zee·koosh
Is there wheelchair access?	Tem acesso para cadeira de rodas? teng a·*se*·soo *pa*·ra ka·*day*·ra de *rro*·dash

Are guide dogs permitted?	É permitida a entrada de cães-guia? e per·mee·*tee*·da a eng·*traa*·da de kaingsh·*gee*·a
How many steps are there?	Quantos degraus há ai? *kwang*·toosh de·*growsh* aa a·ee
Is there an elevator?	Tem elevador? teng e·le·va·*dor*
Are there rails in the bathroom?	Tem corrimão na casa de banho? teng koo·rree·*mowng* na *kaa*·za de *ba*·nyoo
Could you call me a taxi for the disabled?	Pode-me chamar um táxi para deficientes físicos? *po*·de·me sha·*maar* oong *taak*·see *pa*·ra de·fee·see·*eng*·tesh *fee*·zee·koosh
Could you help me cross the street safely?	Pode-me ajudar a atravessar a rua com segurança? *po*·de·me a·zhoo·*daar* a a·tra·ve·*saar* a *rroo*·a kong se·goo·*rang*·sa
Is there somewhere I can sit down?	Há algum lugar onde me possa sentar? aa aal·*goong* loo·*gaar* *ong*·de me *po*·sa *seng*·taar
ramp	rampa **f** *rrang*·pa
walking frame	armação para andar **f** ar·ma·*sowng* *pa*·ra ang·*daar*
walking stick	bengala **f** beng·*gaa*·la
wheelchair	cadeira de rodas **f** ka·*day*·ra de *rro*·dash

Travel with Children

KEY PHRASES

Are children allowed?	É permitida a entrada a crianças?	e per·mee·*tee*·da a eng·*traa*·da a kree·*ang*·sash
Is there a discount for children?	Há desconto para crianças?	aa desh·*kong*·too *pa*·ra kree·*ang*·sash
Is there a baby change room?	Há uma sala reservada para bebés?	aa *oo*·ma *saa*·la rre·zer·*vaa*·da *pa*·ra be·*besh*

Is there a ...?	Há ...?	aa ...
baby change room	uma sala reservada para bebés	*oo*·ma *saa*·la rre·zer·*vaa*·da *pa*·ra be·*besh*
child-minding service	serviço de ama	ser·*vee*·soo de *a*·ma
children's menu	menu para crianças	me·*noo pa*·ra kree·*ang*·sash
crèche	creche	*kre*·she
discount for children	desconto para crianças	desh·*kong*·too *pa*·ra kree·*ang*·sash
family ticket	passagem de família	pa·*saa*·zheng de fa·*mee*·lya

Where can I change a nappy/diaper?	Onde posso mudar a fralda? *ong*·de *po*·soo moo·*daar* a *fraal*·da
I need a/an ...	Preciso de ... pre·*see*·zoo de ...

baby seat	um lugar para bebés	oong loo·*gaar* *pa*·ra be·*besh*
(English-speaking) babysitter	uma ama (que fale inglês)	*oo*·ma *a*·ma (ke *faa*·le eeng·*glesh*)
booster seat	assento de elevação	a·*seng*·too de ee·le·va·*sowng*
cot	cama de grades	*ka*·ma de *graa*·desh
highchair	uma cadeira para crianças	*oo*·ma ka·*day*·ra *pa*·ra kree·*ang*·sash
plastic bag	um saco de plástico	oong *saa*·koo de *plaash*·tee·koo
potty	um bacio	oong ba·*see*·oo
pram/stroller	um carrinho de bebé	oong ka·*rree*·nyoo de be·*be*

Do you sell ...?	Vendem ...? *veng*·deng ...

baby wipes	toalhinhas de bebé	twa·*lyee*·nyash de be·*be*
disposable nappies/diapers	fraldas descartáveis	*fraal*·dash desh·kar·*taa*·vaysh
painkillers for infants	analgésicos infantis	a·naal·*zhe*·zee·koosh eeng·*fang*·teesh
tissues	lenços de papel	*leng*·soosh de pa·*pel*

Where's the nearest ...?	Onde está ... mais próximo/próxima? **m/f**	*ong*·de shtaa ... maish *pro*·see·moo/*pro*·see·ma

park	o parque	oo *paar*·ke
playground	o parque infantil	oo *paar*·ke eeng·fang·*teel*
swimming pool	a piscina	a pesh·*see*·na
theme park	o parque de diversões	oo *paar*·ke de dee·ver·*zoyngsh*
toyshop	a loja de brinquedos	a *lo*·zha de breeng·*ke*·doosh

Could I have some paper and pencils, please?	Pode-me dar papel e lápis, por favor?	*po*·de·me daar pa·*pel* ee *laa*·peesh poor fa·*vor*
Are children allowed?	É permitida a entrada a crianças?	e per·mee·*tee*·da a eng·*traa*·da a kree·*ang*·sash
Is this suitable for ...-year-old children?	Isto é apropriado para crianças de ... anos de idade?	*eesh*·too e a·proo·pree·*aa*·doo *pa*·ra kree·*ang*·sash de ... *a*·noosh de ee·*daa*·de
Do you mind if I breastfeed here?	Importa-se que eu amamente aqui?	eeng·*por*·ta·se ke e·oo a·ma·*meng*·te a·*kee*
Do you know a doctor/ dentist who is good with children?	Conhece algum médico/ dentista bom para crianças?	ko·*nye*·se aal·*goong me*·dee·koo/ deng·*teesh*·ta bong *pa*·ra kree·*ang*·sash

If your child is sick, see **health** (p161).

Social

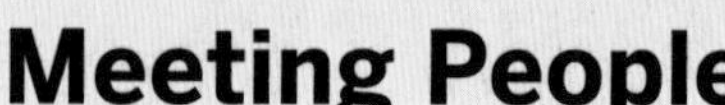

Meeting People

KEY PHRASES

My name is ...	O meu nome é ...	oo *me*·oo *no*·me e ...
I'm from ...	Eu sou de ...	e·oo soh de ...
I work in ...	Trabalho em ...	tra·*baa*·lyoo eng ...
I'm ... years old.	Tenho ... anos.	*ta*·nyoo ... *a*·noosh
And you?	E você?	e vo·*se*

Basics

Yes.	Sim. seeng
No.	Não. nowng
Please.	Por favor. poor fa·*vor*
Thank you (very much).	(Muito) Obrigado. **m** (*mweeng*·too) o·bree·*gaa*·doo (Muito) Obrigada. **f** (*mweeng*·too) o·bree·*gaa*·da
You're welcome.	De nada. de *naa*·da
Excuse me. (to get attention)	Faz favor! faash fa·*vor*
Excuse me. (to get past)	Com licença. kong lee·*seng*·sa
Sorry.	Desculpe. desh·*kool*·pe

Greetings & Goodbyes

Hello./Hi.	Olá. o·*laa*
Good morning/day.	Bom dia. bong *dee*·a
Good afternoon.	Boa tarde. *bo*·a *taar*·de
Good evening.	Boa noite. *bo*·a *noy*·te
Q **How are you?**	Como está? *ko*·moo shtaa
A **Fine, and you?**	Bem, e você? beng e vo·*se*
Q **What's your name?**	Qual é o seu nome? kwaal e oo *se*·oo *no*·me
A **My name is ...**	O meu nome é ... oo *me*·oo *no*·me e ...
I'd like to introduce you to ...	Eu gostava de te apresentar ao/á ... **m/f** e·oo goosh·*taa*·va de te a·pre·zeng·*taar* ow/aa ...

This is ...	Isto é ...	*eesh*·too e ...

I'm pleased to meet you.	Prazer em conhecê-lo/ conhecê-la. **m/f** pra·*zer* eng koo·nye·*se*·lo/ koo·nye·se·la
See you later.	Até logo. a·*te lo*·goo
Goodbye.	Adeus. a·*de*·oosh
Good night.	Boa noite. *bo*·a *noy*·te

Addressing People

Mr	Senhor se·*nyor*
Sir	Cavalheiro ka·va·*lyay*·roo
Mrs/Ms	Senhora se·*nyo*·ra
Miss	Menina me·*nee*·na
Madam	Senhora Dona se·*nyo*·ra *do*·na

Making Conversation

Nice/Awful weather!	Que tempo fantástico/terrível! ke *teng*·poo fang·*taash*·tee·koo/te·*rree*·vel
That's (beautiful), isn't it?	Isto é (lindo), não acha? *eesh*·too e (*leeng*·doo) nowng *aa*·sha
What's this called?	Como se chama isto? *ko*·moo se *sha*·ma *eesh*·too
Do you live here?	Mora aqui? *mo*·ra a·*kee*
Where are you going?	Onde vai? *ong*·de vai
What are you doing?	O que é que está a fazer? oo ke e ke shtaa a fa·*zer*
Q **Do you like it here?**	Gosta daqui? *goosh*·ta da·*kee*
A **I love it here.**	Eu adoro. e·oo a·*do*·roo

Q **How long are you here for?**	Quanto tempo vai cá ficar? *kwang*·too *teng*·poo vai kaa fee·*kaar*
A **I'm here for (four) days/weeks.**	Fico cá (quatro) dias/semanas. *fee*·koo kaa (*kwaa*·troo) *dee*·ash/se·*ma*·nash
Q **Are you here on holiday?**	Está aqui de férias? shtaa a·*kee* de *fe*·ree·ash
A **I'm here for a holiday.**	Estou aqui de férias. shtoh a·*kee* de *fe*·ree·ash
A **I'm here on business.**	Estou aqui em negócios. shtoh a·*kee* eng ne·*go*·syoosh
A **I'm here to study.**	Estou aqui a estudar. shtoh a·*kee* a shtoo·*daar*

Eu adoro.
e·oo a·*do*·roo
I love it here.

Nationalities

Q	**Where are you from?**	De onde é? *dong*·de e
A	**I'm from ...**	Eu sou ... e·oo soh ...

Australia	da Austrália	da owsh·*traa*·lya
Canada	do Canadá	doo ka·na·da
England	da Inglaterra	da eeng·gla·*te*·rra
the USA	dos Estados Unidos	doosh *shtaa*·doosh oo·*nee*·doosh

For more countries, see the **dictionary**.

Age

Q	**How old are you?**	Quantos anos tem? *kwang*·toosh *a*·noosh teng
A	**I'm ... years old.**	Tenho ... anos. *ta*·nyoo ... *a*·noosh
Q	**How old is your daughter?**	Quantos anos tem a sua filha? *kwang*·toosh *a*·noosh teng a *soo*·a *fee*·lya
Q	**How old is your son?**	Quantos anos tem o seu filho? *kwang*·toosh *a*·noosh teng oo *se*·oo *fee*·lyoo
A	**He/She is ... years old.**	Ele/Ela tem ... anos. *e*·le/*e*·la teng ... *a*·noosh
	I'm younger than I look.	Sou mais novo/nova do que pareço. **m/f** soh maish *no*·voo/*no*·va doo ke pa·*re*·soo

I'm older than I look.	Sou mais velho/velha do que pareço. **m/f** soh maish *ve*·lyoo/*ve*·lya doo ke pa·*re*·soo

For your age, see **numbers & amounts** (p30).

Occupations & Studies

Q **What's your occupation?**	Qual é a sua profissão? kwaal e a *soo*·a proo·fee·*sowng*
A **I'm a (teacher).**	Sou (professor/ professora). **m/f** soh (proo·fe·*sor*/ proo·fe·*so*·ra)
A **I work in (health).**	Trabalho em (saúde). tra·*baa*·lyoo eng (sa·*oo*·de)
A **I'm retired.**	Eu estou reformado/ reformada. **m/f** e·oo shtoh rre·for·*maa*·doo/ rre·for·*maa*·da
A **I'm self-employed.**	Eu sou empregado/ empregada por conta própria. **m/f** e·oo soh eng·pre·*gaa*·doo/ eng·pre·*gaa*·da poor *kong*·ta *pro*·pree·a
A **I'm unemployed.**	Eu estou desempregado/ desempregada. **m/f** e·oo shtoh de·zeng·pre·*gaa*·doo/ de·zeng·pre·*gaa*·da
Q **What are you studying?**	O que é que está a estudar? oo ke e ke shtaa a shtoo·*daar*
A **I'm studying humanities.**	Estudo humanísticas. *shtoo*·doo oo·ma·*neesh*·tee·kash

A I'm studying science.	Estudo ciências. *shtoo*·doo see·*eng*·see·ash
A I'm studying Portuguese.	Estudo português. *shtoo*·do poor·too·*gesh*

For more occupations, see the **dictionary**.

Family

Q Do you have a ...?	Tem ...? teng ...
A I (don't) have a ...	Eu (não) tenho ... e·oo (nowng) *ta*·nyoo ...

brother	um irmão	oong eer·*mowng*
daughter	uma filha	oo·ma *fee*·lya
granddaughter	neta	*ne*·ta
grandson	neto	*ne*·too
husband	marido	ma·*ree*·doo
partner	companheiro **m** companheira **f**	kong·pa·*nyay*·roo kong·pa·*nyay*·ra
sister	uma irmã	oo·ma eer·*mang*
son	um filho	oong *fee*·lyoo
wife	esposa	*shpo*·za

Q Are you married?	É casado/casada? **m/f** e ka·*zaa*·doo/ka·*zaa*·da
A I'm married.	Eu sou casado/ casada. **m/f** e·oo soh ka·*zaa*·doo/ ka·*zaa*·da
A I'm divorced.	Eu sou divorciado/ divorciada. **m/f** e·oo soh dee·vor·see·*aa*·doo/ dee·vor·see·*aa*·da

I'm single.	Eu sou solteiro/ solteira. **m/f** *e*·oo soh sol·*tay*·roo/ sol·*tay*·ra
I'm separated.	Eu estou separado/ separada. **m/f** *e*·oo se·pa·*raa*·doo/ se·pa·*raa*·da
I live with someone (a man).	Vivo com o meu namorado. **m** *vee*·voo kong oo *me*·oo na·moo·*raa*·doo
I live with someone (a woman).	Vivo com a minha namorada. **f** *vee*·voo kong a *mee*·nya na·moo·*raa*·da

Talking with Children

When's your birthday?	Quando é que fazes anos? *kwang*·doo e ke *faa*·zesh *a*·noosh
Do you go to school?	Vais à escola? vaish aa *shko*·la
What grade are you in?	Em que ano estás? eng ke *a*·noo shtaash
Do you like (sport)?	Gostas (de desporto)? *goosh*·tash (de desh·*por*·too)
What do you do after school?	O que é que fazes depois da escola? o ke e ke *faa*·zesh de·*poysh* da *shko*·la
Do you learn (English)?	Aprendes (inglês)? a·*preng*·desh (eeng·*glesh*)

Talking about Children

When's the baby due?	Para quando está previsto o nascimento do bebé? *pa*·ra *kwang*·doo shtaa pre·*veesh*·too oo nash·see·*meng*·too doo be·*be*
What are you going to call the baby?	Que nome vai dar ao bebé? ke *no*·me vai daar ow be·*be*
Is this your first child?	É o seu primeiro filho? e oo *se*·oo pree·*may*·roo *fee*·lyoo
How many children do you have?	Quantos filhos tem? *kwang*·toosh *fee*·lyoosh teng
What a beautiful child!	Que linda criança! ke *leeng*·da kree·*ang*·sa
Is it a boy or a girl?	É menino ou menina? e me·*nee*·noo oh me·*nee*·na
How old is he/she?	Quantos anos tem? *kwang*·toosh *a*·noosh teng
What's his/her name?	Como se chama? *ko*·moo se *sha*·ma
Does he/she go to school?	Vai à escola? vai aa *shko*·la

Farewells

Tomorrow is my last day here.	Amanhã é o meu último dia aqui. aa·ma·*nyang* e oo *me*·oo *ool*·tee·moo *dee*·a a·*kee*
It's been great meeting you.	Foi fantástico conhecê-lo/conhecê-la. **m/f** foy fang·*taash*·tee·koo koo·nye·*se*·loo/koo·nye·*se*·la

Keep in touch!	Mantenha-se em contacto! mang·*te*·nya·se eng kong·*taak*·too
If you come to (Scotland), you can stay with me.	Se vier à (Escócia) pode ficar em minha casa. se vee·*er* aa (*shko*·sya) *po*·de fee·*kar* eng *mee*·nya *kaa*·za
Q **What's your address/ email?**	Qual é o seu endereço/email? kwaal e oo *se*·oo eng·de·*re*·soo/ee·*mayl*
Q **What's your phone number?**	Qual é o seu número de telefone? kwaal e oo *se*·oo *noo*·me·roo de te·le·*fo*·ne
A **Here's my ...**	Aqui está o meu ... a·*kee* shtaa oo *me*·oo ...

Well-Wishing

Bless you!	Deus o abençoe! *de*·ooz oo a·beng·*so*·e
Congratulations!	Parabéns! pa·ra·*bengzh*
Good luck!	Boa sorte! *bo*·a *sor*·te
Bon voyage!	Boa viagem! *bo*·a vee·*aa*·zheng
Happy birthday!	Feliz aniversário! fe·*leesh* a·nee·ver·*saa*·ree·oo
Happy New Year!	Feliz Ano Novo! fe·*leesh a*·noo *no*·voo
Merry Christmas!	Feliz Natal! fe·*leesh* na·*taal*

Interests

KEY PHRASES

What do you do in your spare time?	O que faz nos seus tempos livres?	oo ke fazh noosh *se*·oosh *teng*·poosh *lee*·vresh
Do you like ...?	Gosta de ...?	*gosh*·ta de ...
I (don't) like ...	Eu (não) gosto de ...	*e*·oo (nowng) *gosh*·too de ...

Common Interests

What do you do in your spare time?	O que faz nos seus tempos livres? oo ke fazh noosh *se*·oosh *teng*·poosh *lee*·vresh
Q **Do you like ...?**	Gosta de ...? *gosh*·ta de ...
A **I (don't) like ...**	Eu (não) gosto de ... *e*·oo (nowng) *gosh*·too de ...

cooking	cozinhar	koo·zee·*nyaar*
gardening	jardinagem	zhar·dee·*naa*·zheng
hiking	caminhar	ka·mee·*nyaar*
photography	fazer fotografia	fa·*zer* foo·too·gra·*fee*·a
reading	ler	ler
shopping	ir às compras	eer aash *kong*·prash
travelling	viajar	vee·a·*zhaar*

For types of sports, see **sport** (p142), and the **dictionary**.

Music

Do you ...?	Costuma ...? koosh·*too*·ma ...	

dance	ir dançar	eer dang·*saar*
go to concerts	ir a concertos	eer a kong·*ser*·toosh
listen to music	ouvir música	oh·*veer moo*·zee·ka
play an instrument	tocar algum instrumento	too·*kaar* aal·*goong* eeng·shtroo·*meng*·too
sing	cantar	kang·*taar*

Which bands do you like?	De que conjuntos gosta? de ke kong·*zhoong*·toosh *gosh*·ta
Which artists do you like?	De que artistas gosta? de ke ar·*teesh*·tash *gosh*·ta
What music do you like?	De que tipo de música gosta? de ke *tee*·poo de *moo*·zee·ka *gosh*·ta
... music	música **f** *moo*·zee·ka

classical	clássica	*klaa*·see·ka
electronic	electrónica	ee·le·*tro*·nee·ka
folk	popular	poo·poo·*laar*
traditional Portuguese	tradicional portuguesa	tra·dee·syoo·*naal* poor·too·*ge*·za
world	todo o mundo	*to*·doo oo *moong*·doo

Cinema & Theatre

I feel like going to a/an ...	Apetece-me ir ao/à ... m/f *a·pe·te·se·me eer ow/aa ...*	
Q Did you like the ...?	Gostou ...? *goosh·toh ...*	

ballet	do ballet	doo ba·*le*
film	do filme	doo *fil*·me
opera	da ópera	da o·pe·ra
play	da peça (de teatro)	da *pe*·sa (de tee·*aa*·troo)

A I thought it was boring.	Eu achei que era chato/chata. m/f *e·oo a·shay ke e·ra shaa·too/shaa·ta*
A I thought it was excellent.	Eu achei que era excelente. *e·oo a·shay ke e·ra aysh·se·leng·te*
A I thought it was OK.	Eu achei que era razoável. *e·oo a·shay ke e·ra rra·zoo·aa·vel*
What's showing at the cinema/theatre tonight?	O que é que está no cinema/teatro hoje à noite? oo ke e ke shtaa noo see·*ne*·ma/tee·*aa*·troo o·zhe aa *noy*·te
Is it in English?	É em inglês? e eng eeng·*glesh*
Does it have English subtitles?	Tem legendas em inglês? teng le·*zheng*·dash eng eeng·*glesh*
Is there a matinée show?	Há alguma matiné? aa aal·*goo*·ma ma·tee·*ne*
Is this seat taken?	Este lugar está ocupado? *esh*·te loo·*gaar* shtaa o·koo·*paa*·doo

LANGUAGE TIP

Tongue Twisters

Think you've got a bit of a handle on Portuguese? Amuse the locals by reciting one of these little beauties:

Um prato de trigo para três tigres tristes.
oong *praa*·too de *tree*·goo *pa*·ra tresh *tee*·gresh *treesh*·tesh
A plate of wheat for three sad tigers.

Se cá nevasse fazia-se cá esqui.
se kaa ne·*vaa*·se fa·*zee*·a·se kaa shkee
If it snowed here you could ski.

O rato roeu a rolha do garrafão do rei da Rússia.
oo *rraa*·too rroo·*e*·oo a *rro*·lya doo ga·rra·*fowng* doo rray da *rru*·sya
The mouse nibbled the cork of the large wickerwork bottle from the king of Russia.

Have you seen (José e Pilar)?	Já viu a *(José e Pilar)*? zha *vee*·oo a (zho·*ze* e pee·*laar*)
Q **Who's in it?**	Com quem é? kong keng e
A **It stars (José Saramago).**	É com o (José Saramago). e kong oo (zho·*ze* sa·ra·*maa*·goo)
Do you have tickets for ...?	Tem bilhetes para ...? teng bee·*lye*·tesh *pa*·ra ...
I'd like the best tickets.	Eu queria os melhores bilhetes. e·oo ke·*ree*·a oosh me·*lyor*·esh bee·*lye*·tesh
I'd like cheap tickets.	Eu queria bilhetes baratos. e·oo ke·*ree*·a bee·*lye*·tesh ba·*ra*·toosh

I'd like ...	Eu queria ... *e·oo ke·ree·a ...*

1st/2nd balcony seats	lugares no primeiro/ segundo balcão	loo·*gaa*·resh noo pree·*may*·roo/ se·*goong*·doo baal·*kowng*
box seats	um camarote	oong ka·ma·*ro*·te
orchestra seats	lugares na plateia	loo·*gaa*·resh na pla·*tay*·a
wings seats	coxias	koo·*shee*·ash

action movies	filmes de acção **m pl** *feel*·mesh de a·*sowng*
animated films	desenhos animados **m pl** de·*ze*·nyoosh a·nee·*maa*·doosh
comedies	comédias **f pl** koo·*me*·dyash
drama	drama **f** *dra*·ma
documentaries	documentários **m pl** doo·koo·meng·*ta*·ryoosh
horror movies	filmes de terror **m pl** *feel*·mesh de te·*rror*
Portuguese cinema	cinema português **m** see·*ne*·ma poor·too·*gesh*
sci-fi	ficção científica **f** feek·*sowng* see·eng·*tee*·fee·ka
short films	curtas-metragens **f pl** *koor*·tash·me·*traa*·zhengsh
thrillers	filmes de suspense **m pl** *feel*·mesh de soosh·*pengs*
war movies	filmes de guerra **m pl** *feel*·mesh de *ge*·rra

Feelings & Opinions

KEY PHRASES

Are you ...?	Está ...?	shtaa ...
I'm (not) ...	(Não) Estou ...	(nowng) shtoh ...
What do you think of it?	O que é que acha disso?	oo ke e ke *aa*·sha *dee*·soo
I thought it was OK.	Eu achei que razoável.	e·oo a·*shay* ke rra·zoo·*aa*·vel
Did you hear about ...?	Ouviu falar de ...?	oh·*vee*·oo fa·*laar* de ...

Feelings

Q **Are you ...?** — Está ...? / shtaa ...

A **I'm (not) ...** — (Não) Estou ... / (nowng) shtoh ...

cold	com frio	kong *free*·oo
happy	feliz	fe·*leesh*
hot	com calor	kong ka·*lor*
hungry	com fome	kong *fo*·me
in a hurry	com pressa	kong *pre*·sa
sad	triste	*treesh*·te
thirsty	com sede	kong *se*·de
tired	cansado **m** cansada **f**	kang·*saa*·doo kang·*saa*·da
well	bem	beng

What's wrong?	Qual é o problema? kwaal e oo proo·*ble*·ma
What happened?	O que aconteceu? oo ke aa·kong·te·*se*·oo
I'm a little (sad).	Estou um bocadinho (triste). shtoh oon boo·ka·*dee*·nyoo (*treesh*·te)
I feel very (lucky).	Sinto-me com muita (sorte). *seeng*·too·me kong *mweeng*·ta (*sor*·te)
I'm not at all (tired).	Não estou nada (cansado/cansada). **m/f** nowng shtoh *naa*·da (kang·*saa*·doo/kang·*saa*·da)

If you're not feeling well, see **health** (p161).

Opinions

Q **Did you like it?**	Gostou? *gosh*·toh
Q **What do you think of it?**	O que é que acha disso? oo ke e ke *aa*·sha *dee*·soo
A **I thought it was ...**	Eu achei que ... e·oo a·*shay* ke ...
A **It's ...**	É ... e ...

awful	horrível	o·*rree*·vel
beautiful	lindo/linda **m/f**	*leeng*·doo/*leeng*·da
boring	chato/chata **m/f**	*shaa*·too/*shaa*·ta
great	óptimo/óptima **m/f**	*o*·tee·moo/*o*·tee·ma
interesting	interessante	eeng·te·re·*sang*·te
OK	razoável	rra·zoo·*aa*·vel
strange	estranho **m** estranha **f**	*shtra*·nyoo *shtra*·nya

Politics & Social Issues

Q Who do you vote for?	Em que partido vota? eng ke par·*tee*·da *vo*·ta
A I support the ... party.	Eu apoio o ... e·oo a·*poy*·oo oo ...
A I'm a member of the ... party.	Eu sou membro ... e·oo soh *meng*·broo ...
Did you hear about ...?	Ouviu falar de ...? oh·*vee*·oo fa·*laar* de ...
Q Do you agree with it?	Concorda? kong·*kor*·da
A I (don't) agree with ...	Eu (não) concordo com ... e·oo (nowng) kong·*kor*·doo kong ...
How do people feel about ...?	O que é que as pessoas pensam sobre ...? oo ke e ke ash pe·*so*·ash *peng*·sang *so*·bre ...
How can we protest against ...?	Como é que podemos protestar contra ...? *ko*·moo e ke poo·*de*·moosh pro·tesh·*taar kong*·tra ...
How can we support ...?	Como é que podemos apoiar ...? *ko*·moo e ke poo·*de*·moosh a·poy·*aar* ...
immigration	imigração f ee·mee·gra·*sowng*
the economy	a economia f a ee·ko·noo·*mee*·a
the environment	o ambiente m oo ang·bee·*eng*·te
the war in ...	a guerra em ... f a *ge*·rra eng ...

The Environment

Is there a ... problem here?	Há algum problema de ... aqui? aa aal·*goong* pro·*ble*·ma de ... a·*kee*
What should be done about ...?	O que é que deve ser feito em relação ...? oo ke e ke *de*·ve ser *fay*·too eng rre·la·*sowng* ...
pollution	poluição **f** poo·loo·ee·*sowng*
recycling programme	programas de reciclagem **m pl** proo·*gra*·mash de rre·see·*klaa*·zheng
Is this a protected forest/ species?	Esta floresta/espécie está protegida? *esh*·ta flo·*resh*·ta/*shpe*·sye shtaa proo·te·*zhee*·da
Is this a protected park?	Este parque está protegido? *esh*·te *par*·ke shtaa proo·te·*zhee*·doo

LANGUAGE TIP

Masculine & Feminine

In this book, many Portuguese words listed as stand-alone have different masculine and feminine forms, marked with **m** and **f** respectively. When an adjective is used with a noun, its form matches the gender of the noun, eg *parque protegido* *par*·ke proo·te·*zhee*·doo (masculine) vs *floresta protegida* flo·*resh*·ta proo·te·*zhee*·da (feminine). The same applies to saying 'thank you' – the form should match the speaker's gender: *Obrigado* **m** o·bree·*gaa*·doo or *Obrigada* **f** o·bree·*gaa*·da. See also **gender** in the **grammar** chapter (p18).

Going Out

KEY PHRASES

What's on tonight?	O que é que há hoje à noite?	oo ke e ke aa o·zhe aa *noy*·te
Where can I find clubs?	Onde é que há discotecas?	*ong*·de e ke aa deesh·koo·*te*·kash
Would you like to go for a coffee?	Gostava de ir a um café?	goosh·*taa*·va de eer a oong ka·*fe*
Where will we meet?	Onde é que nos encontramos?	*ong*·de e ke noosh eng·kong·*traa*·moosh
What time do you want to meet?	A que horas é que nos encontramos?	a ke *o*·rash e ke noosh eng·kong·*traa*·moosh

Where To Go

What's there to do in the evenings?	O que é que se pode fazer à noite? oo ke e ke se *po*·de fa·*zer* aa *noy*·te
What's on tonight?	O que é que há hoje à noite? oo ke e ke aa *o*·zhe aa *noy*·te
What's on this weekend?	O que é que há este fim-de-semana? oo ke e ke aa *esh*·te feeng·de·se·*ma*·na
Is there a local entertainment guide?	Há um guia local de entertenimento? aa oong *gee*·a loo·*kaal* de eng·ter·te·nee·*meng*·too

I feel like going to a ...	Está-me a apetecer ir a ...	*shtaa*·me a a·pe·te·*ser* eer a ...
bar	um bar	oong bar
bullfight	uma tourada	*oo*·ma toh·*raa*·da
cafe	um café	oong ka·*fe*
concert	um concerto	oong kong·*ser*·too
fado house	uma casa de fados	*oo*·ma *kaa*·za de *faa*·doosh
film	um filme	oong *feel*·me
nightclub	uma discoteca	*oo*·ma deesh·koo·*te*·ka
party	uma festa	*oo*·ma *fesh*·ta
play	uma peça de teatro	*oo*·ma *pe*·sa de tee·*aa*·troo
restaurant	um restaurante	oong rresh·tow·*rang*·te
street party	uma festa de rua	*oo*·ma *fesh*·ta de *rroo*·a

Where can I find ...?	Onde é que há ...?	*ong*·de e ke aa ...
bars	bares	*ba*·resh
clubs	discotecas	deesh·koo·*te*·kash
gay/lesbian venues	lugares de gays/ lésbicas	loo·*gaa*·resh de gaysh/ *lezh*·bee·kash
places to eat	sítios para comer	*see*·tyoosh *pa*·ra koo·*mer*

Invitations

What are you doing tonight?	O que é que vai fazer hoje à noite? oo ke e ke vai fa·*zer* o·zhe aa *noy*·te
What are you doing this weekend?	O que é que vai fazer este fim-de-semana? oo ke e ke vai fa·*zer* *esh*·te feeng·de·se·*ma*·na
Would you like to go (for a) ...?	Gostava de ir ...? goosh·*taa*·va de eer ...
I feel like going (for a) ...	Apetece-me ir ... a·pe·*te*·se·me eer ...

coffee	a um café	a oong ka·*fe*
dancing	dançar	dang·*saar*
drink	beber alguma coisa	be·*ber* aal·*goo*·ma *koy*·za
meal	comer	koo·*mer*
out	sair	sa·*eer*
walk	andar a pé	ang·*daar* a pe

Do you know a good restaurant?	Conhece um bom restaurante? kong·*nye*·se oong bong rresh·tow·*rang*·te
Do you want to come to the concert with me?	Quer vir ao concerto comigo? ker veer ow kong·*ser*·too koo·*mee*·goo
We're having a party.	Vamos dar uma festa. *vaa*·moosh daar *oo*·ma *fesh*·ta
You should come.	Devia vir. de·*vee*·a veer

LOOK FOR

Street numbers follow the name of the street. Often apartments are indicated by floor number as well as by the side of the landing on which they're located — ie *direita* dee·*ray*·ta for right, *esquerda* shker·da for left. For example, *Rua do Rei, no. 15 – 3º drt.* could be translated as '15 King Street, 3rd floor, right side of the landing'.

avenida (av.) f	a·ve·*nee*·da	avenue/boulevard
beco m	*be*·koo	alley
estrada (estd.) f	esh·*traa*·da	road
rua (r.) f	*rroo*·a	street

Responding to Invitations

Yes, I'd love to.	Sim, adorava. seeng a·doo·*raa*·va
That's very kind of you.	É muito simpático da sua parte. e *mweeng*·too seeng·*paa*·tee·koo da *soo*·a *par*·te
Where shall we go?	Onde é que podemos ir? *ong*·de e ke poo·*de*·moosh eer
No, I'm afraid I can't.	Tenho muita pena, mas não posso. *ta*·nyoo *mweeng*·ta *pe*·na mash nowng *po*·soo
Sorry, I can't sing/dance.	Tenho muita pena, mas não sei cantar/dançar. *ta*·nyoo *mweeng*·ta *pe*·na mas nowng say kang·*taar*/dang·*saar*
What about tomorrow?	E que tal amanhã? ee ke taal aa·ma·*nyang*

Arranging to Meet

What time do you want to meet?	A que horas é que nos encontramos? a ke *o*·rash e ke noosh eng·kong·*traa*·moosh
Q Where will we meet?	Onde é que nos encontramos? *ong*·de e ke noosh eng·kong·*traa*·moosh
A Let's meet (at the entrance).	Encontramo-nos (à entrada). eng·kong·*traa*·moo·noosh (aa eng·*traa*·da)
I'll pick you up.	Eu vou buscá-lo/-la. **m/f** e·oo voh boosh·*kaa*·loo/la

Vai ser um prazer.
vai ser oong pra·*zer*
I'm looking forward to it.

I'll be coming later.	Eu vou mais tarde. e·oo voh maish *taar*·de
Where will you be?	Onde é que vais estar? *ong*·de e ke vaish shtaar
Q **Are you ready?**	Está pronto/pronta? **m/f** shtaa *prong*·too/*prong*·ta
A **I'm ready.**	Estou pronto/pronta. **m/f** shtoh *prong*·too/*prong*·ta
I'll see you then.	Até já. a·*te* zhaa
I'm looking forward to it.	Vai ser um prazer. vai ser oong pra·*zer*
Sorry I'm late.	Desculpe o atraso. desh·*kool*·pe oo a·*traa*·zoo

Drugs

Do you want to have a smoke?	Quer um cigarro? ker oong see·*gaa*·rroo
Do you have a light?	Tem lume? teng *loo*·me
I don't take drugs.	Eu não tomo drogas. e·oo nowng *to*·moo *dro*·gash

If the police are talking to you about drugs, see **police** (p158).

Reading Portuguese

A vowel followed by *m* or *n*, or with a tilde (~) above it, is usually nasalised – eg *viagem* vee·*aa*·zheng, *avião* a·vee·*owng*.

The letter *o* is often pronounced oo, especially at the end of a word – eg *gato* *gaa*·too.

The letters *es* at the start of a word, and *s* at the end of a word, are almost always pronounced sh – eg *estômago* *shto*·ma·goo, *crianças* kree·*ang*·sash.

Romance

KEY PHRASES

Would you like to do something?	Queres fazer alguma coisa?	*ke*·resh fa·*zer* aal·*goo*·ma *koy*·za
I love you.	Amo-te.	*a*·moo·te
Leave me alone!	Deixa-me!	*day*·sha·me

Asking Someone Out

Where would you like to go (tonight)?	Onde é que queres ir (hoje à noite)? *ong*·de e ke *ke*·resh eer (*o*·zhe aa *noy*·te)
Q **Would you like to do something (tomorrow)?**	Queres fazer alguma coisa (amanhã)? *ke*·resh fa·*zer* aal·*goo*·ma *koy*·za (aa·ma·*nyang*)
A **Yes, I'd love to.**	Sim, adorava. seeng a·doo·*raa*·va
A **Sorry, I can't.**	Desculpa, mas não posso. desh·*kool*·pa mash nowng *po*·soo

Pick-up Lines

Would you like a drink?	Queres uma bebida? *ke*·resh *oo*·ma be·*bee*·da
You're a fantastic dancer.	Danças muito bem. *daang*·sash *mweeng*·too beng

Can I dance with you?	Posso dançar contigo? *po*·soo dang·*saar* kong·*tee*·goo
Can I sit here?	Posso sentar-me aqui? *po*·soo seng·*taar*·me a·*kee*

Rejections

No, thank you.	Não, obrigado/ obrigada. **m/f** nowng o·bree·*gaa*·doo/ o·bree·*gaa*·da
I'd rather not.	É melhor não. e me·*lyor* nowng
I'm here with my girlfriend.	Estou aqui com a minha namorada. shtoh a·*kee* kong a *mee*·nya na·moo·*raa*·da
I'm here with my boyfriend.	Estou aqui com o meu namorado. shtoh a·*kee* kong oo *me*·oo na·moo·*raa*·doo
Excuse me, I have to go now.	Desculpa, tenho de me ir embora. desh·*kool*·pa *ta*·nyoo de me eer eng·*bo*·ra
Leave me alone!	Deixa-me! *day*·sha·me
Get lost!	Desaparece! de·za·pa·*re*·se

Getting Closer

I really like you.	Eu gosto mesmo de ti. *e*·oo *gosh*·too *mezh*·moo de tee

You're great.	És fantástico/ fantástica. m/f esh fang·*taash*·tee·koo/ fang·*taash*·tee·ka
Can I kiss you?	Posso dar-te um beijo? *po*·soo *dar*·te oong *bay*·zhoo
Do you want to come inside for a while?	Queres entrar? *ke*·resh eng·*traar*
Would you like to stay over?	Queres passar a noite aqui? *ke*·resh pa·*saar* a *noy*·te a·*kee*
Can I stay over?	Posso passar a noite aqui? *po*·soo pa·*saar* a *noy*·te a·*kee*

Sex

Kiss me.	Dá-me um beijo. *daa*·me oong *bay*·zhoo
I want you.	Quero-te. *ke*·roo·te
Q **Do you like this?**	Gostas disto? *gosh*·tash *deesh*·too
A **I (don't) like that.**	Eu (não) gosto disso. e·oo (nowng) *gosh*·too *dee*·soo

LANGUAGE TIP

Multiple Meanings

There's no specific word for 'date' in Portuguese – the Portuguese use the word *encontro* eng·*kong*·troo, which is just a general word for 'meeting'. Be sure you know what kind of meeting you're going to before you turn up with chocolates or flowers!

I think we should stop now.	Acho que é melhor pararmos. *aa*·shoo ke e me·*lyor* pa·*raar*·moosh
Let's go to bed.	Vamos para a cama. *vaa*·moosh *pa*·ra a *kaa*·ma
Do you have a (condom)?	Tens (um preservativo)? tengsh (oong pre·zer·va·*tee*·voo)
Let's use a (condom).	Vamos usar (um preservativo). *vaa*·moosh oo·*zaar* (oong pre·zer·va·*tee*·voo)
I won't do it without protection.	Eu não faço isso sem protecção. e·oo nowng *faa*·soo *ee*·soo seng proo·te·*sowng*
It's my first time.	É a minha primeira vez. e a *mee*·nya pree·*may*·ra vezh
That's great.	Fantástico! fang·*taash*·tee·koo
That was amazing.	Foi extraordinário. foy shtra·or·dee·*naa*·ree·oo
That was romantic.	Foi romântico. foy rroo·*mang*·tee·koo
That was wild.	Foi selvagem. foy sel·*vaa*·zheng

Love

I think we're good together.	Eu acho que nós estamos bem juntos. e·oo *aa*·shoo ke nosh *shta*·moosh beng *zhoong*·toosh

LISTEN FOR

fofa	*fo*·fa	sweetie
meu amor	*me*·oo a·*mor*	my love
querida f	ke·*ree*·da	dear
querido m	ke·*ree*·doo	dear

I love you.	Amo-te. *a*·moo·te
Will you go out with me?	Queres sair comigo? *ke*·resh sa·*eer* koo·*mee*·goo
Will you meet my parents?	Queres conhecer os meus pais? *ke*·resh koo·nye·*ser* oosh *me*·oosh paish
Will you marry me?	Queres casar comigo? *ke*·resh ka·*zaar* koo·*mee*·goo

Leaving

I have to leave (tomorrow).	Vou ter que me ir embora (amanhã). voh ter ke me eer eng·*bo*·ra (aa·ma·*nyang*)
I'll keep in touch.	Eu vou manter-me em contacto. *e*·oo voh mang·*ter*·me eng kong·*taak*·too
I'll miss you.	Eu vou ter saudades tuas. *e*·oo voh ter sow·*daa*·desh *too*·ash
I'll visit you.	Eu vou visitar-te. *e*·oo voh vee·zee·*taar*·te

Beliefs & Culture

KEY PHRASES

What's your religion?	Qual é a sua religião?	kwaal e a *soo*·a rre·lee·zhee·*owng*
I'm ...	Eu sou ...	*e*·oo soh ...
I'm sorry, it's against my beliefs.	Desculpe, mas é contra a minha crença.	desh·*kool*·pe mash e *kong*·tra a *mee*·nya *kreng*·sa

Religion

Q **What's your religion?**
Qual é a sua religião?
kwaal e a *soo*·a rre·lee·zhee·*owng*

A **I'm not religious.**
Não sou religioso/religiosa. **m/f**
nowng soh rre·lee·zhee·*o*·zoo/rre·lee·zhee·*o*·za

A **I'm ...**
Eu sou ...
e·oo soh ...

Buddhist	budista	boo·*deesh*·ta
Christian	cristão **m** cristã **f**	kreesh·*towng* kreesh·*tang*
Hindu	hindu	eeng·*doo*
Jewish	judeu **m** judia **f**	zhoo·*de*·oo zhoo·*dee*·a
Muslim	muçulmano **m** muçulmana **f**	moo·sool·*maa*·noo moo·sool·*maa*·na

I (don't) believe in God.	Eu (não) acredito em Deus. *e*·oo (nowng) a·kre·*dee*·too eng *de*·oosh
Where can I attend a service?	Onde posso assistir a oong serviço religioso? *ong*·de *po*·soo a·seesh·*teer* a oong ser·*vee*·soo rre·lee·zhee·*o*·zoo
Can I pray here?	Posso rezar aqui? *po*·soo rre·*zaar* a·*kee*

Cultural Differences

Is this a local custom?	Este é um costume local? *esh*·te e oong koosh·*too*·me loo·*kaal*
I don't want to offend you.	Não quero ofendê-lo/ ofendê-la. m/f nowng *ke*·roo oo·feng·*de*·lo/ oo·feng·*de*·la
I'm not used to this.	Não estou acostumado/ acostumada a isso. m/f nowngshtoh a·koosh·too·*maa*·doo/ a·koosh·too·*maa*·da a *ee*·soo
I'll try it.	Vou experimentar. voh shpree·meng·*taar*
I'd rather not join in.	Prefiro não tomar parte. pre·*fee*·roo nowng too·*maar paar*·te
I didn't mean to do/ say anything wrong.	Não tive intenção de fazer/dizer nada de mal. nowng *tee*·ve eeng·teng·*sowng* de fa·*zer*/dee·*zeer naa*·da de maal
I'm sorry, it's against my beliefs.	Desculpe, mas é contra a minha crença. desh·*kool*·pe mash e *kong*·tra a *mee*·nya *kreng*·sa

Sports

KEY PHRASES

Which sport do you play?	Que desporto é que pratica?	ke desh·*por*·too e ke pra·*tee*·ka
Who's your favourite team?	Qual é a sua equipa favorita?	kwaal e a *soo*·a e·*kee*·pa fa·voo·*ree*·ta
What's the score?	Qual é o resultado?	kwaal e oo rre·zool·*taa*·doo

Sporting Interests

Q **Which sport do you play?**	Que desporto é que pratica? ke desh·*por*·too e ke pra·*tee*·ka
Q **Which sport do you follow?**	Que desporto é que segue? ke desh·*por*·too e ke *se*·ge
A **I play/do ...**	Eu faço/pratico ... e·oo *faa*·soo/pra·*tee*·koo ...
A **I follow ...**	Eu sigo ... e·oo *see*·goo ...

athletics	atletismo	at·le·*teezh*·moo
basketball	basquetebol	bash·ke·te·*bol*
football (soccer)	futebol	foo·te·*bol*
roller-blading hockey	hóquei em patins	*o*·kay eng pa·*teengsh*
scuba diving	mergulho	mer·*goo*·lyoo
volleyball	voleibol	*vo*·lay·bol

I cycle.	Eu faço ciclismo. e·oo *faa*·soo see·*kleesh*·moo
I run.	Eu corro. e·oo *ko*·rroo
Who's your favourite sportsperson?	Qual é o seu atleta favorito? kwaal e oo *se*·oo at·*le*·ta fa·voo·*ree*·too
Who's your favourite team?	Qual é a sua equipa favorita? kwaal e a *soo*·a e·*kee*·pa fa·voo·*ree*·ta
Q **Do you like (football)?**	Gosta de (futebol)? *gosh*·ta de (foo·te·*bol*)
A **Yes, very much.**	Sim, gosto muito. seeng *gosh*·too *mweeng*·too
A **Not really.**	Nem por isso. neng poor *ee*·soo
A **I like watching it.**	Eu gosto de ver. e·oo *gosh*·too de ver

Going to a Game

Would you like to go to a game?	Quer ir a um jogo? ker eer a oong *zho*·goo
Who are you supporting?	Por quem está? poor keng shtaa
Who's playing?	Quem está a jogar? keng shtaa a zhoo·*gaar*
Who's winning?	Quem está a ganhar? keng shtaa a ga·*nyaar*
What's the score?	Qual é o resultado? kwaal e oo rre·zool·*taa*·doo

CULTURE TIP

Bullfighting

The ancient rite of bullfighting (*tourada* toh·*raa*·da) remains one of Portugal's most popular spectator sports. It's a bit different from the Spanish version. The bull (*touro* *toh*·roo) first faces a horseman (*cavaleiro* ka·va·*lay*·roo), who must plant a number of barbs into the bull's neck muscle. The bull's horns are cut (so as not to have sharp points) and padded with leather. A crew of foot soldiers (*forcados* foor·*kaa*·doosh) then enters the ring, taunts the bull into charging forcefully, and eventually wrestles him to a standstill. The bull doesn't die in the ring but is almost always killed just afterwards by a butcher.

That was a bad game!	Foi um mau jogo! foy oong mow *zho*·goo
That was a great game!	Foi um jogo óptimo! foy oong *zho*·goo *o*·tee·moo
That was a boring game!	Foi um jogo chato! foy oong *zho*·goo *shaa*·too

Playing Sport

Some of the phrases in this section are in the informal form, as people tend to be casual in the middle of a game. See **grammar** (p20), for more details on polite and informal forms.

Q **Can I join in?**	Posso entrar? *po*·soo eng·*traar*
Q **Do you want to play?**	Quer jogar? ker zhoo·*gaar*
A **That would be great.**	Isso era óptimo. *ee*·soo *e*·ra *o*·tee·moo
A **I can't.**	Não posso. nowng *po*·soo

LISTEN FOR

bola de partida	*bo*·la de par·*tee*·da	match-point
empate	eng·*paa*·te	draw/even
nada	*naa*·da	love (zero)
zero	*ze*·roo	nil (zero)

A I have an injury.	Estou lesado/lesada. **m/f** shtoh le·*zaa*·doo/le·*zaa*·da
Your/My point.	O ponto é teu/meu. oo *pong*·too e *te*·oo/*me*·oo
Kick/Pass it to me!	Passa! *paa*·sa
You're a good player.	És um bom jogador. **m** esh oong bong zhoo·ga·*dor* És uma boa jogadora. **f** esh *oo*·ma *bo*·a zhoo·ga·*do*·ra
Thanks for the game.	Obrigado/Obrigada pelo jogo. **m/f** o·bree·*gaa*·doo/o·bree·*gaa*·da *pe*·loo *zho*·goo
Where's the nearest golf course/tennis court?	Onde é que é o campo de golfe/ténis mais próximo? *ong*·de e ke e oo *kang*·poo de *gol*·fe/*te*·neesh maish *pro*·see·moo
Where's the nearest gym?	Onde é que é o ginásio mais próximo? *ong*·de e ke e oo zhee·*naa*·zyoo maish *pro*·see·moo

Where's the nearest swimming pool?	Onde é que é a piscina mais próxima? *ong*·de e ke e a pesh·*see*·na maish *pro*·see·ma
What's the charge per ...?	Quanto se paga por ...? *kwang*·too se *paa*·ga poor ...

day	dia	*dee*·a
game	jogo	*zho*·goo
hour	hora	*o*·ra
visit	visita	vee·*zee*·ta

Can I hire a ...?	Pode-se alugar ...? *po*·de·se a·loo·*gaar* ...

ball	uma bola	*oo*·ma *bo*·la
bicycle	uma bicicleta	*oo*·ma bee·see·*kle*·ta
court	um campo	oong *kang*·poo
racquet	uma raquete	*oo*·ma rra·*ke*·te

Where's a good place to ...?	Onde é que há um bom lugar para ...? *ong*·de e ke aa oong bong loo·*gaar pa*·ra ...

fish	pescar	pesh·*kaar*
go horseriding	andar a cavalo	ang·*daar* a ka·*vaa*·loo
run	correr	koo·*rrer*
ski	esquiar	shkee·*aar*
snorkel	fazer snorkel	fa·*zer snor*·kel
surf	fazer surf	fa·*zer* sarf

Do I have to be a member to attend?	Tenho de ser membro para entrar? *ta*·nyoo de ser *meng*·broo *pa*·ra eng·*traar*
Is there a women-only session?	Há alguma sessão só para mulheres? aa aal·*goo*·ma se·*sowng* so *pa*·ra moo·*lye*·resh
Where are the changing rooms?	Onde são os balneários? *ong*·de sowng oosh bal·nee·*aa*·ree·oosh

Football/Soccer

Who plays for (Porto)?	Quem joga no (Porto)? keng *zho*·ga noo (*por*·too)
He's a great (player).	Ele é um grande (jogador). e·le e oong *grang*·de (zhoo·ga·*dor*)
He played brilliantly in the match against (Italy).	Ele jogou muito bem contra (a Itália). e·le zho·*goh mweeng*·too beng *kong*·tra (a ee·*taa*·lya)
Which team is at the top of the league?	Qual é a equipa que vai à frente no campeonato? kwaal e a e·*kee*·pa ke vai aa *freng*·te noo kang·pee·oo·*naa*·too
What a great/terrible team!	Que equipa fantástica/ horrível! ke e·*kee*·pa fang·*taash*·tee·ka/ o·*rree*·vel

LISTEN FOR

árbitro m	*ar*·bee·troo	referee
atacante m	a·ta·*kang*·te	striker
baliza f	ba·*lee*·za	goal (structure)
bola f	*bo*·la	ball
canto m	*kang*·too	corner (kick)
cartão m **amarelo**	kar·*towng* a·ma·*re*·loo	yellow card
cartão m **vermelho**	kar·*towng* ver·*me*·lyoo	red card
falta f	*faal*·ta	foul
fora-de-jogo	*fo*·ra·de·*zho*·goo	offside
grande f **penalidade**	*grang*·de pe·na·lee·*daa*·de	penalty
guarda-redes m	*gwaar*·da·*rre*·desh	goalkeeper
jogador m	zhoo·ga·*dor*	player
lançamento m **lateral**	lang·sa·*meng*·too la·te·*raal*	throw-in
livre m	*lee*·vre	free kick
treinador m	tray·na·*dor*	coach

What a ...! Que ...!
ke ...

goal	golo	*go*·loo
hit	pancada	pang·*kaa*·da
kick	pontapé	pong·ta·*pe*
pass	passe	*paa*·se
performance	actuação	a·too·a·*sowng*

Off to see a match? Check out **buying tickets** (p42), and **going to a game** (p143).

Outdoors

KEY PHRASES

Where can I buy supplies?	Onde é que posso comprar mantimentos?	*ong*·de e ke *po*·soo kong·*praar* mang·tee·*meng*·toosh
Do we need a guide?	Precisamos de um guia?	pre·see·*za*·moosh de oong *gee*·a
Is it safe?	É seguro?	e se·*goo*·roo
I'm lost.	Estou perdido/perdida. m/f	shtoh per·*dee*·doo/per·*dee*·da
What's the weather like?	Como está o tempo?	*ko*·moo shtaa oo *teng*·poo

Hiking

Where can I ...? Onde é que posso ...? *ong*·de e ke *po*·soo ...

buy supplies	comprar mantimentos	kong·*praar* mang·tee·*meng*·toosh
find someone who knows this area	encontrar alguém que conheça esta área	eng·kong·*traar* aal·*geng* ke koo·*nye*·sa *esh*·ta *aa*·re·a
get a map	arranjar um mapa	a·rrang·*zhaar* oong *maa*·pa
hire hiking gear	alugar equipamento de caminhada	a·loo·*gaar* e·kee·pa·*meng*·too de ka·mee·*nyaa*·da

How high is the climb?	Qual é a altura da escalada? kwaal e a aal·*too*·ra da shka·*laa*·da
How long is the trail?	Qual é o comprimento do atalho? kwaal e oo kong·pree·*meng*·too doo a·*taa*·lyoo
Is it safe?	É seguro? e se·*goo*·roo
Are there guided treks?	Há caminhadas com guia? aa ka·mee·*nyaa*·dash kong *gee*·a
Do we need a guide?	Precisamos de um guia? pre·see·*za*·moosh de oong *gee*·a
Do we need to take food/water?	Precisamos de levar comida/água? pre·see·*za*·moosh de le·*vaar* koo·*mee*·da/*aa*·gwa
Is the track (well-) marked?	O trilho está (bem) sinalizado? oo *tree*·lyoo shtaa (beng) see·na·lee·*zaa*·doo
Is the track open?	O trilho está aberto? oo *tree*·lyoo shtaa a·*ber*·too
Which is the easiest/ shortest route?	Qual é a rota mais fácil/ curta? kwaal e a *rro*·ta maish *faa*·seel/ *koor*·ta
Does this path go to ...?	Este caminho leva a ...? *esh*·te ka·*mee*·nyoo *le*·va a ...
Can I go through here?	Posso ir por aqui? *po*·soo eer poor a·*kee*
I'm lost.	Estou perdido/perdida. **m/f** shtoh per·*dee*·doo/per·*dee*·da

Where can I find the ...?	Onde ...? ong·de ...

campsite	é o parque de campismo	e oo *par*·ke de kang·*peesh*·moo
nearest village	é a aldeia mais próxima	e a aal·*day*·a maish *pro*·see·ma
showers	são os chuveiros	sowng oosh shoo·*vay*·roosh
toilets	são as casas de banho	sowng ash *kaa*·zash de *ba*·nyoo

When does it get dark?	A que horas fica escuro? a ke *o*·rash *fee*·ka *shkoo*·roo
Is there a hut?	Há alguma cabana? aa aal·*goo*·ma ka·*ba*·na

Onde é que é a melhor praia?

ong·de e ke e a me·*lyor prai*·a

Where's the best beach?

Do we need to take a sleeping bag?	Precisamos de levar saco-cama? pre·see·*za*·moosh de le·*vaar* *saa*·koo·*kaa*·ma
Is the water OK to drink?	Pode-se beber esta água? *po*·de·se be·*ber* *esh*·ta *aa*·gwa

Beach

Where's the ... beach?	Onde é que é a ...? *ong*·de e ke e a ...

best	melhor praia	me·*lyor* *prai*·a
nearest	praia mais próxima	*prai*·a maish *pro*·see·ma
nudist	praia de nudismo	*prai*·a de noo·*deesh*·moo
public	praia pública	*prai*·a *poo*·blee·ka

Is it safe to dive/swim here?	É seguro mergulhar/nadar aqui? e se·*goo*·roo mer·goo·*lyaar*/na·*daar* a·*kee*
What time is high/low tide?	A que horas é a maré alta/baixa? a ke *o*·rash e a ma·*re* *aal*·ta/*bai*·sha

LISTEN FOR

Cuidado com a corrente!	kwee·*daa*·doo kong a koo·*rreng*·te Be careful of the undertow!
É perigoso!	e pree·*go*·zoo It's dangerous!

Não Mergulhar	nowng mer·goo·*lyaar*	No Diving
Não Nadar	nowng na·*daar*	No Swimming

How much to rent a ...? Quanto custa para alugar ...? *kwang*·too *koosh*·ta *pa*·ra a·loo·*gaar* ...

chair	uma cadeira	*oo*·ma ka·*day*·ra
hut	uma cabana	*oo*·ma ka·*ba*·na
sun umbrella	um guarda-sol	oong gwaar·da·*sol*
wind stopper	um pára-vento	oong *paa*·ra·*veng*·too

Weather

What's the weather like? Como está o tempo? *ko*·moo shtaa oo *teng*·poo

What will the weather be like tomorrow? Como vai estar o tempo amanhã? *ko*·moo vai shtaar oo *teng*·poo aa·ma·*nyang*

It's ... Está ... shtaa ...

cloudy	enublado	e·noo·*blaa*·doo
(very) cold	(muito) frio	(*mweeng*·too) *free*·oo
raining	a chover	a shoo·*ver*
snowing	a nevar	a ne·*vaar*
sunny	sol	sol
warm	quente	*keng*·te
windy	ventoso	veng·*to*·zoo

Where can I buy a rain jacket?	Onde é que posso comprar uma gabardina? *ong*·de e ke *po*·soo kong·*praar* *oo*·ma ga·baar·*dee*·na
Where can I buy an umbrella?	Onde é que posso comprar um guarda-chuva? *ong*·de e ke *po*·soo kong·*praar* oong gwaar·da·*shoo*·va

Flora & Fauna

What ... is that?	Que ...? ke ...

animal	animal é aquele	aa·nee·*maal* e a·*ke*·le
flower	flor é aquela	flor e a·*ke*·la
plant	planta é aquela	*plang*·ta e a·*ke*·la
tree	árvore é aquela	*aar*·vo·re e a·*ke*·la

Is it dangerous?	É perigoso/perigosa? **m/f** e pree·*go*·zoo/pree·*go*·za
Is it poisonous?	É venenoso/venenosa? **m/f** e ve·ne·*no*·zoo/ve·ne·*no*·za
Is it protected?	É protegido/protegida? **m/f** e proo·te·*zhee*·doo/proo·te·*zhee*·da
What's it used for?	Para que é que é usado/usada? **m/f** *pa*·ra ke e ke e oo·*zaa*·doo/oo·*zaa*·da
Can you eat the fruit?	Pode-se comer esta fruta? *po*·de·se koo·*mer* *esh*·ta *froo*·ta

For names of plants and animals, see the **dictionary**.

Safe Travel

Emergencies

KEY PHRASES

Help!	Socorro!	soo·*ko*·rroo
There's been an accident.	Houve um acidente.	*oh*·ve oong a·see·*deng*·te
It's an emergency.	É uma emergência.	e *oo*·ma ee·mer·*zheng*·sya

Help!	Socorro! soo·*ko*·rroo
Stop!	Stop! stop
Go away!	Vá-se embora! *vaa*·se eng·*bo*·ra
Thief!	Ladrão! la·*drowng*
Fire!	Fogo! *fo*·goo
Watch out!	Cuidado! kwee·*daa*·doo
Call a doctor.	Chame um médico. *shaa*·me oong *me*·dee·koo
Call an ambulance.	Chame uma ambulância. *shaa*·me *oo*·ma ang·boo·*lang*·sya
Call the police.	Chame a polícia. *shaa*·me a poo·*lee*·sya
It's an emergency.	É uma emergência. e *oo*·ma ee·mer·*zheng*·sya

LOOK FOR

Esquadra da Polícia	*shkwaa*·dra da poo·*lee*·sya	Police Station
Hospital	osh·pee·*taal*	Hospital
Polícia	poo·*lee*·sya	Police
Urgências	oor·*zheng*·syash	Emergency Department

There's been an accident.	Houve um acidente. *oh*·ve oong a·see·*deng*·te
Could you please help?	Pode ajudar, por favor? *po*·de a·zhoo·*daar* poor fa·*vor*
Can I use your phone?	Posso usar o seu telefone? *po*·soo oo·*zaar* oo *se*·oo te·le·*fo*·ne
I'm lost.	Estou perdido/perdida. **m/f** shtoh per·*dee*·doo/per·*dee*·da
Where are the toilets?	Onde é a casa de banho? *ong*·de e a *kaa*·za de *ba*·nyoo
Is it safe ...?	É seguro ...? e se·*goo*·roo ...

at night	à noite	aa *noy*·te
for gay people	para gays	*pa*·ra gaysh
for travellers	para turistas	*pa*·ra too·*reesh*·tash
for women	para mulheres	*pa*·ra moo·*lye*·resh
on your own	ir sozinho/sozinha **m/f**	eer so·*zee*·nyoo/so·*zee*·nya

Police

KEY PHRASES

Where's the police station?	Onde é a esquadra da polícia?	*ong*·de e a *shkwaa*·dra da poo·*lee*·sya
I want to contact my embassy.	Eu quero contactar com a minha embaixada.	e·oo *ke*·roo kong·tak·*taar* kong a *mee*·nya eng·bai·*shaa*·da
My bag was stolen.	Roubaram o meu saco.	rroh·*baa*·rang oo *me*·oo *saa*·koo

Where's the police station?	Onde é a esquadra da polícia? *ong*·de e a *shkwaa*·dra da poo·*lee*·sya
I want to report an offence.	Eu quero denunciar um crime. e·oo *ke*·roo de·noong·see·*aar* oong *kree*·me
It was him/her.	Foi ele/ela. foy e·le/e·la
I've been (assaulted).	Eu fui (agredido/ agredida). **m/f** e·oo fwee (a·gre·*dee*·doo/ a·gre·*dee*·da)
He/She has been (raped).	Ele/Ela foi (violado/ violada). **m/f** e·le/e·la foy (vee·oo·*laa*·doo/ vee·oo·*laa*·da)

My ... was/were stolen.	Roubaram ... rroh·*baa*·rang ...
I've lost my ...	Eu perdi ... e·oo per·*dee* ...

backpack	a minha mochila	a *mee*·nya mo·*shee*·la
bag	o meu saco	oo *me*·oo *saa*·koo
handbag	a minha bolsa	a *mee*·nya *bol*·sa
jewellery	as minhas jóias	ash *mee*·nyash *zhoy*·ash
money	o meu dinheiro	oo *me*·oo dee·*nyay*·roo
papers	os meus papeís	oosh *me*·oosh pa·*paysh*
passport	o meu passaporte	oo *me*·oo paa·sa·*por*·te
wallet	a minha carteira	a *mee*·nya kar·*tay*·ra

I didn't realise I was doing anything wrong.	Eu não percebi que estava a fazer algo errado. e·oo nowng per·se·*bee* ke *shtaa*·va a fa·*zer aal*·goo e·*rraa*·doo
I didn't do it.	Eu não fiz isso. e·oo nowng feez *ee*·soo
What am I accused of?	De que sou acusado/acusada? **m/f** de ke soh a·koo·*zaa*·doo/a·koo·*zaa*·da
I want to contact my embassy.	Eu quero contactar com a minha embaixada. e·oo *ke*·roo kong·tak·*taar* kong a *mee*·nya eng·bai·*shaa*·da
Can I make a phone call?	Posso fazer um telefonema? *po*·soo fa·*zer* oong te·le·foo·*ne*·ma

LISTEN FOR

agressão — *a·gre·sowng* — assault

distúrbio da ordem pública — *deesh·toor·byoo da or·deng poo·blee·ka* — disturbing the peace

excesso de velocidade — *aysh·se·soo de ve·loo·see·daa·de* — speeding

multa de estacionamento — *mool·ta de shta·syoo·na·meng·too* — parking fine

não ter um visto legal — *nowng ter oong veesh·too le·gaal* — not having a visa

pequeno furto — *pe·ke·noo foor·too* — shoplifting

posse (de substâncias ilegais) — *po·se (de su·be·shtang·syash ee·le·gaish)* — possession (of illegal substances)

roubo — *rroh·boo* — theft

ter visto expirado — *ter veesh·too aysh·pee·raa·doo* — overstaying a visa

Can I have a lawyer (who speaks English)?	Posso ter acesso a um advogado (que fale inglês)? *po·soo ter a·se·soo a oong a·de·voo·gaa·doo (que faa·le eeng·glesh)*
I have insurance.	Eu estou coberto/coberta pelo seguro. **m/f** *e·oo shtoh koo·ber·too/koo·ber·ta pe·loo se·goo·roo*
I have a prescription for this drug.	Eu tenho uma receita para esta droga. *e·oo ta·nyoo oo·ma rre·say·ta pa·ra esh·ta dro·ga*

Health

KEY PHRASES

Where's the nearest hospital?	Qual é o hospital mais perto?	kwaal e oo osh·pee·*taal* maish *per*·too
I'm sick.	Estou doente.	shtoh doo·*eng*·te
I need a doctor.	Eu preciso de um médico.	*e*·oo pre·*see*·zoo de oong *me*·dee·koo
I'm on medication for ...	Eu estou a tomar medicamentos para ...	*e*·oo shtoh a too·*maar* me·dee·ka·*meng*·toosh *pa*·ra ...
I'm allergic to ...	Eu sou alérgico/ alérgica a ... **m/f**	*e*·oo soh a·*ler*·zhee·koo/ a·*ler*·zhee·ka a ...

Doctor

Address doctors and dentists as *Senhor Doutor* se·*nyor* doh·*tor* (men) or *Senhora Doutora* se·*nyo*·ra doh·*to*·ra (women).

Where's the nearest ...? Qual é ... mais perto/perta?
kwaal e ... maish *per*·too/*per*·ta

dentist	o dentista	oo deng·*teesh*·ta
doctor	o médico **m** a médica **f**	oo *me*·dee·koo a *me*·dee·ka
hospital	o hospital	oo osh·pee·*taal*
optometrist	o oculista	oo o·koo·*leesh*·ta
(night) pharmacist	a farmácia (de serviço)	a far·*maa*·sya (de ser·*vee*·soo)

I need a doctor (who speaks English).	Eu preciso de um médico (que fale inglês). *e·oo pre·see·zoo de oong me·dee·koo (que faa·le eeng·glesh)*
Could I see a female doctor?	Posso ser visto/vista por uma médica? m/f *po·soo ser veesh·too/veesh·ta poor oo·ma me·dee·ka*
I've run out of my medication.	Os meus medicamentos acabaram. *oosh me·oosh me·dee·ka·meng·toosh a·ka·baa·rowng*
My prescription is ...	A minha receita é ... *a meeng·nya rre·say·ta e ...*
What's the correct dosage?	Qual é a dose correcta? *kwaal e a do·ze koo·rre·ta*
I don't want a blood transfusion.	Eu não quero uma transfusão sanguínea. *e·oo nowng ke·roo oo·ma trangsh·foo·zowng sang·gwee·nee·a*
Please use a new syringe.	Por favor use uma seringa nova. *poor fa·vor oo·ze oo·ma se·reeng·ga no·va*
I've been vaccinated against (hepatitis A/B/C).	Eu tenho as vacinas de (hepatite A/B/C). *e·oo ta·nyoo ash va·see·nash de (e·pa·tee·te a/be/se)*
He has been vaccinated against (tetanus).	Ele foi vacinado contra (tétano). *e·la foy va·see·naa·da kong·tra (te·ta·noo)*

LISTEN FOR

Onde é que dói?	*ong*·de e ke doy Where does it hurt?
Tem febre?	teng *fe*·bre Do you have a temperature?
É alérgico/alérgica a alguma coisa? m/f	e a·*ler*·zhee·koo/ a·*ler*·zhee·ka a aal·*goo*·ma *koy*·za Are you allergic to anything?
Está a tomar alguma coisa?	shtaa a too·*maar* aal·*goo*·ma *koy*·za Are you on medication?
Há quanto tempo tem estes sintomas?	aa *kwang*·too *teng*·poo teng *esh*·tesh seeng·*to*·mash How long have you been like this?

She has been vaccinated against (typhoid).	Ela foi vacinada contra (febre tifóide). e·la foy va·see·*naa*·da kong·tra (*fe*·bre tee·*foy*·de)
I need new contact lenses.	Eu preciso de lentes de contacto novas. e·oo pre·*see*·zoo de *leng*·tesh de kong·*taak*·too *no*·vash
I need new glasses.	Eu preciso de óculos novos. e·oo pre·*see*·zoo de o·koo·loosh *no*·voosh

Symptoms & Conditions

I'm sick.	Estou doente. shtoh doo·*eng*·te

I've been (vomiting).	Eu tenho estado (a vomitar). *e·oo ta·nyoo shtaa·doo (a voo·mee·taar)*
He/She has been (injured).	Ele/Ela tem estado (magoado/magoada). **m/f** *e·le/e·la teng shtaa·doo (ma·goo·aa·doo/ ma·goo·aa·da)*
I feel ...	Eu sinto-me ... *e·oo seeng·too·me ...*

dizzy	tonto/tonta **m/f**	*tong·too/tong·ta*
hot and cold	com suores frios	*kong soo·o·resh free·oosh*
nauseous	enjoado **m** enjoada **f**	*eng·zhoo·aa·doo* *eng·zhoo·aa·da*
shivery	a tremer	*a tre·mer*
weak	fraco/fraca **m/f**	*fraa·koo/fraa·ka*

It hurts here.	Dói-me aqui. *doy·me a·kee*
I'm dehydrated.	Estou desidratado/ desidratada. **m/f** *shtoh de·zee·dra·taa·doo/ de·zee·dra·taa·da*
I can't sleep.	Não consigo dormir. *nowng kong·see·goo dor·meer*
I'm on medication for ...	Eu estou a tomar medicamentos para ... *e·oo shtoh a too·maar me·dee·ka·meng·toosh pa·ra ...*
I've noticed a lump here.	Notei um alto aqui. *no·tay oong aal·too a·kee*

LISTEN FOR

Bebe?	*be*·be Do you drink?
Fuma?	*foo*·ma Do you smoke?
Toma drogas?	*to*·ma *dro*·gash Do you take drugs?
É sexualmente activo/activa? m/f	e sek·soo·al·*meng*·te a·*tee*·voo/a·*tee*·va Are you sexually active?
Alguma vez praticou sexo sem protecção?	aal·*goo*·ma vezh pra·tee·*koh* *sek*·soo seng proo·te·*sowng* Have you had unprotected sex?

I have (a/an) ...	Eu tenho ... *e*·oo *ta*·nyoo ...
food poisoning	intoxicação alimentar **f** eeng·tok·see·ka·*sowng* a·lee·meng·*taar*
sore throat	dores de garganta **f pl** *do*·resh de gar·*gang*·ta

Women's Health

(I think) I'm pregnant.	(Eu acho que) estou grávida. (*e*·oo *aa*·shoo ke) shtoh *graa*·vee·da
I haven't had my period for (six) weeks.	Eu já não tenho o período há (seis) semanas. *e*·oo zha nowng *ta*·nyoo oo pe·*ree*·o·doo aa (saysh) se·*ma*·nash

LISTEN FOR

Está com o período?	shtaa kong oo pe·*ree*·o·doo Are you menstruating?
Quando foi a última vez que teve o período?	*kwang*·doo foy a *ool*·tee·ma vezh ke *te*·ve oo pe·*ree*·oo·doo When did you last have your period?
Usa contraceptivos?	*oo*·za kong·tra·se·*tee*·voosh Are you using contraception?
Está grávida?	shtaa *graa*·vee·da Are you pregnant?
Está grávida.	shtaa *graa*·vee·da You're pregnant.

I'm on the Pill.	Eu tomo a pílula. *e*·oo *to*·moo a *pee*·loo·la
I need contraception.	Eu preciso de contraceptivos. *e*·oo pre·*see*·zoo de kong·tra·se·*tee*·voosh
I need the morning-after pill.	Eu preciso da pílula do dia seguinte. *e*·oo pre·*see*·zoo da *pee*·loo·la doo *dee*·a se·*geeng*·te
I need a pregnancy test.	Eu preciso de um teste de gravidez. *e*·oo pre·*see*·zoo de oong *tesh*·te de gra·vee·*desh*
period pain	dores do período **f pl** *do*·resh doo pe·*ree*·o·doo
yeast infection	infecção vaginal **f** eeng·fe·*sowng* va·zhee·*naal*

Parts of the Body

My ... hurts.	O meu ... está a doer-me. **m** oo *me*·oo ... shtaa a doo·*er*·me A minha ... está a doer-me. **f** a *meeng*·nya ... shtaa a doo·*er*·me
I can't move my ...	Eu não consigo mexer o meu ... **m** e·oo nowng kong·*see*·goo me·*sher* oo *me*·oo ... Eu não consigo mexer a minha ... **f** e·oo nowng kong·*see*·goo me·*sher* a *meeng*·nya ...

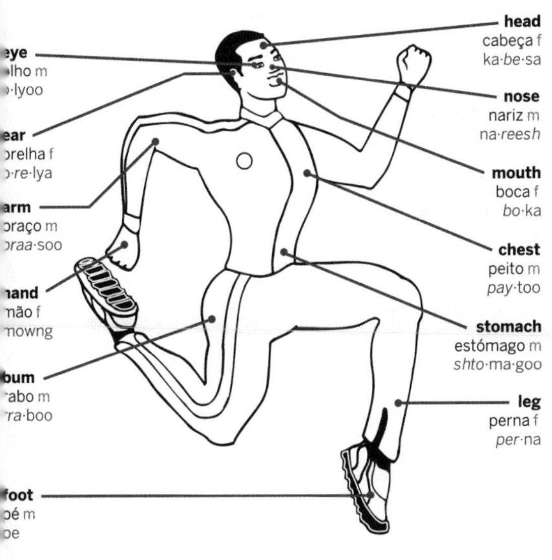

I have a cramp in my ...	Eu tenho uma cãibra no meu ... **m** *e·oo ta·nyoo oo·ma ka·eeng·bra noo me·oo ...* Eu tenho uma cãibra na minha ... **f** *e·oo ta·nyoo oo·ma ka·eeng·bra na meeng·nya ...*
My ... is swollen.	O meu ... está inchado. **m** oo *me*·oo ... shtaa eeng·*shaa*·doo A minha ... está inchada. **f** a *meeng*·nya ... shtaa eeng·*shaa*·da

Allergies

I have a skin allergy.	Eu tenho uma alergia da pele. *e*·oo *ta*·nyoo *oo*·ma a·ler·*zhee*·a da *pe*·le
I'm allergic to ...	Eu sou alérgico/alérgica a ... **m/f** *e*·oo soh a·*ler*·zhee·koo/ a·*ler*·zhee·ka a ...
He/She is allergic to ...	Ele/Ela é alérgico/alérgica a ... **m/f** *e*·le/*e*·la e a·*ler*·zhee·koo/ a·*ler*·zhee·ka a ...
anti-inflammatories	anti-inflamatórios **m pl** ang·tee·eeng·fla·ma·*to*·ryoosh
codeine	codeína **f** ko·de·*ee*·na
penicillin	penicilina **f** pe·nee·see·*lee*·na
sulphur-based drugs	medicamentos à base de enxofre **m pl** me·dee·ka·*meng*·toosh aa *baa*·ze de eng·*sho*·fre

For food-related allergies, see **special diets & allergies** (p192).

Pharmacist

I need something for (a headache).	Eu preciso de alguma coisa para (as dores de cabeça). *e·oo pre·see·zoo de aal·goo·ma koy·za pa·ra (ash do·resh de ka·be·sa)*
Do I need a prescription for (antihistamines)?	Necessito de uma receita para (antihistamínicos)? *ne·se·see·too de oo·ma rre·say·ta pa·ra (ang·tee·eesh·ta·mee·nee·koosh)*
I have a prescription.	Eu tenho uma receita. *e·oo ta·nyoo oo·ma rre·say·ta*
How many times a day?	Quantas vezes por dia? *kwang·tash ve·zesh poor dee·a*
Will it make me drowsy?	Vou ficar sonolento/sonolenta? m/f *voh fee·kaar soo·noo·leng·too/soo·noo·leng·ta*
This is my usual medicine.	Estes são os meus medicamentos habituais. *esh·tesh sowng oosh me·oosh me·dee·ka·meng·toosh a·bee·too·aish*

LISTEN FOR

Antes/Depois de comer.	*ang·tesh/de·poysh de koo·mer* Before/After food.
Já tomou isto alguma vez?	*zhaa to·moh eesh·too aal·goo·ma vezh* Have you taken this before?
Tem que levar o tratamento até ao fim.	*teng ke le·vaar oo tra·ta·meng·too a·te ow feeng* You must complete the course.

LISTEN FOR

Abra bem a boca.	*aa*·bra beng a *bo*·ka	Open wide.
Morda isto.	*mor*·da *eesh*·too	Bite down on this.
Bocheche.	boo·*she*·she	Rinse.

Dentist

I have a broken tooth.	Eu tenho um dente partido. e·oo *ta*·nyoo oong *deng*·te par·*tee*·doo
I have a cavity.	Eu tenho uma cárie. e·oo *ta*·nyoo *oo*·ma *kaa*·ree·e
I have a toothache.	Eu tenho uma dor de dentes. e·oo *ta*·nyoo oong *oo*·ma dor de *deng*·tesh
I need a filling.	Eu preciso de um chumbo. e·oo pre·*see*·zoo de oong *shoong*·boo
My dentures are broken.	A minha dentadura está partida. a *mee*·nya deng·ta·*doo*·ra shtaa par·*tee*·da
My gums hurt.	As minhas gengivas doem-me. aash *meeng*·nyash zheng·*zhee*·vash do·*eng*·me
I don't want it extracted.	Eu não quero extrair o dente. e·oo nowng *ke*·roo aysh·tra·*eer* oo *deng*·te
I need an anaesthetic.	Eu preciso de anestesia. e·oo pre·*see*·zoo de a·nesh·te·*zee*·a

Food

Eating Out

KEY PHRASES

Can you recommend a restaurant?	Pode-me recomendar um restaurante?	*po*·de·me rre·koo·meng·*daar* oong rresh·tow·*rang*·te
A table for two, please.	Uma mesa para dois, por favor.	*oo*·ma *me*·za *pa*·ra doysh poor fa·*vor*
I'd like the menu, please.	Queria um menu, por favor.	ke·*ree*·a oong me·*noo* poor fa·*vor*
I'd like a beer, please.	Eu queria uma cerveja, por favor.	*e*·oo ke·*ree*·a *oo*·ma ser·*ve*·zha poor fa·*vor*
Please bring the bill.	Pode-me trazer a conta.	*po*·de·me tra·*zer* a *kong*·ta

Basics

Breakfast is a quick affair in Portugal, usually consisting of a coffee with toast or a pastry. Lunch (usually taken around 1pm) is the main meal of the day, and generally includes meat or fish, vegetables, and rice or potatoes – plus wine, cheese, olives and bread. Dinner is generally lighter and is eaten around 8 or 9pm – even later on weekends.

breakfast	pequeno almoço **m** pe·*ke*·noo aal·*mo*·soo
lunch	almoço **m** aal·*mo*·soo
dinner	jantar **m** zhang·*taar*
snack	lanche **m** *lang*·she

eat v	comer koo·*mer*
drink v	beber be·*ber*
I'd like ...	Eu queria ... *e*·oo ke·*ree*·a ...
I'm starving!	Estou esfomeado/ esfomeada! **m/f** shtoh shfo·mee·*aa*·doo/ shfo·mee·*aa*·da

Finding a Place to Eat

Can you recommend a ...?	Pode-me recomendar ...? *po*·de·me rre·koo·meng·*daar* ...

bar	um bar	oong bar
beer house	uma cervejaria	*oo*·ma ser·ve·zha·*ree*·a
cafe	um café	oong ka·*fe*
grill restaurant	uma churrasqueira	*oo*·ma shoo·rraash·*kay*·ra
neighbourhood restaurant	uma tasca	*oo*·ma *taash*·ka
pastry shop	uma pastelaria	*oo*·ma pash·te·la·*ree*·a
restaurant	um restaurante	oong rresh·tow·*rang*·te
tavern	uma taberna	*oo*·ma ta·*ber*·na
tea house	uma casa de chá	*oo*·ma *kaa*·za de shaa

Where would you go for a celebration?	Onde é que iria para festejar? *ong*·de e ke ee·*ree*·a *pa*·ra fesh·te·*zhaar*
Where would you go for a cheap meal?	Onde é que iria para uma refeição barata? *ong*·de e ke ee·*ree*·a *pa*·ra *oo*·ma rre·fay·*sowng* ba·*raa*·ta
Where would you go for local specialities?	Onde é que iria para especialidades locais? *ong*·de e ke ee·*ree*·a *pa*·ra shpe·see·a·lee·*daa*·desh lo·*kaish*
I'd like to reserve a table for (five) people.	Eu queria reservar uma mesa para (cinco) pessoas. e·oo ke·*ree*·a rre·zer·*vaar* *oo*·ma *me*·za *pa*·ra (*seeng*·ko) pe·*so*·ash
I'd like to reserve a table for (8pm).	Eu queria reservar uma mesa para as (oito da noite). e·oo ke·*ree*·a rre·zer·*vaar* *oo*·ma *me*·za *pa*·ra ash (*oy*·too da *noy*·te)

CULTURE TIP

Bacalhau

It's famed as being in so many recipes that you could eat it a different way every day for a year. It's white, hard as a rock and it smells decidedly fishy ... Yes, it's *bacalhau* ba·ka·*lyow*, considered by many to be the Portuguese national food. The word is often translated as simply 'cod', but if that conjures up images involving five minutes with a frypan and a slice of lemon, you'll have to leave them behind – this is salted and dried fish, and needs serious soaking.

LISTEN FOR

Estamos fechados.	*shta*·moosh fe·*shaa*·doosh	We're closed.
Estamos cheios.	*shta*·moosh *shay*·oosh	We're full.
Um momento.	oong moo·*meng*·too	One moment.

Are you still serving food?	Ainda servem comida? a·*eeng*·da *ser*·veng koo·*mee*·da
How long is the wait?	Quanto tempo é que se tem de estar à espera? *kwang*·too *teng*·poo e ke se teng de shtaar aa *shpe*·ra

At the Restaurant

In Portugal restaurants usually have what is called *couvert* koo·*ver* – bread, butter, paté, olives and sometimes prosciutto at the tables. If you eat them you'll be charged a (normally small) fee.

I'd like a (non)smoking table, please.	Queria uma mesa de (não) fumador, por favor. ke·*ree*·a *oo*·ma *me*·za de (nowng) foo·ma·*dor* poor fa·*vor*
I'd like a table for (two), please.	Queria uma mesa para (dois), por favor. ke·*ree*·a *oo*·ma *me*·za *pa*·ra (doysh) poor fa·*vor*

For two, please.	Para dois, por favor.	*pa*·ra doysh poor fa·*vor*

LISTEN FOR

Onde é que se quer/ querem sentar? sg/pl	*ong*·de e ke se ker/ *ke*·reng seng·*taar* Where would you like to sit?
Já decidiram?	zha de·see·*dee*·rowng What can I get for you?
Gosta/Gostam de ...? sg/pl	*goosh*·ta/*goosh*·towng de ... Do you like ...?
Eu aconselho ...	*e*·oo a·kong·*sa*·lyoo ... I suggest the ...
Bem passado ou mal passado?	beng pa·*saa*·doo oh mal pa·*saa*·doo How would you like that cooked?
Aqui está!	a·*kee* shtaa Here you go!
Bom apetite.	bong a·pe·*tee*·te Enjoy your meal.

What would you recommend?	O que é que recomenda? oo ke e ke rre·koo·*meng*·da
What's in that dish?	Quais são os ingredientes daquele prato? kwaish sowng oosh eeng·gre·dee·*eng*·tesh da·*ke*·le *praa*·too
What's that called?	Como é que se chama aquilo? *ko*·moo e ke se *shaa*·ma a·*kee*·loo
I'll have that.	Eu quero aquilo. eu *ke*·roo a·*kee*·loo
Does it take long to prepare?	Demora muito tempo a preparar? de·*mo*·ra *mweeng*·too *teng*·poo a pre·pa·*raar*

Eating Out

Can I see the menu, please?

Posso ver o menu, por favor?

po·soo ver oo me·*noo* poor fa·*vor*

What would you recommend for ...?

O que você recomenda para ...?

oo ke vo·*se* rre·koo·*meng*·da *pa*·ra ...

the main meal
o prato principal
oo *praa*·too preeeng·see·*paal*

dessert
sobremesa
soo·bre·*me*·za

drinks
bebidas
be·*bee*·dash

Can you bring me some ..., please?

Pode-me trazer ...

po·de·me tra·*zer* ...

I'd like the bill, please.

Queria a conta, por favor.

ke·*ree*·a a *kong*·ta poor fa·*vor*

Can you recommend a good local wine?	Pode-me recomendar um bom vinho daqui da zona?	*po*·de·me rre·koo·meng·*daar* oong bong *vee*·nyoo da·*kee* daa *zo*·na
I'd like (a/the) ..., please.	Queria ..., por favor.	ke·*ree*·a ... poor fa·*vor*

children's menu	o menu das crianças	oo me·*noo* dash kree·*ang*·sash
drink list	a lista das bebidas	a *leesh*·ta dash be·*bee*·dash
local speciality	uma especialidade local	*oo*·ma shpe·see·a·lee·*daa*·de loo·*kaal*
menu (in English)	um menu (em inglês)	oong me·*noo* (eng eeng·*lesh*)
wine list	uma lista dos vinhos	*oo*·ma *leesh*·ta doosh *vee*·nyoosh

Menu, please.	O menu, por favor.	oong me·*noo* poor fa·*vor*

Requests

Please bring (a/the) ...	Pode-me trazer ...	*po*·de·me tra·*zer* ...

cutlery	os talheres	oosh ta·*lye*·resh
(wine)glass	um copo (de vinho)	oong *ko*·poo (de *vee*·nyoo)
napkin	o guardanapo	oo gwar·da·*naa*·poo
tablecloth	a toalha de mesa	a *twaa*·lya de *me*·za

I'd like it ...	Eu queria ...	e·oo ke·*ree*·a ...
I don't want it ...	Eu não quero ...	e·oo nowng *ke*·roo ...

boiled	cozido **m** cozida **f**	koo·*zee*·doo koo·*zee*·da
broiled/grilled	grelhado **m** grelhada **f**	gre·*lyaa*·doo gre·*lyaa*·da
(deep-)fried	frito **m** frita **f**	*free*·too *free*·ta
mashed	esmagado **m** esmagada **f**	shma·*gaa*·doo shma·*gaa*·da
medium	nem bem nem mal-passado/ mal-passada **m/f**	neng beng neng maal·pa·*saa*·doo/ maal·pa·*saa*·da
rare	mal-passado **m** mal-passada **f**	maal·pa·*saa*·doo maal·pa·*saa*·da
reheated	reaquecido **m** reaquecida **f**	rre·a·ke·*see*·doo rre·a·ke·*see*·da
steamed	cozido/ cozida a vapor **m/f**	koo·*zee*·doo/ koo·*zee*·da a va·*por*
well-done	bem-passado **m** bem-passada **f**	beng·pa·*saa*·doo beng·pa·*saa*·da
with the dressing on the side	o molho da salada à parte	oo *mo*·lyoo da sa·*laa*·da aa *paar*·te
without ...	sem ...	seng ...

I'd like it with/without ...	Eu queria com/sem ... *e·oo ke·ree·a kong/seng ...*

cheese	queijo	*kay*·zhoo
chilli	píri-píri	*pee*·ree·*pee*·ree
garlic	alho	*aa*·lyoo
nuts	oleaginosas	o·lee·a·zhee·*no*·zash
pepper	pimenta	pee·*meng*·ta
salt	sal	saal
tomato sauce	molho de tomate	*mo*·lyoo de too·*maa*·te

For other specific meal requests, see **vegetarian & special meals** (p192).

Compliments & Complaints

I love this dish.	Eu adoro este prato. e·oo a·*do*·roo *esh*·te *praa*·too
I love the local cuisine.	Eu adoro a comida local. e·oo a·*do*·roo a koo·*mee*·da loo·*kaal*
That was delicious!	Isto estava delicioso! *eesh*·too *shtaa*·va de·lee·see·*o*·zoo
This is hitting the spot.	Está a saber-me mesmo bem. shtaa a sa·*ber*·me *mesh*·moo beng
My compliments to the chef.	Os meus parabéns ao cozinheiro chefe. oosh *me*·oosh pa·ra·*bengzh* ow koo·zee·*nyay*·roo *she*·fe
I'm full.	Estou cheio/cheia. **m/f** shtoh *shay*·oo/*shay*·a

LOOK FOR

Petiscos	pe·*teesh*·koosh	Appetisers
Sopas	*so*·pash	Soups
Entradas	eng·*traa*·dash	Entrées
Saladas	sa·*laa*·dash	Salads
Pratos Principais	*praa*·toosh preeng·see·*paish*	Main Courses
Extras	*aysh*·trash	Side Dishes
Sobremesa	soo·bre·*me*·za	Desserts
Bebidas	be·*bee*·dash	Drinks
Aperitivos	a·pe·ree·*tee*·voosh	Apéritifs
Espirituosos	shpee·ree·too·*o*·zoosh	Spirits
Cerveja	ser·*ve*·zha	Beers
Refrigerantes	rre·free·zhee·*rang*·tesh	Soft Drinks
Vinhos Espumantes	*vee*·nyoosh shpoo·*mang*·tesh	Sparkling Wines
Vinhos Brancos	*vee*·nyoosh *brang*·koosh	White Wines
Vinhos Tintos	*vee*·nyoosh *teeng*·toosh	Red Wines
Digestivos	dee·zhesh·*tee*·voosh	Digestifs

See also the **menu decoder** (p194).

This is ... Isto está ... *eesh*·too shtaa ...

burnt	queimado	kay·*maa*·doo
cold	frio	*free*·oo
(too) spicy	(demasiado) picante	(de·ma·zee·*aa*·doo) pee·*kang*·te
stale	duro	*doo*·roo
superb	magnífico	maag·*nee*·fee·koo

Paying the Bill

Please bring the bill.	Pode-me trazer a conta. *po*·de·me tra·*zer* a *kong*·ta
Bill, please.	A conta, por favor. a *kong*·ta poor fa·*vor*
There's a mistake in the bill.	Há um erro na conta. aa oong *e*·rroo na *kong*·ta

Nonalcoholic Drinks

coffee	café **m** ka·*fe*
orange juice	sumo de laranja natural **m** *soo*·moo de la·*rang*·zha na·too·*raal*
soft drink	refrigerante **m** rre·free·zhe·*rang*·te

sparkling mineral water	água mineral com gás **f** *aa*·gwa mee·ne·*raal* kong gaash
still mineral water	água mineral sem gás **f** *aa*·gwa mee·ne·*raal* seng gaash

CULTURE TIP

Coffee

The Portuguese make pretty decent coffee. As in Italy, if you just order a *café* ka·*fe* what you'll get is an espresso or short black – strong black coffee in a demitasse (small cup). The variations on the basic espresso are numerous, but the main terms are listed below. Just beware, if you ask for decaffeinated coffee (*café sem cafeína* ka·*fe* seng ka·fe·*ee*·na), a sachet of instant coffee will usually arrive with a pot of hot water for you to make yourself.

um café/ cimbalino/ expresso	oong ka·*fe*/ seeng·ba·*lee*·noo/ *shpre*·soo	an espresso
um café com leite	oong ka·*fe* kong *lay*·te	half espresso, half milk in a large cup (caffe latte)
um café duplo	oong *ka*·fe *doo*·ploo	a double espresso
um carioca	oong ka·ree·o·ka	a weak espresso
um galão	oong ga·*lowng*	an espresso with hot milk served in a tall glass
um garoto	oong ga·*ro*·too	an espresso with a dash of milk
uma bica	*oo*·ma *bee*·ka	an espresso
uma bica dupla	*oo*·ma *bee*·ka *doo*·pla	a double espresso

tea	chá **m** shaa
(hot) water	água (quente) **f** *aa*·gwa (*keng*·te)
with (milk)	com (leite) kong (*lay*·te)
without (sugar)	sem (açúcar) seng (a·*soo*·kar)

Alcoholic Drinks

beer	cerveja **f** ser·*ve*·zha
a shot of ...	um copinho de ... oong koo·*pee*·nyoo de ...

firewater	água-ardente	*aa*·gwaar·*deng*·te
gin	gin	zheeng
rum	rum	rroong
whisky	uísque	oo·*eesh*·kee

a bottle of ... wine	uma garrafa de vinho ... *oo*·ma ga·*rraa*·fa de *vee*·nyoo ...
a glass of ... wine	um copo de vinho ... oong *ko*·poo de *vee*·nyoo ...

dessert	de sobremesa	de soo·bre·*me*·za
red	tinto	*teeng*·too
rosé	rosé	rro·*ze*
sparkling	espumante	shpoo·*mang*·te
white	branco	*brang*·koo
young (green)	verde	*ver*·de

LISTEN FOR

à pressão	aa pre·*sowng*	draft
um fino	oong *fee*·noo	small (20cl) draft beer (in the centre and north of Portugal)
um jarro	oong *zhaa*·roo	a jug of beer
um quartilho	oong kwar·*tee*·lyoo	a pint of beer
uma caneca	*oo*·ma ka·*ne*·ka	larger (33cl) draft beer
uma garrafa de cerveja	*oo*·ma ga·*rraa*·fa de ser·*ve*·zha	large bottle of beer
uma imperial	*oo*·ma eeng·pree·*aal*	small (20cl) draft beer (in the south, including Lisbon)
uma mini	*oo*·ma *mee*·nee	small bottle of beer

For additional items, see the **menu decoder** (p194), and the **dictionary**.

In the Bar

Excuse me!	Desculpe! desh·*kool*·pe
I'm next.	Eu sou a seguir. e·oo soh a se·*geer*
Q **What would you like?**	O que é que quer? oo ke e ke ker
A **I'll have (a beer).**	Eu queria (uma cerveja). e·oo ke·*ree*·a (*oo*·na ser·*ve*·zha)

LISTEN FOR

O que é que vão comer/ tomar?	oo ke e ke vowng koo·*mer*/ too·*maar* What are you having to eat/ drink?
Eu acho que já bebeu demais.	e·oo *aa*·shoo ke zhaa be·*be*·oo de·*maish* I think you've had enough.
Últimos pedidos.	*ool*·tee·moosh pe·*dee*·doosh Last orders.

Same again, please.	O mesmo, por favor. oo *mezh*·moo poor fa·*vor*
No ice, thanks.	Sem gelo, por favor. seng *zhe*·loo poor fa·*vor*
I'll buy you a drink.	Eu pago-lhe uma bebida. e·oo *paa*·goo·lye *oo*·ma be·*bee*·da
I don't drink alcohol.	Eu não bebo álcool. e·oo nowng *be*·boo *aal*·koo·ol
It's my round.	É a minha rodada. e a *mee*·nya rroo·*daa*·da
Do you serve meals here?	Vocês servem refeições aqui? vo·*sesh ser*·veng rre·fay·*soyngsh* a·*kee*
Are these complimentary?	Isto é gratuito? *eesh*·too e gra·*twee*·too

Drinking Up

Cheers!	À nossa! aa *no*·sa

I feel fantastic!	Estou a sentir-me mesmo bem. shtoh a seng·*teer*·me *mesh*·moo beng
I think I've had one too many.	Acho que bebi demais. *aa*·shoo ke be·*bee* de·*maish*
I'm feeling drunk.	Estou a sentir-me bêbado/bêbada. **m/f** shtoh a seng·*teer*·me *be*·ba·doo/*be*·ba·da
I feel ill.	Sinto-me mal. *seeng*·too·me maal
Where's the toilet?	Onde é a casa de banho? *ong*·de e a *kaa*·za de *ba*·nyoo
I'm tired, I'd better go home.	Estou cansado/cansada, é melhor ir para casa. **m/f** shtoh kang·*saa*·doo/kang·*saa*·da e me·*lyoor* eer *pa*·ra *kaa*·za
Can you call a taxi for me?	Pode chamar-me um táxi? *po*·de sha·*maar*·me oong *taak*·see
I don't think you should drive.	Eu acho que não devia conduzir. e·oo *aa*·shoo ke nowng de·*vee*·a kong·doo·*zeer*

Self-Catering

KEY PHRASES

What's the local speciality?	Qual é a especialidade local?	kwaal e a shpe·see·a·lee·*daa*·de loo·*kaal*
Where can I find the ... section?	Onde é que é a secção de ...?	*ong*·de e ke e a sek·*sowng* de ...
I'd like some ...	Eu queria uns/umas ... **m/f**	e·oo ke·*ree*·a oongsh/*oo*·mash ...

Buying Food

What's the local speciality?	Qual é a especialidade local? kwaal e a shpe·see·a·lee·*daa*·de loo·*kaal*
What's that?	O que é aquilo? oo ke e a·*kee*·loo
Do you have other kinds?	Há de outros tipos? aa de *oh*·troosh *tee*·poosh
Can I taste it?	Posso provar? *po*·soo proo·*vaar*
Can I have a bag, please?	Pode-me dar um saco, por favor? *po*·de·me daar oong *saa*·koo poor fa·*vor*
How much is (a kilo of cheese)?	Quanto é (um quilo de queijo)? *kwang*·too e (oong *kee*·loo de *kay*·zhoo)

I'd like ...	Eu queria ... *e*·oo ke·*ree*·a ...

(200) grams	(duzentos) gramas	(doo·*zeng*·toosh) *graa*·mash
half a dozen	meia dúzia	*may*·a *doo*·zya
a dozen	uma dúzia	*oo*·ma *doo*·zya
half a kilo	meio quilo	*may*·oo *kee*·loo
a kilo	um quilo	oong *kee*·loo
(two) kilos	(dois) quilos	(doysh) *kee*·loosh
a bottle	uma garrafa	*oo*·ma ga·*rraa*·fa
a jar	um frasco	oong *fraash*·koo
a packet	um pacote	oong pa·*ko*·te
a piece	uma peça	*oo*·ma *pe*·sa
(three) pieces	(três) peças	(tresh) *pe*·sash
a slice	uma fatia	*oo*·ma fa·*tee*·a
(six) slices	(seis) fatias	(saysh) fa·*tee*·ash
a tin (can)	uma lata	*oo*·ma *laa*·ta
some	uns/umas **m/f**	oongsh/*oo*·mash
that one	aquele **m** aquela **f**	a·*ke*·le a·*ke*·la
this one	este/esta **m/f**	*esh*·te/*esh*·ta

Less.	Menos. *me*·noosh
A bit more.	Um pouco mais. oong *poh*·koo maish
Enough.	Chega. *she*·ga
Do you have anything cheaper?	Há alguma coisa mais barata? aa aal·*goo*·ma *koy*·za maish ba·*raa*·ta

Where can I find the ... section?	Onde é que é ...?	*ong*·de e ke e ...
dairy	a secção de produtos lácteos	a sek·*sowng* de proo·*doo*·toosh *laak*·tee·oosh
fish	a peixaria	a pay·sha·*ree*·a
frozen goods	os congelados	oosh kong·zhe·*laa*·doosh
fruit and vegetable	a fruta e vegetais	a *froo*·ta e ve·zhe·*taish*
meat	a carne	a *kaar*·ne

Cooking

Could I please borrow a ...?	Podia-me emprestar ...?	poo·*dee*·a·me eng·presh·*taar* ...
I need a ...	Preciso de uma ...	pre·*see*·zoo de *oo*·ma ...
chopping board	tábua para cortar	*taa*·boo·a *pa*·ra kor·*taar*
frying pan	frigideira	free·gee·*day*·ra
knife	faca	*faa*·ka
saucepan	caçarola	ka·sa·*ro*·la
cooked	cozinhado/cozinhada **m/f**	koo·zee·*nyaa*·doo/koo·zee·*nyaa*·da
cured	curado/curada **m/f**	koo·*raa*·doo/koo·*raa*·da
dried	seco/seca **m/f**	*se*·koo/*se*·ka

Há de outros tipos?
aa de *oh*·troosh *tee*·poosh
Do you have other kinds?

resh	fresco/fresca **m/f** *fresh*·koo/*fresh*·kaa
rozen	congelado/ congelada **m/f** kong·zhe·*laa*·doo/ kong·zhe·*laa*·da
aw	cru/crua **m/f** kroo/*kroo*·a
moked	fumado/fumada **m/f** foo·*maa*·doo/foo·*maa*·da

or more cooking implements, see the **dictionary**.

Vegetarian & Special Meals

KEY PHRASES

Do you have vegetarian food?	Tem comida vegetariana?	teng koo·*mee*·da ve·zhe·ta·ree·*a*·na
Could you prepare a meal without ...?	Pode preparar sem ...?	*po*·de pre·pa·*raar* seng ...
I'm allergic to ...	Eu sou alérgico/ alérgica a ... **m/f**	e·oo soh a·*ler*·zhee·koo/ a·*ler*·zhee·ka a ...

Special Diets & Allergies

Is there a (vegetarian) restaurant near here?	Há algum restaurante (vegetariana) perto daqui? *aa aal·goong rresh·tow·rang·t (ve·zhe·ta·ree·aa·na) per·too da·kee*
I'm on a special diet.	Eu tenho uma dieta especial. *e·oo ta·nyoo oo·ma dee·e·ta shpe·see·aal*
I don't eat ...	Eu não como ... *e·oo nowng ko·moo ...*
I'm a vegan.	Eu sou vegan. *e·oo soh vee·gang*
I'm a vegetarian.	Eu sou vegetariano/ vegetariana. **m/f** *e·oo soh ve·zhe·ta·ree·a·noo ve·zhe·ta·ree·a·na*

I'm allergic to ...	Eu sou alérgico/ alérgica a ... **m/f** e·oo soh a·*ler*·zhee·koo/ a·*ler*·zhee·ka a ...

dairy produce	produtos lácteos	pro·*doo*·toosh *laak*·tee·oosh
eggs	ovos	*o*·voosh
honey	mel	mel
nuts	oleaginosas	o·lee·a·zhee·*no*·zash
peanuts	amendoins	a·meng·doo·*eengsh*
seafood	marisco	ma·*reesh*·koo
shellfish	crustáceos	kroosh·*taa*·se·oosh

Ordering Food

Do you have halal/ kosher food?	Tem comida halal/kosher? teng koo·*mee*·da a·*laal/ko*·sher
Do you have vegetarian food?	Tem comida vegetariana? teng koo·*mee*·da ve·zhe·ta·ree·*a*·na
Is it cooked with ...?	Leva ...? *le*·va ...
Could you prepare a meal without ...?	Pode preparar sem ...? *po*·de pre·pa·*raar* seng ...

butter	manteiga	mang·*tay*·ga
fish	peixe	*pay*·she
(red) meat	carne (vermelha)	*kaar*·ne (ver·*me*·lya)
oil	óleo	*o*·lee·oo
pork	carne de porco	*kaar*·ne de *por*·koo
poultry	aves	*aa*·vesh

A

Menu DECODER

livro de culinária

This miniguide to Portuguese cuisine is designed to help you navigate menus and get the most out of your gastronomic experience in Portugal. Portuguese nouns, and adjectives affected b gender, have their gender indicated by ⓜ and/or ⓕ. If it's a plural noun, you'll also see pl.

~ A ~

abacate ⓜ a·ba·*kaa*·te avocado
abóbora ⓕ a·*bo*·boo·ra pumpkin
abobrinha ⓕ a·boo·*bree*·nya zucchini
açafrão ⓜ a·sa·*frowng* saffron
acepipes ⓜ pl a·se·*pee*·pesh delicacies • hors d'oeuvres • titbits
achigã ⓜ a·shee·*gang* black bass
ácido/ácida ⓜ/ⓕ *aa*·see·doo/ *aa*·see·da sour
açorda ⓕ a·*sor*·da bread-based thick soup, often flavoured with garlic, coriander & olive oil
— de bacalhau de ba·ka·*lyow* **açorda** with shredded salt cod
— de gambas de *gang*·bash **açorda** containing prawns
— de marisco de ma·*reesh*·koo **açorda** with prawns, mussels & cockles
— de sável de *saa*·vel spicy **açorda** flavoured with shad (fish) broth
açúcar ⓜ a·*soo*·kar sugar
— amarelo a·ma·*re*·loo brown sugar
— granulado gra·noo·*laa*·doo granulated or refined sugar
agriões ⓜ pl a·gree·*oyngsh* watercress
água-ardente ⓕ *aa*·gwaar·*deng*·te brandy-like spirit
— de cana de *ka*·na sugar-cane spir
— de figo de *fee*·goo fig brandy
— de medronho de me·*dro*·nyoo brandy made from arbutus berry
— velha *ve*·lya fine brandy
aipo ⓜ *ai*·poo celery
alcachofra ⓕ aal·ka·*sho*·fra artichok
alecrim ⓜ a·le·*kreeng* rosemary
Alentejana, à a·leng·te·*zha*·na, aa Alentejo style – dish made with garlic, olive oil, paprika, usually pork & small cockles
alface ⓕ aal·*faa*·se lettuce
alheiras ⓕ pl a·*lyay*·rash sausage c bread, garlic, chilli & meats
alho ⓜ *aa*·lyoo garlic
— francês frang·*sesh* leek
— porro *po*·rroo leek
almôndegas ⓕ pl aal·*mong*·de·gas beef or pork meatballs
alperce ⓜ aal·*per*·se apricot
amanteigado ⓜ a·mang·tay·*gaa*·dc 'buttery' – describes creamy cheese

MENU DECODER

marguinha ⓕ a·mar·*gee*·nya
ımond-flavoured liqueur
mêijoas ⓕ pl a·may·*zhoo*·ash
ockles
- à Bulhão Pato aa boo·*lyowng*
aa·too broth of small cockles in
oriander, white wine & garlic sauce
- ao natural ow na·too·*raal*
teamed cockles
- na cataplana na ka·ta·*pla*·na
mall cockles cooked with onion,
hopped **chouriço**, ham and red &
reen capsicum
meixa ⓕ a·*may*·sha plum
meixas de Elvas ⓕ pl a·*may*·shash
e *el*·vash 'plums of Elvas' – sweet
essert plums preserved in sugar
meixa seca ⓕ a·*may*·sha *se*·ka
rune
mêndoa ⓕ a·*meng*·doo·a almond
mendoim ⓜ a·meng·doo·*eeng*
eanut
mora ⓕ a·*mo*·ra blackberry
nanás ⓜ a·na·*naash* pineapple
nho ⓜ *a*·nyoo lamb (see also
orrego)
nis ⓜ a·*neesh* aniseed
nona ⓕ a·*no*·na custard apple
reias ⓕ pl a·*ray*·ash sweet biscuit
avoured with lemon
renque ⓜ a·*reng*·ke herring
rjamolho ⓜ ar·zha·*mo*·lyoo Algarve
ame for **gaspacho**
rrepiadas ⓕ pl a·rre·pee·*aa*·dash
iced almonds, held together with
ıeringue
rroz ⓜ a·*rrosh* rice
- árabe *aa*·ra·be rice with raisins,
uts & sometimes chopped dried fruit
- à valenciana aa va·leng·see·*a*·na
saffron-flavoured rice dish similar
paella
- cozido koo·*zee*·doo boiled rice
- de bacalhau de ba·ka·*lyow*
omato-flavoured rice with shredded
alt cod

— de berbigão de ber·bee·*gowng*
rice with cockles, seasoned with
coriander
— de bucho de *boo*·shoo creamy
rice cooked in pork broth
— de cabidela de ka·bee·*de*·la
chicken & rice casserole with fresh
chicken blood
— de ervilhas de er·*vee*·lyash rice
with peas
— de espigos de *shpee*·goosh rice
with cabbage
— de feijão de fay·*zhowng* rice with
red beans
— de forno de *for*·noo baked rice
with onion & prosciutto or **salpicão**
— de grelos de *gre*·loosh rice with
cabbage
— de lampreia de lang·*pray*·a
lamprey & rice stew with onion,
parsley, white wine, **chouriço** &
lamprey blood
— de langueirão de lang·gay·*rowng*
rice with razor clams & onion,
seasoned with garlic & parsley
— de lapas de *laa*·pash rice with
limpets
— de marisco de ma·*reesh*·koo
casserole of seafood & rice in tomato
sauce
— de pato de *paa*·too baked or
braised casserole of rice with
shredded duck & sausage slices
— de polvo de *pol*·voo chunks of
octopus & onion in a tomato-rice stew
— de sarrabulho de sa·rra·*boo*·lyoo
stew with rice, pork, beef, chicken &
sauce made of onion & pig's blood
— de tamboril de tang·boo·*reel*
tomato-rice stew with frog-fish chunks
— de tomate de too·*maa*·te rice
cooked in a tomato broth, often
served with fried fish
— doce *do*·se creamy rice sprinkled
with cinnamon
— integral eeng·te·*graal* brown rice

B

arrufadas de Coimbra ⓕ pl a·rroo·*faa*·dash de *koyng*·bra dome-shaped, cinnamon-flavoured bread
asa ⓕ *aa*·za wing
— de frango de *frang*·goo chicken wing
— de perú de pe·*roo* turkey wing
assado/assada ⓜ/ⓕ a·*saa*·doo/a·*saa*·da roast
assado de peixe ⓜ a·*saa*·doo de *pay*·she mixture of different roasted or baked fish
atum ⓜ a·*toong* tuna
— de escabeche de shka·*be*·she raw tuna 'pickled' or 'cooked' in vinegar
avelã ⓕ a·ve·*lang* hazelnut
aves ⓕ pl *aa*·vesh poultry
avestruz ⓜ&ⓕ a·vesh·*troosh* ostrich
azeite ⓜ a·*zay*·te olive oil
azeitonas ⓕ pl a·zay·*to*·nash olives
— pretas *pre*·tash black olives
— recheadas rre·shee·*aa*·dash stuffed olives
— sem caroço seng ka·*ro*·soo pitted olives
— verdes *ver*·desh green olives
azevias ⓕ pl a·ze·*vee*·ash fried puff pastry with a sweet chickpea filling

~ B ~

baba de camelo ⓕ *baa*·ba de ka·*me*·loo 'camel drool' – caramel mousse made with condensed milk
bacalhau ⓜ ba·ka·*lyow* dried salt cod
— à Assis aa a·*sees* crumbled salt cod cooked in olive oil with vegetables, mixed with eggs & parsley, then baked
— à Brás aa braas flaked cod fried with egg, potato & olives
— à cozinha velha aa koo·*zee*·nya *ve*·lya chopped salt cod, onions & carrots fried in olive oil & cooked in a white sauce, covered with breadcrumbs, then baked
— à Gomes de Sá aa *go*·mes de saa flaked salt cod soaked in milk & browned in the oven with vegetables & eggs
— albardado aal·bar·*daa*·doo salt cod fried in a doughy batter
— assado com batatas a murro a·*saa*·doo kong ba·*taa*·tash a *moo*·rroo baked or roasted salt cod with smashed baked potatoes, garlic & olive oil
— assado com pão de centeio a·*saa*·doo kong powng de seng·*tay*·oo baked salt cod steak sprinkled with garlic, olive oil & crumbled rye bread
— com todos kong *to*·doosh boiled salt cod served with boiled egg & vegetables
— cozido koo·*zee*·doo boiled salt cod
— cru desfiado kroo desh·fee·*aa*·doo shredded raw salt cod in an olive oil & vinegar dressing
— desfiado desh·fee·*aa*·doo fine strips of raw salt cod served with chopped onion & garlic
— guisado gee·*zaa*·doo stewed salt cod steaks with olive oil, tomatoes, onion, potatoes, butter, herbs & spices
— no borralho noo boo·*rraa*·lyoo salt cod steak in cabbage leaves & bacon cooked in burning embers
— no forno noo *for*·noo baked salt cod, often smothered in an onion & olive oil sauce
— roupa-velha rroh·pa·*ve*·lya mixture of cabbage, salt cod & potatoes, sautéed in olive oil & garlic
bagaço ⓜ ba·*gaa*·soo **água-ardente** often drunk with an espresso coffee
banha ⓕ *baa*·nya lard
barriga-de-freira ⓕ ba·*rree*·ga·de·*fray*·ra sponge cake or bread covered in a sugary syrup with eggs & a hint of lemon
barrinhas de pescada ⓕ pl ba·*rree*·nyash de pesh·*kaa*·da fish sticks

atata doce ⓕ ba·*taa*·ta *do*·se weet potato
atatas ⓕ pl ba·*taa*·tash potatoes
– a murro *a moo*·rroo baked otatoes with the skin on, smashed & easoned with olive oil & garlic
– cozidas koo·*zee*·dash boiled otatoes
– fritas *free*·tash potato chips/crisps
atido ⓜ ba·*tee*·doo milk/fruit shake
aunilha ⓕ bow·*nee*·lya vanilla
ebida ⓕ be·*bee*·da beverage
– (não) alcoólica (nowng) al·koo·o·lee·ka (non)alcoholic drink
– espirituosa shpee·ree·too·o·za pirit
– fria *free*·a cold beverage
– quente *keng*·te hot beverage
erbigão ⓜ ber·bee·*gowng* cockle
eringela ⓕ be·reeng·*zhe*·la ubergine • eggplant
esugo ⓜ be·*zoo*·goo sea bream
eterraba ⓕ be·te·*rraa*·ba beetroot
ica ⓕ *bee*·ka espresso coffee
– cheia *shay*·a espresso topped with ot water
– com uma pinga kong *oo*·ma *eeng*·ga espresso topped with **gua-ardente** (drunk as a digestive)
ifana no pão ⓕ bee·*fa*·na noo owng thin pork steak sandwich
ifana no prato ⓕ bee·*fa*·na noo *raa*·too thin pork steak
ife ⓜ *bee*·fe fillet • steak of beef, ther meats, poultry or fish
– à café aa ka·*fe* thick rump steak erved with sauce of milk, lemon uice & mustard
– à casa aa *kaa*·za thin, pan-fried teak with a fried egg on top
– à cerveja aa ser·*ve*·zha steak with eer-based, buttery sauce
– alto *aal*·too thick steak
– à Marrare aa ma·*rraa*·re thick rump teak served with cream sauce & epper
— à pimenta aa pee·*meng*·ta steak with whole peppercorns
— bem passado beng pa·*saa*·doo well-done steak
— com ovo a cavalo kong *o*·voo a ka·*vaa*·loo fried steak marinated with fresh garlic, served with a fried egg on top
— da alcatra da aal·*kaa*·tra rump steak
— de atum de a·*toong* tuna steak
— do vazio doo va·*zee*·oo sirloin steak
— mal passado maal pa·*saa*·doo rare steak
bifinho ⓜ bee·*fee*·nyoo thin, boneless slices of meat
biscoitos ⓜ pl beesh·*koy*·toosh biscuits • cookies
— de Alcanena de aal·ka·*ne*·na light, airy biscuit made with olive oil
— de azeite de a·*zay*·te light, airy biscuit made with olive oil
bitoque ⓜ bee·*to*·ke small steak or fillet usually served with a fried egg on top
bola ⓕ *bo*·la breadroll
— de Berlim com/sem creme de ber·*leeng* kong/seng *kre*·me plain doughnut with/without custard filling
— de carne de *kaar*·ne baked meat pie with bread dough pastry
— de presunto de pre·*zoong*·too **bola de carne** with a layer of prosciutto
— de sardinhas de sar·*dee*·nyash **bola** with a layer of sardines
bolachas ⓕ pl boo·*laa*·shash biscuits • cookies • crackers
bolachos ⓜ pl boo·*laa*·shoosh pig's blood made into a dumpling, served with the fatty cooking juices of **rojões**
boleima ⓕ boo·*lay*·ma small cakes made of bread dough filled with apple slices or chopped walnuts

bolinhos ⓜ pl boo·*lee*·nyoosh biscuits
— de amêndoa de a·*meng*·doo·a almond marzipan moulded into many shapes: animals, fruit, vegetables
— de Jerimu de zhe·ree·*moo* pumpkin cakes flavoured with cinnamon
— de pinhão de pee·*nyowng* pine nut cakes
bolo ⓜ *bo*·loo pastry • sweet cake
— de arroz de a·*rrosh* cake made with rice & wheat flour topped with sugar
— de bolacha de boo·*laa*·sha biscuits layered with sweetened butter-cream frosting to form a cake
— de caco de *kaa*·koo griddle bread (bread toasted on an iron sheet on the stove or over coals) served hot with garlic butter, sometimes cooked with a spicy **chouriço** inside
— de coco de *ko*·koo coconut custard-filled pastry tart • coconut macaroon
— de Dom Rodrigo de dong rroo·*dree*·goo candy-like, soft confection made of real eggs, **ovos moles** & ground almonds
— de laranja de la·*rang*·zha orange cake
— de mel de mel rich molasses & spice cake with candied fruit & almonds
— de noz de nosh walnut cake
— de sertã de ser·*tang* corn biscuits cooked in a frying-pan
— do caco doo *kaa*·koo flat bread-rolls baked on a stone or cement slab
— lêvedo *le*·ve·doo light scone cooked in a frying-pan
— real rree·*aal* dense cake made with lots of eggs, grated almonds, pumpkin jam, cinnamon & lemon
— rei rray Christmas bread in the shape of a ring, studded with walnuts & pine nuts, with a gift and a broad bean inside
bonito ⓜ boo·*nee*·too bonito (fish)
borrachões ⓜ pl boo·rra·*shoyngsh* fried ring-shaped biscuits flavoured with brandy or white wine & cinnamon
borrachos ⓜ pl boo·*rraa*·shoosh breadcrumb fritters in a syrup of white **vinho verde**, lemon & cinnamon
borrego ⓜ boo·*rre*·goo lamb
— assado a·*saa*·doo roast lamb
broa ⓕ *bro*·a sweet potato & almond cakes
— de milho de *mee*·lyoo corn bread
— serrana se·*rra*·na highland bread (corn or rye bread)
broas de mel ⓕ pl *bro*·ash de mel soft biscuit made of honey & flour
bróculos ⓜ pl *bro*·koo·loosh broccoli
broínhas (de Natal) ⓕ pl bro·*eeng*·nyash (de na·*taal*) muffin-like pastry with raisins, pine nuts & walnuts
bucho de porco ⓜ *boo*·shoo de *por*·koo pig stomach
bucho recheado ⓜ *boo*·shoo rre·shee·*aa*·doo pig's belly stuffed with pork, bread or rice & cloves or cumin – served sliced
burras ⓕ pl *boo*·rrash roast pig cheeks

~ C ~

cabeça de xara ⓕ ka·*be*·sa de *shaa*·ra pig's head cooked with garlic, herbs & white wine, served sliced
de cabidela de ka·bee·*de*·la any dish made with blood
cabrito ⓜ ka·*bree*·too kid (goat)
caça ⓕ *kaa*·sa game
cacau ⓜ ka·*kow* cocoa
cacholeira ⓕ ka·shoo·*lay*·ra pork liver sausage
café ⓜ ka·*fe* coffee • espresso coffee
— em grão eng growng coffee beans
— instantâneo eeng·shtang·*taa*·nee·oo instant coffee
— moído moo·*ee*·doo ground coffee

— **torrado** too·*rraa*·doo roast coffee
cajú ⓜ ka·*zhoo* cashew
calda (de açúcar) ⓕ *kaal*·da (de a·soo·kar) syrup
caldeirada ⓕ kaal·day·*raa*·da soup-like stew, usually with fish
caldo ⓜ *kaal*·doo broth • soup • stock
camarão ⓜ ka·ma·*rowng* shrimp
canela ⓕ ka·*ne*·la cinnamon
canja/caldo de galinha ⓕ *kaang*·zha/*kaal*·doo de ga·*lee*·nya chicken broth
canja/sopa de conquilhas ⓕ *kaang*·zha/*so*·pa de kong·*kee*·lyash cockle soup
caracóis ⓜ pl ka·ra·*koysh* snails
caracol ⓜ ka·ra·*kol* similar to a Danish pastry but with raisins or candied fruit
caril ⓜ ka·*reel* curry (powder)
carne ⓕ *kaar*·ne meat
— **assada** a·*saa*·da roast meat
— **de cavalo** de ka·*vaa*·loo horse meat
— **de porco** de *por*·koo pork
— **de porco à Portuguesa** de *por*·koo aa poor·too·*ge*·za pork Alentejo-style without baby cockles
— **de vaca** de *vaa*·ka beef
— **do alguidar** doo aal·gee·*daar* chunks of cooked pork preserved in pork lard, served as an appetiser
— **picada/passada** pee·*kaa*·da/pa·*saa*·da ground meat (mince)
carneiro ⓜ kar·*nay*·roo lamb • mutton
carnes frias ⓕ pl *kaar*·nesh *free*·ash cold meats
castanhas ⓕ pl kash·*taa*·nyash chestnuts
cavacas ⓕ pl ka·*vaa*·kash sweet biscuit with white sugar icing
cavalas ⓕ pl ka·*vaa*·lash mackerel
cebola ⓕ se·*bo*·la onion
cenoura ⓕ se·*noh*·ra carrot
cereja ⓕ se·*re*·zha cherry
cerveja ⓕ ser·*ve*·zha beer
— **à pressão** aa pre·*sowng* beer on tap
— **loura** *loh*·ra 'blonde beer' – regular beer, as opposed to stout
— **preta** *pre*·ta dark beer • stout
chá ⓜ shaa tea
— **de ervas** de *er*·vash herbal tea
— **de limão** de lee·*mowng* glass or cup of boiling water with lemon rind
champanhe ⓜ shang·*pa*·nye champagne
chanfana ⓕ shang·*fa*·na hearty stew with goat or mutton in heavy red wine sauce
charros alimados ⓜ pl *shaa*·rroosh a·lee·*maa*·doosh skinned mackerel in olive oil & vinegar (or lemon) dressing, served with sliced onion, garlic & parsley
chila ⓕ *shee*·la spaghetti squash
chispe com feijão branco ⓜ *sheesh*·pe kong fay·*zhowng* *brang*·koo trotters with white beans, **chouriço**, pig's ear, kale & potatoes
chouriço ⓜ shoh·*ree*·soo garlicky pork sausage flavoured with red pepper paste
— **assado** a·*saa*·doo grilled sausage
— **de sangue** de *sang*·ge blood sausage
churrasco ⓜ shoo·*rraash*·koo barbecued • grilled on a spit or skewer
cidra ⓕ *see*·dra cider
coco ⓜ *ko*·koo coconut
codorniz ⓕ koo·door·*nees* quail
coelho ⓜ koo·e·lyoo rabbit
— **à caçador** aa ka·sa·*dor* rabbit stewed with wine & tomato
— **em vinha d'alho** eng *vee*·nya *daa*·lyoo baked rabbit with slices of fried bread & onion, drizzled with port or white wine
coentrada ⓕ kweng·*traa*·da sauce with abundant amounts of coriander
coentros ⓜ pl *kweng*·troosh coriander
cogumelos ⓜ pl koo·goo·*me*·loosh mushrooms

colorau ⓜ koo·loo·*row* sweet paprika
cominhos ⓜ pl koo·*mee*·nyoosh cumin
com todos kong *to*·doosh 'with everything' – a dish with the lot
conquilha ⓕ kong·*kee*·lya cockle
cordeiro ⓜ cor·*day*·roo lamb
coscurões ⓜ pl koosh·koo·*royngsh* orange- & brandy-flavoured biscuit
costeleta ⓕ koosh·te·*le*·ta chop
couve ⓕ *koh*·ve cabbage
— de Bruxelas de broo·*she*·lash Brussels sprout
— flor flor cauliflower
coxa de galinha ⓕ *ko*·sha de ga·*lee*·nya fried, savoury chicken thigh
cozido/cozida ⓜ/ⓕ koo·*zee*·doo/koo·*zee*·da boiled
cozido à Portuguesa ⓜ koo·*zee*·doo aa poor·too·*ge*·za hearty meal made with chunks of different meats & sausages, vegetables, beans & rice
creme (de pasteleiro) ⓜ *kre*·me (de pash·te·*lay*·roo) egg, flour, water & sugar paste used to fill cakes

~ D ~

delícia de batata ⓕ de·*lee*·sya de ba·*taa*·ta little cakes of mashed potato mixed with almonds & cinnamon
dobrada ⓕ doo·*braa*·da tripe with white beans & rice
doce ⓜ *do*·se dessert • jam • sweet
— de amêndoa de a·*meng*·doo·a marzipan sweets
duchesse ⓕ doo·*shes* puff pastry filled with whipped cream & topped with fruit or thin threads of sugar & egg paste

~ E ~

empada ⓕ eng·*paa*·da miniature pot pie
empadão ⓜ eng·pa·*downg* dish similar to shepherd's pie
encharcada ⓕ eng·shar·*kaa*·da cooked egg yolks in a sugary syrup, decorated with cinnamon
enchido ⓜ eng·*shee*·doo any variety of sausage
engarrafado por ⓜ eng·ga·rra·*faa*·doo poor bottled by (winery name)
enguia ⓕ eng·*gee*·a eel
ensopado ⓜ eng·soo·*paa*·doo stew served on toasted or deep-fried bread
entrecosto ⓜ eng·tre·*kosh*·too pork ribs
ervilhas ⓕ pl er·*vee*·lyash peas
— com ovos escalfados kong *o*·voosh shkal·*faa*·doosh peas & sliced **chouriço** cooked with lard, olive oil, onions & parsley, served with poached eggs
— de vagem ⓕ de *vaa*·zheng snow peas
escabeche ⓜ shka·*be*·she raw meat or fish pickled in olive oil, vinegar, garlic & bay leaf
escalfado/escalfada ⓜ/ⓕ shkaal·*faa*·doo/shkaal·*faa*·da poached
escalopes ⓜ pl shka·*lo*·pesh medallion-shaped cuts of boneless meat
espanhola, à shpa·*nyo*·la, aa dish in tomato & onion sauce
espargos ⓜ pl *shpar*·goosh asparagus
esparguete ⓜ shpar·*ge*·te spaghetti
espetada ⓕ shpe·*taa*·da kebab
espinafres ⓜ pl shpee·*naa*·fresh spinach
estopeta de atum ⓕ shtoo·*pe*·ta de a·*toong* tuna, onion, tomatoes & green capsicum in an olive oil & vinegar dressing

~ F ~

faisão ⓜ fai·*zowng* pheasant
farinha ⓕ fa·*ree*·nya flour

farinheira ⓕ fa·ree·*nyay*·ra sausage stuffed with spiced, flour-based mix
farófias ⓕ pl fa·*ro*·fee·ash dessert of beaten egg whites in a custard sauce
farripas de laranja ⓕ pl fa·*rree*·pash de la·*rang*·zha chocolate-covered strips of orange peel
farturas ⓕ pl far·*too*·rash deep-fried dough swirls rolled in sugar & cinnamon, usually found at fairs
fataça na telha ⓕ fa·*taa*·sa na *te*·lya mullet seasoned with chopped onion, parsley, paprika & bacon, cooked between two clay roof tiles buried in embers
fatias ⓕ pl fa·*tee*·ash slices
— da China/Tomar da *shee*·na/too·*maar* steam-cooked loaf made of whipped egg yolks & sugar
— douradas doh·*raa*·dash slices of bread soaked in milk & eggs, fried, smothered in sugar & topped with cinnamon
favada à Portuguesa ⓕ fa·*vaa*·da aa poor·too·*ge*·za stew of fava beans, sausage & sometimes poached eggs
fava-rica ⓕ fa·va·*rree*·ka fava bean soup with garlic & vinegar
favas ⓕ *faa*·vash broad bean
— à Algarvia ⓕ pl *faa*·vash aa aal·gar·*vee*·a fava beans cooked with blood sausage, bacon, sometimes **chouriço** & mint
febras ⓕ pl *fe*·brash pork cutlets
feijão ⓜ fay·*zhowng* bean
feijoada ⓕ fay·*zhwaa*·da bean stew with sausages or other meat
ferraduras ⓕ pl fe·rra·*doo*·rash horseshoe-shaped pastry, sometimes layered with candied fruit
fiambre ⓜ fee·*ang*·bre cold meat • ham
fígado ⓜ *fee*·ga·doo liver
figo ⓜ *fee*·goo fig
focinho de porco ⓜ foo·*see*·nyoo de *por*·koo pig's snout
folar ⓜ foo·*laar* brioche dough baked with chicken, spicy sausages & **presunto**, eaten at Easter
folhado ⓜ foo·*lyaa*·doo puff pastry
formigos ⓜ pl for·*mee*·goosh sweetmeats – thick paste of soaked hard bread or biscuit with egg yolks, sugar, honey, milk, cinnamon & wine, cooked slowly over low heat
framboesa ⓕ frang·*bwe*·za raspberry
francesinha ⓕ frang·se·*zee*·nya ham, sausage & cheese in a tomato-cream sauce, on slices of bread
frango ⓜ *frang*·goo chicken
frito/frita ⓜ/ⓕ *free*·too/*free*·ta fried
fruta ⓕ *froo*·ta fruit
frutas secas ⓕ pl *froo*·tash *se*·kash dried fruit

~ G ~

galão ⓜ ga·*lowng* an espresso with hot milk served in a tall glass
galinha ⓕ ga·*lee*·nya hen
— do campo doo *kaang*·poo free-range chicken
gambas ⓕ pl *gang*·bash prawns
garoto ⓜ ga·*ro*·too ready-made filter coffee topped with warm or hot milk
gaspacho ⓜ gash·*paa*·shoo chilled tomato & garlic bread soup flavoured with olive oil, vinegar & oregano
gelado ⓜ zhe·*laa*·doo ice cream
geleia ⓕ zhe·*lay*·a jelly
gengibre ⓜ zheng·*zhee*·bre ginger
gila ⓕ *zhee*·la spaghetti squash
ginja ⓕ *zheeng*·zha sour cherry
goiaba ⓕ goy·*aa*·ba guava
grão (de bico) ⓜ growng (de *bee*·koo) chickpeas • garbanzo beans
guardanapo ⓜ gwar·da·*naa*·poo a jelly roll cake cut into squares & folded in half, filled with **creme de pasteleiro**
guisado/guisada ⓜ/ⓕ gee·*za*·doo/gee·*za*·da stewed

~ H ~

hortaliça ⓕ or·ta·*lee*·sa vegetables
hortelã ⓕ or·te·*lang* mint

~ I ~

iogurte ⓜ yo·*goor*·te yogurt
iscas ⓕ pl *eesh*·kash pork liver

~ J ~

jaquinzinhos ⓜ pl zha·keeng·*zee*·nyoosh small fried horse-mackerel
jardineira ⓕ zhar·dee·*nay*·ra hearty beef & vegetable stew
jardineira, à zhar·dee·*nay*·ra, aa a type of beef & vegetable stew
javali ⓜ zha·va·*lee* wild boar
jesuítas ⓜ pl zhe·zoo·*ee*·tash puff pastry with baked meringue icing

~ L ~

lagosta ⓕ la·*gosh*·ta lobster
lagostim ⓜ la·goosh·*teeng* crayfish
laranja ⓕ la·*rang*·zha orange
lebre ⓕ *le*·bre hare
— com feijão branco kong fay·*zhowng* *brang*·koo hare & white bean stew
legumes ⓜ pl le·*goo*·mesh vegetables
leitão ⓜ lay·*towng* roasted suckling pig
leite ⓜ *lay*·te milk
— condensado kong·deng·*saa*·doo condensed milk
— gordo *gor*·doo whole milk
— magro *maa*·groo skim milk
lentilha ⓕ leng·*tee*·lya lentil
licor ⓜ lee·*kor* liqueur
lima ⓕ *lee*·ma lime
limão ⓜ lee·*mowng* lemon
limonada ⓕ lee·moo·*naa*·da lemonade
língua ⓕ *leeng*·gwa tongue
— de gato de *gaa*·too very small, hard vanilla biscuit
linguiça ⓕ leeng·*gwee*·sa thin, long garlicky sausage
lombinhos de porco ⓜ pl long·*bee*·nyoosh de *por*·koo thinly sliced pork tenderloin
lombo de porco assado ⓜ *long*·boo de *por*·koo a·*saa*·doo roast pork loin
lulas ⓕ pl *loo*·lash squid
— à Sevilhana aa se·vee·*lya*·na fried squid rings served with mayonnaise
— recheadas rre·shee·*aa*·dash small squid stuffed with a mixture of rice, tomatoes, **presunto** & parsley

~ M ~

maçã ⓕ ma·*sang* apple
Madeirense, à ma·day·*reng*·se, aa Madeira-style – a dish cooked with tomatoes, onion & garlic (and sometimes bananas or Madeira wine)
malagueta ⓕ ma·la·*ge*·ta red hot chilli peppers, also called **piripiri**
mal cozido/cozida ⓜ/ⓕ maal koo·*zee*·doo/koo·*zee*·da soft-boiled
manga ⓕ *mang*·ga mango
manjar branco ⓜ mang·*zhaar* *brang*·koo coconut-milk pudding with prunes, with syrup poured over the top
manteiga ⓕ mang·*tay*·ga butter
mão de vaca guisada ⓜ mowng de *vaa*·ka gee·*zaa*·da stew of cow's feet, chickpeas, tomatoes, onion, garlic **chouriço**, parsley & white wine
maracujá ⓜ ma·ra·koo·*zhaa* passionfruit
maranhos ma·*ra*·nyoosh pork belly stuffed with lamb, **presunto**, **chouriço**, wine & rice
marisco ⓜ ma·*reesh*·koo shellfish
marmelada ⓕ mar·me·*laa*·da quince paste
massas ⓕ pl *maa*·sash noodles • pasta
mel ⓜ mel honey

melancia ⓕ me·lang·*see*·a watermelon
melão ⓜ me·*lowng* (honeydew) melon
— com presunto kong pre·*zoong*·too slices of honeydew melon topped with slices of **presunto**
meloa ⓕ me·*lo*·a cantaloupe • rockmelon
melosa ⓕ me·*lo*·za mixed drink of brandy & honey
merengue ⓜ me·*reng*·ge meringue
mexido/mexida ⓜ/ⓕ me·*shee*·doo/ me·*shee*·da scrambled
mexilhões ⓜ pl me·shee·*lyoyngsh* mussels
migas ⓕ pl *mee*·gash a side dish, usually made of bread flavoured with olive oil, garlic & spices & fried
— de bacalhau de ba·ka·*lyow* **migas** made with bread, salt cod, onion, tomatoes, garlic, red capsicum paste & coriander, served with grilled eels
— de batata de ba·*taa*·ta side dish of mashed potatoes flavoured with bacon, sausage & garlic, shaped into round balls
mil folhas ⓜ pl meel *fo*·lyash layers of flaky pastry with custard filling
milho ⓜ *mee*·lyoo corn
— frito ⓜ *free*·too cubes of fried white cornmeal served with skewers of grilled meat or poultry
miolos (de porco) ⓜ pl mee·*o*·loosh (de *por*·koo) (pork) brains
miudezas ⓕ pl myoo·de·*zash* giblets
moelas ⓕ pl mo·e·lash chicken gizzards
molho ⓜ *mo*·lyoo dressing • gravy • sauce
morangos ⓜ pl moo·*rang*·goosh strawberries
morcela ⓕ moor·*se*·la blood sausage
morgados ⓜ pl mor·*gaa*·doosh sweetmeats made with almonds & figs
moscatel ⓜ moosh·ka·*tel* topaz-coloured, sweet dessert wine
mostarda ⓕ moosh·*taar*·da mustard

~ N ~

nabiça ⓕ na·*bee*·sa turnip greens
nabo ⓜ *naa*·boo turnip
na púcara ⓕ na *poo*·ka·ra chicken or duck cooked in a clay pot with **presunto**, tomatoes, onion, port, brandy, white wine, bay leaves & garlic
natas ⓕ pl *naa*·tash cream (from milk)
negro ⓜ *ne*·groo type of sausage made from blood rather than meat
nêspera ⓕ *nesh*·pe·ra loquat
novilho ⓜ noo·*vee*·lyoo veal
noz ⓕ nos walnut

~ O ~

oleaginosa ⓕ o·lee·a·zhee·*no*·za nut
óleo ⓜ *o*·lee·oo oil
orelha de porco de coentrada ⓕ o·re·lya de *por*·koo de kweng·*traa*·da sliced pig's ear seasoned with garlic & coriander, in olive oil & vinegar dressing, served cold
ostra ⓕ *osh*·tra oyster
ovo ⓜ *o*·voo egg
— cozido koo·*zee*·doo boiled egg
— de chocolate de shoo·koo·*laa*·te chocolate Easter egg
— escalfado shkal·*faa*·doo poached egg
— estrelado shtre·*laa*·doo fried egg
— mexido me·*shee*·doo scrambled egg
ovos moles ⓜ pl *o*·voosh *mo*·lesh sweetened egg yolks
ovos verdes ⓜ pl *o*·voosh *ver*·desh boiled eggs stuffed with a mixture of egg yolks, butter & parsley, coated in flour & fried

~ P ~

pá ⓕ paa front leg of an animal
paio ⓜ *pai*·oo smoked pork tenderloin sausage
panado ⓜ pa·*naa*·doo breaded pork cutlet
pão ⓜ powng bread
— de centeio de seng·*tay*·oo light rye bread
— de leite de *lay*·te sweet roll made with wheat flour, eggs & milk
— de milho de *mee*·lyoo corn bread
— integral eeng·te·*graal* wholegrain bread
papas ⓕ pl *paa*·pash gruel • porridge
papos-de-anjo ⓜ pl *paa*·poosh·de·*ang*·zhoo little egg-based puffs in a sugar syrup
papo-seco ⓜ *paa*·poo·*se*·koo most common type of bread roll
passas ⓕ pl *paa*·sash raisins • sultanas
pastéis ⓜ pl pash·*taysh* pastries
— de bacalhau de ba·ka·*lyow* deep-fried savouries made of mashed potato, onion, parsley & salt cod
— de feijão de fay·*zhowng* rich lima bean & almond mixture in flaky pastry shells
— de massa tenra de *ma*·sa *teng*·ra meat-filled fried pastries
— de nata/Belém de *na*·ta/be·*leng* egg custard tarts with flaky pastry shell
— de Tentúgal de teng·*too*·gaal flaky pastries with a filling of creamy egg yolk & sugar paste
pastel ⓜ pash·*tel* pastry
pataniscas de bacalhau ⓕ pl pa·ta·*neesh*·kash de ba·ka·*lyow* seasoned salt cod fritters
paté ⓜ paa·*te* paté
pato ⓜ *paa*·too duck
peito de frango ⓜ *pay*·too de *frang*·goo chicken breast
peixe ⓜ *pay*·she fish
pepino ⓜ pe·*pee*·noo cucumber
pêra ⓕ *pe*·ra pear
perdiz ⓕ per·*deez* partridge
pernil no forno ⓜ per·*neel* noo *for*·noo roast leg of pork
peru ⓜ pe·*roo* turkey
pescadinhas de rabo na boca ⓕ pl pesh·ka·*dee*·nyash de *rraa*·boo na *bo*·ka small whiting fried with their tails in their mouths
pêssego ⓜ *pe*·se·goo peach
petingas ⓕ pl pe·*teeng*·gash small sardines
pezinhos de porco *pe*·zee·nyoosh de *por*·koo pig's feet flavoured with coriander, garlic & onion
picante ⓜ&ⓕ pee·*kang*·te spicy/hot
pimenta ⓕ pee·*meng*·ta pepper
pimento ⓜ pee·*meng*·too capsicum
pipis ⓜ pl pee·*peesh* stewed chicken giblets, flavoured with garlic, onion, paprika, white wine & chilli
piri piri *pee*·ree *pee*·ree red hot chilli peppers (also called **malagueta**) • sauce made from red hot chilli peppers
pito de Santa Luzia ⓜ *pee*·too de *sang*·ta loo·*zee*·a sweet made from yeast dough filled with sugar, cinnamon & pumpkin
polvo ⓜ *pol*·voo octopus
porco ⓜ *por*·koo pork
posta ⓕ *posh*·ta steak slice
prato de grão ⓜ *praa*·too de growng chickpea stew flavoured with tomato, garlic, bay leaf & cumin
pratos completos ⓜ pl *praa*·toosh kong·*ple*·toosh a dish with all the elements that would constitute a meal in itself
prego no pão ⓜ *pre*·goo noo powng small steak sandwich

presunto ⓜ pre·*zoong*·too prosciutto • smoked ham
pudim ⓜ poo·*deeng* pudding
— de café de ka·*fe* coffee-flavoured pudding
— de leite de *lay*·te custard-like pudding with lemon-flavoured caramel sauce
— de ovos de *o*·voosh very eggy, baked custard-like pudding
— do Abade de Priscos doo a·*baa*·de de *preesh*·koosh pudding made of egg yolks, sliced smoked bacon, port, lemon & cinnamon
— flan flang caramel custard
— molotov mo·lo·*tov* poached meringue with caramel sauce
puré de batata ⓜ poo·*re* de ba·*taa*·ta mashed potatoes

~ Q ~

queijada ⓕ kay·*zhaa*·da small tarts with sweet, dense filling
queijo ⓜ *kay*·zhoo cheese
— da Serra/Estrela da *se*·rra/*shtre*·la popular creamy cheese made from sheep's milk
— de Azeitão de a·zay·*towng* soft, creamy cheese made from sheep's milk near the town of Azeitão
— de cabra de *kaa*·bra goat's milk cheese
— de ovelha de oo·*ve*·lya sheep's milk cheese
— de vaca de *vaa*·ka cow's milk cheese
— saloio sa·*loy*·oo firm cow's milk cheese
— seco *se*·koo dry cheese similar in texture to parmesan
queimado/queimada ⓜ/ⓕ kay·*maa*·doo/kay·*maa*·da burnt
queque *ke*·ke plain yellow cupcake
quivi kee·vee kiwi(fruit)

~ R ~

rabanadas ⓕ pl rra·ba·*naa*·dash see **fatias douradas**
rabanete ⓜ rra·ba·*ne*·te radish
rancho ⓜ *rrang*·shoo hearty stew of chickpeas, onion, potatoes, macaroni, veal trotters, pork belly, **chouriço** & beef
rebento de feijão ⓕ rre·*beng*·too de fay·*zhowng* bean sprout
regueifas ⓕ pl rre·*gay*·fash cinnamon- & saffron-flavoured biscuit rings
rendinhas ⓕ pl rreng·*dee*·nyash almond nougat which resembles lace
repolho ⓜ rre·*po*·lyoo cabbage
requeijada ⓕ rre·kay·*zhaa*·da tart made with **requeijão**
requeijão ⓜ rre·kay·*zhowng* fresh, ricotta-style cheese
rim ⓜ rreeng kidney • kidney-shaped eclair
rissol ⓜ rree·*sol* fried pastry • rissole
robalo ⓜ rroo·*baa*·loo rock bass
rocha ⓕ *rro*·sha large, soft spice biscuit
rojões ⓜ pl rroo·*zhoyngsh* spiced & marinated chunks of fried pork
rolo de carne ⓜ *rro*·loo de *kaar*·ne meatloaf
rosbife ⓜ rrosh·*bee*·fe roast beef

~ S ~

safio ⓜ sa·*fee*·oo conger eel • sea eel
sal ⓜ saal salt
— fino *fee*·noo refined salt
— grosso *gro*·soo rock salt
salada ⓕ sa·*laa*·da salad
— de alface de aal·*fa*·se lettuce salad
— de atum de a·*toong* salad of tuna, potato, peas, carrots & boiled eggs in an olive oil & vinegar dressing

— de bacalhau com feijão frade de ba·ka·*lyow* kong fay·*zhowng fraa*·de salad of uncooked salt cod & black-eyed beans in olive oil & vinegar dressing
— de feijão frade de fay·*zhowng fraa*·de black-eyed bean salad flavoured with onion, garlic, olive oil & vinegar, sprinkled with chopped boiled egg & parsley
— de frutas de *froo*·tash fruit salad
— de tomate de too·*maa*·te tomato & onion salad, often flavoured with oregano
— mista *meesh*·ta tomato, lettuce & onion salad
— russa *rroo*·sa potato salad with peas, carrots & mayonnaise
salame de chocolate ⓜ sa·*la*·me de shoo·koo·*laa*·te dense chocolate fudge roll studded with bits of biscuits, served sliced
salgadinho ⓜ saal·ga·*dee*·nyoo small savoury pastry
salgado/salgada ⓜ/ⓕ saal·*gaa*·doo/saal·*gaa*·da salty • small savoury pastry
salmão ⓜ saal·*mowng* salmon
— fumado foo·*maa*·doo smoked salmon
salmonete ⓜ saal·moo·*ne*·te red mullet
salpicão ⓜ saal·pee·*kowng* smoked pork sausage flavoured with garlic, bay leaf & sometimes wine
salsa ⓕ *saal*·sa flat-leaf parsley • parsley
salsicha ⓕ saal·*see*·sha sausage
— fresca *fresh*·ka fresh pork sausage
salteado/salteada ⓜ/ⓕ saal·tee·*aa*·doo/saal·tee·*aa*·da sautéed
sálvia ⓕ *saal*·vee·a sage
sandes ⓕ *sang*·desh sandwich
sanduiche ⓕ sang·*dwee*·she sandwich (see also **sandes**)
sardinha ⓕ sar·*dee*·nya sardine
sarrabulho ⓜ sa·rra·*boo*·lyoo variety of meats cooked in pig's blood
sável ⓜ *saa*·vel shad (fish)
— na telha na *te*·lya **fataça na telha** made with shad
sericá/sericaia ⓕ se·ree·*ka*/se·ree·*kay*·a soft cake with an almost creamy texture served with a stewed plum in syrup
simples ⓜ&ⓕ *seeng*·plesh plain • with no ccompaniments, filling or icing
sobremesa ⓕ soo·bre·*me*·za dessert • jam • sweet
sonhos ⓜ pl *so*·nyoosh sweet fried dough, sprinkled with sugar & cinnamon
sopa ⓕ *so*·pa soup
— de pedra de *pe*·dra vegetable soup with red beans, onions, potatoes, pig's ear, bacon & sausages
— do dia doo *dee*·a soup of the day
sumo ⓜ *soo*·moo juice
— de laranja natural de la·*rang*·zha na·too·*raal* freshly squeezed orange juice

~ T ~

tâmara ⓕ *taa*·ma·ra date (fruit)
tangerina ⓕ tang·zhe·*ree*·na mandarin
tarte ⓕ *tar*·te pie
tecolameco ⓜ te·koo·la·*me*·koo rich & sweet orange & almond cake, well loved around Portalegre
tigelada ⓕ tee·zhe·*laa*·da firm egg custard flavoured with vanilla, lemon or cinnamon
tomate ⓜ too·*maa*·te tomato
tomilho ⓜ too·*mee*·lyoo thyme
toranja ⓕ to·*rang*·zha grapefruit
tornedó ⓜ tor·ne·*do* thick, tender steak
torrada ⓕ too·*rraa*·da toast

torresmos ⓜ pl too·*rrezh*·moosh pork cracklings served as a snack
torta ⓕ *tor*·ta tart with filling
— de laranja de la·*rang*·zha rolled orange-flavoured tart made with lots of eggs & little flour
— de Viana de vee·*aa*·na tart filled with jam • tart with egg yolk icing
tortulhos ⓜ pl tor·*too*·lyoosh sheep's tripe stuffed with more sheep's tripe
tosta ⓕ *tosh*·ta pieces of toast
— mista *meesh*·ta toasted ham & cheese sandwich
toucinho ⓜ toh·*see*·nyoo uncured bacon
— rançoso rrang·*so*·zoo cake made with almonds & egg yolks, sprinkled with sugar & cinnamon
— salgado saal·*gaa*·doo salt-cured bacon
trança ⓕ *trang*·sa type of pastry topped with coconut mixture & chopped nuts
Transmontana, à aa trangsh·mong·*ta*·na, aa Trás-os-Montes style – hearty dish usually flavoured with sausages & other meat, garlic & onion
tremoços ⓜ pl tre·*mo*·soosh salted, preserved yellow lupins eaten as a snack
tripas ⓕ pl *tree*·pash tripe
— à moda do Porto aa *mo*·da doo *por*·too slow-cooked dried beans, trotters, tripe, chicken, vegetables, sausages & cumin
trouxas de ovos ⓕ pl *troh*·shash de *o*·voosh beaten egg poached in sugar syrup
truta ⓕ *troo*·ta trout
— de escabeche de shka·*be*·she trout prepared **escabeche**, fried & prepared with a garlic, onion & parsley dressing, served cold with boiled potatoes
túberas com ovos ⓕ pl *too*·be·rash kong *o*·voosh sliced mushrooms fried with onion, bay leaf & eggs

~ U ~

uvas ⓕ pl *oo*·vash grapes

~ V ~

veado ⓜ vee·*aa*·doo venison
velhoses ⓕ pl ve·*lyo*·zesh orange- & brandy-flavoured pumpkin fritters
verde ⓜ&ⓕ *ver*·de unripe (fruit)
vinagre ⓜ vee·*naa*·gre vinegar
vinha d'alhos ⓕ *vee*·nya *daa*·lyoosh meat marinated in wine or vinegar, olive oil, garlic & bay leaf
vinho ⓜ *vee*·nyoo wine
— branco *brang*·koo white wine
— da casa da *kaa*·za house wine
— da região da rre·zhee·*owng* local wine
— do Porto doo *por*·too port
— do Porto branco doo *por*·too *brang*·koo dry white port
— espumante shpoo·*mang*·te sparkling wine
— rosé rro·*ze* rosé wine
— tinto *teeng*·too red wine
— verde *ver*·de young wine – light sparkling red, white or rosé wine
vitela (assada) ⓕ vee·*te*·la (a·*saa*·da) (roast) veal

~ X ~

xerém ⓜ she·*reng* cornmeal porridge, served with shellfish, **chouriço**, pork or other meat

Dictionary

ENGLISH *to* PORTUGUESE

inglês – português

Portuguese nouns have their gender indicated with ⓜ (masculine) and ⓕ (feminine). Where adjectives or nouns have separate masculine and feminine forms, these are divided by a slash and marked ⓜ/ⓕ. You'll also see words marked as v (verb), n (noun), a (adjective), pl (plural), sg (singular), inf (informal) and pol (polite) where necessary. Verbs are given in the infinitive – for details on how to change verbs for use in a sentence, see **grammar** (p25). For food and drink terms, see the **menu decoder** (p194).

A

aboard a bordo a *bor*·doo
abortion aborto ⓜ a·*bor*·too
about cerca de *ser*·ka de
above por cima de poor *see*·ma de
abroad no estrangeiro noo shtrang·*zhay*·roo
accident acidente ⓜ a·see·*deng*·te
accommodation hospedagem ⓕ osh·pe·*daa*·zheng
account (bill) conta ⓕ *kong*·ta
across através a·tra·*vesh*
activist activista ⓜ&ⓕ aa·tee·*veesh*·ta
actor actor/actriz ⓜ/ⓕ aa·*tor*/aa·*treesh*
adaptor adaptador ⓜ a·da·pe·ta·*dor*
addiction vício ⓜ *vee*·syoo
address endereço ⓜ eng·de·*re*·soo
administration administração ⓕ a·de·mee·neesh·tra·*sowng*
admission entrada ⓕ eng·*traa*·da
admit v admitir a·de·mee·*teer*
adult n&a adulto/adulta ⓜ/ⓕ a·*dool*·too/a·*dool*·ta
advertisement anúncio ⓜ a·*noong*·syoo
advice conselho ⓜ kong·*se*·lyoo
after depois de·*poysh*
afternoon tarde ⓕ *taar*·de
again novamente no·va·*meng*·te
age idade ⓕ ee·*daa*·de
agree concordar kong·koor·*daar*
agriculture agricultura ⓕ a·gree·kool·*too*·ra
ahead em frente eng *freng*·te
AIDS SIDA ⓕ *see*·da
air ar ⓜ aar
air conditioning ar condicionado ⓜ aar kong·dee·syoo·*naa*·doo
airline companhia aérea ⓕ kong·pa·*nyee*·a a·e·ree·a
airmail via aérea ⓕ *vee*·a a·e·ree·a
airplane avião ⓜ a·vee·*owng*
airport aeroporto ⓜ a·e·ro·*por*·too
airport tax taxa de aeroporto ⓕ *taa*·sha de a·e·ro·*por*·too

aisle coxia ⓜ koo·*shee*·a
alarm clock despertador ⓜ desh·per·ta·*dor*
all todo/toda ⓜ/ⓕ *to*·doo/*to*·da
allergy alergia ⓕ a·ler·*zhee*·a
almost quase *kwaa*·ze
alone sozinho/sozinha ⓜ/ⓕ so·*zee*·nyoo/so·*zee*·nya
already já zhaa
also também tang·*beng*
altitude altitude ⓕ aal·tee·*too*·de
always sempre *seng*·pre
ambassador embaixador/embaixatriz ⓜ/ⓕ eng·bai·sha·*dor*/eng·bai·sha·*treesh*
ambulance ambulância ⓕ ang·boo·*lang*·sya
anaemia anemia ⓕ a·ne·*mee*·a
anarchist anarquista ⓜ&ⓕ a·nar·*keesh*·ta
ancient antigo/antiga ⓜ/ⓕ ang·*tee*·goo/ang·*tee*·ga
and e e
angry zangado/zangada ⓜ/ⓕ zang·*gaa*·doo/zang·*gaa*·da
animal animal ⓜ&ⓕ a·nee·*maal*
ankle tornozelo ⓜ toor·noo·*ze*·loo
another um outro/uma outra ⓜ/ⓕ oong *oh*·troo/oo·ma *oh*·tra
answer resposta ⓕ rresh·*posh*·ta
antibiotics antibióticos ⓜ pl ang·tee·bee·*o*·tee·koosh
antique antiguidade ⓕ ang·tee·gwee·*daa*·de
antiseptic antiséptico ⓜ ang·tee·*se*·tee·koo
apartment apartamento ⓜ a·par·ta·*meng*·too
appendix (body) apêndice ⓜ a·*peng*·dee·se
appointment consulta ⓕ kong·*sool*·ta
architect arquitecto/arquitecta ⓜ/ⓕ ar·kee·*te*·too/ar·kee·*te*·ta
architecture arquitectura ⓕ ar·kee·te·*too*·ra
argue discutir deesh·koo·*teer*
arm (body) braço ⓜ *braa*·soo

aromatherapy aromaterapia ⓕ a·ro·ma·te·ra·*pee*·a
arrest prender preng·*der*
arrival chegada ⓕ she·*gaa*·da
arrive chegar she·*gaar*
art arte ⓕ *aar*·te
art gallery galeria de arte ⓕ ga·le·*ree*·a de *aar*·te
artist artista ⓜ&ⓕ ar·*teesh*·ta
ashtray cinzeiro ⓜ seeng·*zay*·roo
ask (a question) perguntar per·goong·*taar*
ask (for something) pedir pe·*deer*
aspirin aspirina ⓕ ash·pee·*ree*·na
asthma asma ⓕ *ash*·ma
at à a
athletics atletismo ⓜ at·le·*teesh*·moo
atmosphere atmosfera ⓕ at·moosh·*fe*·ra
aunt tia ⓕ *tee*·a
Australia Austrália ⓕ owsh·*traa*·lya
ATM caixa automático ⓜ *kai*·sha ow·too·*maa*·tee·koo
avenue avenida ⓕ a·ve·*nee*·da
awful horrível o·*rree*·vel

B

B&W (film) preto e branco *pre*·too e *brang*·koo
baby bebé ⓜ&ⓕ be·*be*
baby food comida de bebé ⓕ koo·*mee*·da de be·*be*
baby powder pó de talco ⓜ po de *taal*·koo
babysitter ama ⓕ *a*·ma
back (body) costas ⓕ pl *kosh*·tash
back (position) atrás a·*traash*
backpack mochila ⓕ moo·*shee*·la
bad mau/má ⓜ/ⓕ *ma*·oo/maa
bag saco ⓜ *saa*·koo
baggage bagagem ⓕ ba·*gaa*·zheng
baggage allowance limite de peso ⓜ lee·*mee*·te de *pe*·zoo
baggage claim balcão de bagagens ⓜ bal·*kowng* de ba·*gaa*·zhengsh
bakery padaria ⓕ paa·da·*ree*·a
balance (account) saldo ⓜ *saal*·doo

B

balcony varanda ⓕ va·*rang*·da
ball (sport) bola ⓕ *bo*·la
band (music) grupo ⓜ *groo*·poo
bandage ligadura ⓕ lee·ga·*doo*·ra
Band-Aid penso ⓜ *peng*·soo
bank banco ⓜ *bang*·koo
bank account conta bancária ⓕ *kong*·ta bang·*kaa*·rya
banknote nota bancária ⓕ *no*·ta bang·*kaa*·rya
baptism baptismo ⓜ ba·*teezh*·moo
bar bar ⓜ baar
barber barbeiro ⓜ bar·*bay*·roo
bar work trabalho num bar ⓜ tra·*baa*·lyoo noong baar
basket cesto ⓕ *sesh*·too
basketball basquetebol ⓜ bash·ke·te·*bol*
bath banho ⓜ *ba*·nyoo
bathroom casa de banho ⓕ *kaa*·za de *ba*·nyoo
battery pilha ⓕ *pee*·lya
be (ongoing) ser ser
be (temporary) estar shtaar
beach praia ⓕ *prai*·a
beach volleyball vóleibol de praia ⓜ *vo*·lay·bol de *prai*·a
beautiful bonito/bonita ⓜ/ⓕ boo·*nee*·too/boo·*nee*·ta
beauty salon salão de beleza ⓜ sa·*lowng* de be·*le*·za
bed cama ⓕ *ka*·ma
bedding lençóis e mantas ⓕ pl leng·*soysh* ee *mang*·tash
bedroom quarto ⓜ *kwaar*·too
bee abelha ⓕ a·*be*·lya
beer cerveja ⓕ ser·*ve*·zha
beer house cervejaria ⓕ ser·ve·zha·*ree*·a
before antes *ang*·tesh
beggar pedinte ⓜ&ⓕ pe·*deeng*·te
behind atrás a·*traash*
below abaixo a·*bai*·shoo
beside ao lado de ow *laa*·doo de
best o/a melhor ⓜ/ⓕ oo/a me·*lyor*
bet aposta ⓕ a·*posh*·ta
better melhor me·*lyor*
between entre *eng*·tre
bicycle bicicleta ⓕ bee·see·*kle*·ta
big grande *grang*·de
bike bicicleta ⓕ bee·see·*kle*·ta
bike chain corrente de bicicleta ⓕ koo·*rreng*·te de bee·see·*kle*·ta
bike lock cadeado de bicicleta ⓜ ka·dee·*aa*·doo de bee·see·*kle*·ta
bike path caminho de bicicleta ⓕ ka·*mee*·nyoo de bee·see·*kle*·ta
bike shop loja de ciclismo ⓕ *lo*·zha de see·*kleesh*·moo
bill (restaurant) conta ⓕ *kong*·ta
binoculars binóculos ⓜ pl bee·*no*·koo·loosh
bird pássaro ⓜ *paa*·sa·roo
birth certificate certidão de nascimento ⓕ ser·tee·*downg* de nash·see·*meng*·too
birthday aniversário ⓜ a·nee·ver·*saa*·ryoo
bite (dog) mordedura ⓕ moor·de·*doo*·ra
bite (insect) mordida (por um insecto) ⓕ mor·*dee*·da (poor oong eeng·*se*·too)
bitter amargo/amarga ⓜ/ⓕ a·*maar*·goo/a·*maar*·ga
black preto/preta ⓜ/ⓕ *pre*·too/*pre*·ta
bladder bexiga ⓕ be·*shee*·ga
blanket cobertor ⓜ koo·ber·*tor*
blind cego/cega ⓜ/ⓕ *se*·goo/*se*·ga
blister bolha ⓕ *bo*·lya
blocked bloqueado/bloqueada ⓜ/ⓕ blo·kee·*aa*·doo/blo·kee·*aa*·da
blood sangue ⓜ *sang*·ge
blood pressure tensão arterial ⓕ teng·*sowng* ar·te·ree·*aal*
blood test análise de sangue ⓕ a·*naa*·lee·ze de *sang*·ge
blood type grupo sanguíneo ⓜ *groo*·poo sang·*gwee*·nee·oo
blue azul a·*zool*
board subir a bordo soo·*beer* a *bor*·doo
boarding house pensão ⓕ peng·*sowng*

boarding pass cartão de embarque ⓜ kar·*towng* de eng·*baar*·ke
boat barco ⓜ *baar*·koo
body corpo ⓜ *kor*·poo
bone osso ⓜ *o*·soo
book livro ⓜ *lee*·vroo
book (reserve) reservar rre·zer·*vaar*
booked out esgotado/esgotada ⓜ/ⓕ shgoo·*taa*·doo/shgoo·*taa*·da
bookshop livraria ⓕ lee·vra·*ree*·a
boots botas ⓕ *bo*·tash
border fronteira ⓕ frong·*tay*·ra
bored aborrecido/aborrecida ⓜ/ⓕ a·boo·rre·*see*·doo/a·boo·rre·*see*·da
boring chato/chata ⓜ/ⓕ *shaa*·too/*shaa*·ta
borrow pedir emprestado pe·*deer* eng·presh·*taa*·doo
botanic garden jardim botânico ⓜ zhar·*deeng* boo·*ta*·nee·koo
both ambos/ambas ⓜ/ⓕ *ang*·boosh/*ang*·bash
bottle garrafa ⓕ ga·*rraa*·fa
bottle opener saca-rolhas ⓜ *saa*·ka·*rro*·lyash
bottle shop loja de bebidas ⓕ *lo*·zha de be·*bee*·dash
bottom (body) nádegas ⓕ pl *naa*·de·gash
bottom (position) fundo ⓕ *foong*·doo
bowl tigela ⓕ tee·*zhe*·la
box caixa ⓕ *kai*·sha
boxing boxe ⓜ *bok*·se
boy menino ⓜ me·*nee*·noo
boyfriend namorado ⓜ na·moo·*raa*·doo
bra soutien ⓜ soo·tee·*eng*
brake (car) travão ⓜ tra·*vowng*
brave corajoso/corajosa ⓜ/ⓕ koo·ra·*zho*·zoo/koo·ra·*zho*·za
bread pão ⓜ powng
break quebrar ke·*braar*
break down (car) avariar a·va·ree·*aar*
breakfast pequeno almoço ⓜ pe·*ke*·noo aal·*mo*·soo
breast peito ⓜ sg *pay*·too
breasts seios ⓜ *say*·oosh
breathe respirar rresh·pee·*raar*
bribe suborno ⓜ soo·*bor*·noo
bridge (structure) ponte ⓕ *pong*·te
briefcase pasta ⓕ *pash*·ta
bring trazer tra·*zer*
brochure brochura ⓕ broo·*shoo*·ra
broken quebrado/quebrada ⓜ/ⓕ ke·*braa*·doo/ke·*braa*·da
broken down (car, etc) avariado/avariada ⓜ/ⓕ a·va·ree·*aa*·doo/a·va·ree·*aa*·da
bronchitis bronquite ⓕ brong·*kee*·te
brother irmão ⓜ eer·*mowng*
brown castanho/castanha ⓜ/ⓕ kash·*ta*·nyoo/kash·*ta*·nya
bruise nódoa negra ⓕ *no*·doo·a *ne*·gra
brush escova ⓕ *shko*·va
bucket balde ⓜ *baal*·de
Buddhist n&a budista ⓜ&ⓕ boo·*deesh*·ta
budget orçamento ⓜ or·sa·*meng*·too
buffet bufete ⓜ boo·*fe*·te
bug bicho ⓜ *bee*·shoo
build construir kong·shtroo·*eer*
builder construtor ⓜ kong·shtroo·*tor*
building prédio ⓜ *pre*·dyoo
bull touro ⓜ *toh*·roo
bullfight tourada ⓕ toh·*raa*·da
bullfighter cavaleiro ⓜ ka·va·*lay*·roo
bullring praça de touros ⓕ *praa*·sa de *toh*·roosh
burn queimadura ⓕ kay·ma·*doo*·ra
bus autocarro ⓜ ow·to·*kaa*·roo
business negócios ⓜ pl ne·*go*·syoosh
business class classe executiva ⓕ *klaa*·se ee·zhe·koo·*te* e·va
businessperson homem/mulher de negócios ⓜ/ⓕ o·meng/moo·*lyer* de ne·*go*·syoosh
business trip viagem de negócios ⓕ vee·*aa*·zheng de ne·*go*·syoosh
busker artista de rua ⓜ&ⓕ ar·*teesh*·ta de *rroo*·a

bus station/stop paragem de autocarros Ⓕ pa·*raa*·zheng de ow·to·*kaa*·rroosh
busy ocupado/ocupada Ⓜ/Ⓕ o·koo·*paa*·doo/o·koo·*paa*·da
but mas mash
button botão Ⓜ boo·*towng*
buy comprar kong·*praar*

C

cabin camarote Ⓜ ka·ma·*ro*·te
cake shop pastelaria Ⓕ pash·te·la·*ree*·a
calculator calculadora Ⓕ kaal·koo·la·*do*·ra
calendar calendário Ⓜ ka·leng·*daa*·ryoo
call (telephone) telefonar te·le·foo·*naar*
camera máquina fotográfica Ⓕ *maa*·kee·na foo·too·*graa*·fee·ka
camera shop loja de equipamentos fotográficos Ⓕ *lo*·zha de e·kee·pa·*meng*·toosh foo·too·*graa*·fee·koosh
camp acampar a·kang·*paar*
camping ground acampamento Ⓜ a·kang·pa·*meng*·too
camping store loja de campismo Ⓕ *lo*·zha de kang·*peezh*·moo
campsite parque de campismo Ⓜ *paar*·ke de kang·*peezh*·moo
can (tin) lata Ⓕ *laa*·ta
can poder poo·*der*
Canada Canadá Ⓜ ka·na·*daa*
cancel cancelar kang·se·*laar*
cancer cancro Ⓜ *kang*·kroo
candle vela Ⓕ *ve*·la
can opener abre latas Ⓜ *aa*·bre *laa*·tash
captain capitão Ⓜ ka·pee·*towng*
car carro Ⓜ *kaa*·rroo
caravan caravana Ⓕ ka·ra·*va*·na
cards (playing) cartas Ⓕ pl *kaar*·tash
care (for someone) gostar goosh·*taar*
car hire aluguer de automóvel Ⓜ a·loo·*ger* de ow·too·*mo*·vel
car owner's title título de registo do automóvel Ⓜ *tee*·too·loo de rre·*zheesh*·too doo ow·too·*mo*·vel
car park parque de estacionamento Ⓜ *paar*·ke de shta·syoo·na·*meng*·too
car registration registo automóvel Ⓜ rre·*zheesh*·too ow·too·*mo*·vel
carry carregar ka·rre·*gaar*
carton caixa de papelão Ⓕ *kai*·sha de pa·pe·*lowng*
cash dinheiro dee·*nyay*·roo
cash (a cheque) levantar (um cheque) le·vang·*taar* (oong *she*·ke)
cash register caixa registadora Ⓕ *kai*·sha rre·zheesh·ta·*do*·ra
cassette cassete Ⓕ kaa·*se*·te
castle castelo Ⓜ kash·*te*·loo
casual work trabalho temporário Ⓜ tra·*baa*·lyoo teng·poo·*raa*·ryoo
cat gato/gata Ⓜ/Ⓕ *gaa*·too/*gaa*·ta
cathedral catedral Ⓕ ka·te·*draal*
Catholic n&a católico/católica Ⓜ/Ⓕ ka·*to*·lee·koo/ka·*to*·lee·ka
cave caverna Ⓕ ka·*ver*·na
celebration comemoração Ⓕ koo·me·moo·ra·*sowng*
cell phone telemóvel Ⓜ te·le·*mo*·vel
cemetery cemitério Ⓜ se·mee·*te*·ryoo
cent cêntimo Ⓜ *seng*·tee·moo
centimetre centímetro Ⓜ seng·*tee*·me·troo
centre centro Ⓜ *seng*·troo
certificate certificado Ⓜ ser·tee·fee·*kaa*·doo
chain (bike) corrente Ⓕ koo·*rreng*·te
chair cadeira Ⓕ ka·*day*·ra
chairlift teleférico Ⓜ te·le·*fe*·ree·koo
championships campeonatos Ⓜ pl kang·pe·oo·*naa*·toosh
chance oportunidade Ⓕ o·poor·too·nee·*daa*·de
change mudança Ⓕ moo·*dang*·sa
change (coins) troco Ⓜ *tro*·koo
change (money) trocar troo·*kaar*
changing room sala de provas Ⓕ *saa*·la de *pro*·vash

charming charmoso/charmosa ⓜ/ⓕ shar·*mo*·zoo/shar·*mo*·za
chat up dar conversa daar kong·*ver*·sa
cheap barato/barata ba·*raa*·too/ ba·*raa*·ta
cheat enganar eng·ga·*naar*
check verificar ve·ree·fee·*kaar*
check (banking) cheque ⓜ *she*·ke
check (bill) conta ⓕ *kong*·ta
check-in check-in ⓜ shek·*eeng*
checkpoint ponto de controle ⓜ *pong*·too de kong·*tro*·le
chef cozinheiro/cozinheira chefe ⓜ/ⓕ koo·zee·*nyay*·roo/koo·zee·*nyay*·ra *she*·fe
cheque (banking) cheque ⓜ *she*·ke
chess xadrez ⓜ sha·*dresh*
chess board tabuleiro de xadrez ⓜ ta·boo·*lay*·roo de sha·*dresh*
chest (body) peito ⓜ *pay*·too
chewing gum pastilha elástica ⓕ pash·*tee*·lya e·*laash*·tee·ka
chicken galinha ⓕ ga·*lee*·nya
chicken pox bechigas ⓕ pl be·*shee*·gash
child criança ⓜ&ⓕ kree·*ang*·sa
childminding (service) ama ⓕ *a*·ma
child seat cadeira de criança ⓕ ka·*day*·ra de kree·*ang*·sa
children crianças ⓜ&ⓕ pl kree·*ang*·sash
chocolate chocolate ⓜ shoo·koo·*laa*·te
choose escolher shkoo·*lyer*
Christian n&a Cristão/Cristã ⓜ/ⓕ kreesh·*towng*/kreesh·*tang*
Christmas Natal ⓜ na·*taal*
church igreja ⓕ ee·*gre*·zha
cigar charuto ⓜ sha·*roo*·too
cigarette cigarro ⓜ see·*gaa*·rroo
cigarette lighter isqueiro ⓜ eesh·*kay*·roo
cinema cinema ⓜ see·*ne*·ma
circus circo ⓜ *seer*·koo
city cidade ⓕ see·*daa*·de
city centre centro da cidade ⓜ *seng*·troo da see·*daa*·de

civil rights direitos civis ⓜ pl dee·*ray*·toosh *see*·veesh
class (category) classe ⓕ *klaa*·se
class system sistema de classes ⓜ seesh·*te*·ma de *klaa*·sesh
clean limpo/limpa ⓜ/ⓕ *leeng*·poo/ *leeng*·pa
clean limpar leeng·*paar*
cleaning limpeza ⓕ leeng·*pe*·za
client cliente ⓜ&ⓕ klee·*eng*·te
cliff penhasco ⓜ pe·*nyaash*·koo
climb subir soo·*beer*
cloakroom bengaleiro ⓜ beng·ga·*lay*·roo
clock relógio ⓜ rre·*lo*·zhyoo
close perto *per*·too
close fechar fe·*shaar*
closed fechado/fechada ⓜ/ⓕ fe·*shaa*·doo/fe·*shaa*·da
clothesline estendal da roupa ⓕ shteng·*daal* da *rroh*·pa
clothing roupas ⓕ pl *rroh*·pash
clothing store loja de roupas ⓕ *lo*·zha de *rroh*·pash
cloud nuvem ⓕ noo·*veng*
cloudy nublado/nublada ⓜ/ⓕ noo·*blaa*·doo/noo·*blaa*·da
clutch (car) embraiagem ⓕ eng·brai·*aa*·zheng
coach (bus) autocarro ⓜ ow·to·*kaa*·rroo
coach (trainer) treinador/ treinadora ⓜ/ⓕ tray·na·*dor*/ tray·na·*do*·ra
coat casaco ⓜ ka·*zaa*·koo
cockroach barata ⓕ ba·*raa*·ta
coffee café ⓜ ka·*fe*
coins moedas ⓕ pl moo·e·dash
cold frio/fria ⓜ/ⓕ *free*·oo/*free*·a
cold (illness) constipação ⓕ kong·shtee·pa·*sowng*
colleague colega ⓜ&ⓕ koo·*le*·ga
collect call ligação a cobrar ⓕ lee·ga·*sowng* a koo·*braar*
college universidade ⓕ oo·nee·ver·see·*daa*·de
colour cor ⓕ kor

C

comb pente ⓜ *peng*·te
come vir veer
comedy comédia ⓕ koo·*me*·dya
comfortable confortável kong·for·*taa*·vel
commission comissão ⓕ koo·mee·*sowng*
communion comunhão ⓕ koo·moo·*nyowng*
communist n&a comunista ⓜ&ⓕ koo·moo·*neesh*·ta
company (firm) empresa ⓕ eng·*pre*·za
compass bússola ⓕ *boo*·soo·la
complain reclamar rre·kla·*maar*
complaint reclamação ⓕ rre·kla·ma·*sowng*
complimentary grátis *graa*·teesh
computer computador ⓜ kong·poo·ta·*dor*
concert concerto ⓜ kong·*ser*·too
concussion abalo cerebral ⓜ a·*baa*·loo se·re·*braal*
conditioner (hair) amaciador ⓜ a·ma·see·a·*dor*
condom preservativo ⓜ pre·zer·va·*tee*·voo
conference (big) conferência ⓕ kong·fe·*reng*·sya
conference (small) colóquio ⓜ koo·*lo*·kyoo
confession confissão ⓕ kong·fee·*sowng*
confirm confirmar kong·feer·*maar*
conjunctivitis conjuntivite ⓕ kong·zhoong·tee·*vee*·te
connection ligação ⓕ lee·ga·*sowng*
constipation prisão de ventre ⓕ pree·*zowng* de *ven*·tre
consulate consulado ⓜ kong·soo·*laa*·doo
contact lenses lentes de contacto ⓜ pl *leng*·tesh de kong·*taak*·too
contact lens solution líquido para lentes de contacto ⓜ *lee*·kee·doo *pa*·ra *leng*·tesh de kong·*taak*·too

contraceptives contraceptivo ⓜ kong·tra·se·*tee*·voo
contract contrato ⓜ kong·*traa*·too
convenience store loja de conveniência ⓕ *lo*·zha de kong·ve·*nyeng*·sya
cook cozinheiro/cozinheira ⓜ/ⓕ koo·zee·*nyay*·roo/koo·zee·*nyay*·ra
cook cozinhar koo·zee·*nyaar*
cooking cozinha ⓕ koo·*zee*·nya
cool (cold) fresco/fresca ⓜ/ⓕ *fresh*·koo/*fresh*·ka
cool (exciting) fixe ⓜ&ⓕ *fee*·she
corkscrew saca-rolhas ⓜ *saa*·ka·*rro*·lyash
corner esquina ⓕ *shkee*·na
corrupt corrupto/corrupta ⓜ/ⓕ koo·*rroop*·too/koo·*rroop*·ta
cost custar koosh·*taar*
cotton algodão ⓜ aal·goo·*downg*
cotton balls bolas de algodão ⓕ pl *bo*·lash de aal·goo·*downg*
cotton buds cotonete ⓜ ko·to·*ne*·te
cough tossir too·*seer*
cough medicine xarope ⓜ sha·*ro*·pe
count contar kong·*taar*
counter (at bar) balcão ⓜ baal·*kowng*
country país ⓜ pa·*eesh*
countryside interior do país ⓜ eeng·te·ree·*or* doo pa·*eesh*
coupon cupão ⓜ koo·*powng*
court (legal) tribunal ⓜ tree·boo·*naal*
court (sport) campo ⓜ *kang*·poo
cover charge consumo obrigatório ⓜ kon·*soo*·moo o·bree·ga·*to*·ree·oo
cow vaca ⓕ *vaa*·ka
crafts artesanato ⓜ ar·te·za·*naa*·too
crash (car) acidente ⓜ a·see·*deng*·te
crazy louco/louca ⓜ/ⓕ *loh*·koo/*loh*·ka
cream creme ⓜ *kre*·me
crèche infantário ⓜ eeng·fang·*taa*·ree·oo
credit crédito ⓜ *kre*·dee·too
credit card cartão de crédito ⓜ kar·*towng* de *kre*·dee·too

DICTIONARY

cross (religious) cruz ⓕ kroosh
crowded cheio/cheia ⓜ/ⓕ *shay*·oo/*shay*·a
cup chávena ⓕ *shaa*·ve·na
cupboard armário ⓜ ar·*maa*·ryoo
currency exchange câmbio ⓜ *kang*·byoo
current (electricity) corrente ⓕ koo·*rreng*·te
current affairs assuntos do dia ⓜ pl a·*soong*·toosh doo *dee*·a
custom costume ⓜ koosh·*too*·me
customs alfândega ⓕ aal·*fang*·de·ga
cut cortar koor·*taar*
cutlery talheres ⓜ pl ta·*lye*·resh
CV CV ⓜ se·*ve*
cycle andar de bicicleta ang·*daar* de bee·see·*kle*·ta
cycling ciclismo ⓜ see·*kleesh*·moo
cyclist ciclista ⓜ&ⓕ see·*kleesh*·ta
cystitis cistite ⓕ seesh·*tee*·te

D

daily diário/diária ⓜ/ⓕ dee·*aa*·ryoo/dee·*aa*·rya
dance dançar dang·*saar*
dancing dança ⓕ *dang*·sa
dangerous perigoso/perigosa ⓜ/ⓕ pe·ree·*go*·zoo/pe·ree·*go*·za
dark (colour/night) escuro/escura ⓜ/ⓕ *shkoo*·roo/*shkoo*·ra
date (appointment) encontro ⓜ eng·*kong*·troo
date (day) data ⓕ *daa*·ta
date (a person) namorar na·moo·*raar*
date of birth data de nascimento ⓕ *daa*·ta de nash·see·*meng*·too
daughter filha ⓕ *fee*·lya
dawn madrugada ⓕ ma·droo·*gaa*·da
day dia ⓜ *dee*·a
dead morto/morta ⓜ/ⓕ *mor*·too/*mor*·ta
deaf surdo/surda ⓜ/ⓕ *soor*·doo/*soor*·da
decide decidir de·see·*deer*
(car) deck convés (de automóveis) ⓜ kong·*vesh* (de ow·too·*mo*·vaysh)
deep profundo/profunda ⓜ/ⓕ proo·*foong*·doo/proo·*foong*·da
deforestation desflorestação ⓜ desh·floo·resh·ta·*sowng*
degrees (temperature) graus ⓜ pl growsh
delay atraso ⓜ a·*traa*·zoo
delicatessen charcutaria ⓕ shar·koo·ta·*ree*·a
deliver entregar eng·tre·*gaar*
democracy democracia ⓕ de·moo·kra·*see*·a
demonstration manifestação ⓕ ma·nee·fesh·ta·*sowng*
dental dam protector de borracha ⓜ proo·te·*tor* de boo·*rraa*·sha
dental floss fio dental ⓜ *fee*·oo deng·*taal*
dentist dentista ⓜ&ⓕ deng·*teesh*·ta
deodorant desodorizante ⓜ de·zo·doo·ree·*zang*·te
depart partir par·*teer*
departure partida ⓕ par·*tee*·da
departure gate porta de partida ⓕ *por*·ta de par·*tee*·da
deposit (bank) depósito ⓜ de·*po*·zee·too
desert deserto ⓜ de·*zer*·too
design design ⓜ dee·*zain*
dessert sobremesa ⓕ soo·bre·*me*·za
destination destino ⓜ desh·*tee*·noo
details detalhes ⓜ pl de·*taa*·lyesh
diabetes diabetes ⓕ dee·a·*be*·tesh
dial tone sinal da linha telefónica ⓜ see·*naal* da *lee*·nya te·le·*fo*·nee·ka
diaper fralda ⓕ *fraal*·da
diaphragm diafragma ⓜ dee·a·*fraa*·ge·ma
diarrhoea diarreia ⓕ dee·a·*rray*·a
diary diário ⓜ dee·*aa*·ryoo
dice dados ⓜ pl *daa*·doosh
dictionary dicionário ⓜ dee·syoo·*naa*·ryoo
die morrer moo·*rrer*
diet dieta ⓕ dee·*e*·ta
different diferente dee·fe·*reng*·te
difficult difícil dee·*fee*·seel

dining car vagão restaurante ⓜ *va·gowng* rresh·tow·*rang*·te
dinner jantar ⓜ zhang·*taar*
direct directo/directa ⓜ/ⓕ dee·*re*·too/dee·*re*·ta
direct-dial ligação directa ⓕ lee·ga·*sowng* dee·*re*·ta
direction direcção ⓕ dee·re·*sowng*
director director/directora ⓜ/ⓕ dee·re·*tor*/dee·re·*to*·ra
dirty sujo/suja ⓜ/ⓕ *soo*·zhoo/*soo*·zha
disabled deficiente de·fee·see·*eng*·te
disco disco ⓜ *deesh*·koo
discount desconto ⓜ desh·*kong*·too
discrimination discriminação ⓕ deesh·kree·mee·na·*sowng*
disease doença ⓕ doo·*eng*·sa
dish prato ⓜ *praa*·too
diving mergulho ⓜ mer·*goo*·lyoo
diving equipment equipamento de mergulho ⓜ e·kee·pa·*meng*·too de mer·*goo*·lyoo
divorced divorciado/divorciada ⓜ/ⓕ dee·vor·see·*aa*·doo/dee·vor·see·*aa*·da
dizzy tonto/tonta ⓜ/ⓕ *tong*·too/*tong*·ta
do fazer fa·*zer*
doctor médico/médica ⓜ/ⓕ *me*·dee·koo/*me*·dee·ka
documentary documentário ⓜ doo·koo·meng·*taa*·ryoo
dog cão ⓜ kowng
dole (welfare) assistência social ⓕ a·seesh·*teng*·sya soo·see·*aal*
doll boneco/boneca ⓜ/ⓕ boo·*ne*·koo/boo·*ne*·ka
double duplo/dupla ⓜ/ⓕ *doo*·ploo/*doo*·pla
double bed cama de casal ⓕ *ka*·ma de ka·*zaal*
double room quarto de casal ⓜ *kwaar*·too de ka·*zaal*
down baixo *bai*·shoo
downhill para baixo *pa*·ra *bai*·shoo
dream sonho ⓜ *so*·nyoo
dress vestido ⓜ vesh·*tee*·doo
dried seco/seca ⓜ/ⓕ *se*·koo/*se*·ka
drink bebida ⓕ be·*bee*·da
drink (alcoholic) bebida alcoólica ⓕ be·*bee*·da aal·koo·o·lee·ka
drink beber be·*ber*
drive conduzir kong·doo·*zeer*
drivers licence carta de condução ⓕ *kaar*·ta de kong·doo·*sowng*
drug droga ⓕ *dro*·ga
drug addiction vício da droga ⓜ *vee*·syoo da *dro*·ga
drug dealer traficante de drogas ⓜ&ⓕ tra·fee·*kang*·te de *dro*·gash
drug trafficking tráfico de drogas ⓜ *traa*·fee·koo de *dro*·gash
drug user toxicodependente ⓜ&ⓕ *tok*·see·ko·de·peng·*deng*·te
drunk bêbado/bêbada ⓜ/ⓕ *be*·ba·doo/*be*·ba·da
dry seco/seca ⓜ/ⓕ *se*·koo/*se*·ka
dry secar se·*kaar*
dummy (pacifier) chupeta ⓕ shoo·*pe*·ta

E

each cada *ka*·da
ear orelha ⓕ o·*re*·lya
early cedo *se*·doo
earn ganhar ga·*nyaar*
earplugs tampões para os ouvidos ⓜ pl tang·*poyngsh pa*·ra oosh oh·*vee*·doosh
earrings brincos ⓜ pl *breeng*·koosh
earthquake terramoto ⓜ te·rra·*mo*·too
Easter Páscoa ⓕ *paash*·kwa
easy fácil *faa*·seel
eat comer koo·*mer*
economy class classe económica ⓕ *klaa*·se ee·koo·*no*·mee·ka
education educação ⓕ e·doo·ka·*sowng*
election eleição ⓕ e·lay·*sowng*
electrical store loja de aparelhos eléctricos ⓕ *lo*·zha de a·pa·*re*·lyoosh ee·*le*·tree·koosh

electricity electricidade ⓕ ee·le·tree·see·*daa*·de
elevator elevador ⓜ ee·le·va·*dor*
embassy embaixada ⓕ eng·bai·*shaa*·da
emergency emergência ⓕ ee·mer·*zheng*·sya
emotional sensível seng·*see*·vel
employee empregado/empregada ⓜ/ⓕ eng·pre·*gaa*·doo/eng·pre·*gaa*·da
employer patrão/patroa ⓜ/ⓕ pa·*trowng*/pa·*tro*·a
empty vazio/vazia ⓜ/ⓕ va·*zee*·oo/va·*zee*·a
end fim ⓜ feeng
engaged (phone) ocupado ⓜ o·koo·*paa*·doo
engaged comprometido/comprometida ⓜ/ⓕ kong·proo·me·*tee*·doo/kong·proo·me·*tee*·da
engagement noivado ⓜ noy·*vaa*·doo
engine motor ⓜ moo·*tor*
engineering engenharia ⓕ eng·zhe·nya·*ree*·a
England Inglaterra ⓕ eeng·gla·*te*·rra
English inglês ⓜ eeng·*glesh*
enjoy (oneself) divertir-se dee·ver·*teer*·se
enough suficiente soo·fee·see·*eng*·te
enter entrar eng·*traar*
entertainment guide guia de espectáculos ⓜ *gee*·a de shpe·*taa*·koo·loosh
entry entrada ⓕ eng·*traa*·da
envelope envelope ⓜ eng·ve·*lo*·pe
environment ambiente ⓜ ang·bee·*eng*·te
epilepsy epilepsia ⓕ e·pee·le·pe·*see*·a
equality igualdade ⓕ ee·gwal·*daa*·de
equal opportunity igualdade de oportunidades ⓕ ee·gwal·*daa*·de de o·poor·too·nee·*daa*·desh
equipment equipamento ⓜ e·kee·pa·*meng*·too
escalator escada rolante ⓕ *shkaa*·da rroo·*lang*·te
estate agency agência de imobiliário ⓕ a·*zheng*·sya de ee·mo·bee·*lyaa*·ryoo
euro euro ⓜ *e*·oo·roo
evening da noite ⓜ da *noy*·te
every todo/toda ⓜ/ⓕ *to*·doo/*to*·da
everyone todos/todas ⓜ/ⓕ *to*·doosh/*to*·dash
everything tudo ⓜ *too*·doo
exactly exactamente e·za·ta·*meng*·te
example exemplo ⓜ e·*zeng*·ploo
excellent excelente ay·she·*leng*·te
exchange câmbio ⓜ *kang*·byoo
exchange trocar troo·*kaar*
exchange rate taxa de câmbio ⓕ *taa*·sha de *kang*·byoo
excluded excluído/excluída ⓜ/ⓕ aysh·kloo·*ee*·doo/aysh·kloo·*ee*·da
exhaust (car) exaustor ⓜ ee·zowsh·*tor*
exhibition exposição ⓕ shpoo·zee·*sowng*
exit saída ⓕ saa·*ee*·da
expensive caro/cara ⓜ/ⓕ *kaa*·roo/*kaa*·ra
experience experiência ⓕ shpe·ree·*eng*·sya
exploitation exploração ⓕ shplo·ra·*sowng*
express expresso/expressa ⓜ/ⓕ *shpre*·soo/*shpre*·sa
express mail correio azul ⓜ koo·*rray*·oo a·*zool*
extension (visa) extensão ⓕ shteng·*sowng*
eye olho ⓜ *o*·lyoo
eye drops colírio ⓜ koo·*lee*·ree·oo

F

fabric tecido ⓜ te·*see*·doo
face rosto ⓜ *rrosh*·too
face cloth toalha de rosto ⓕ *twaa*·lya de *rrosh*·too
factory fábrica ⓕ *faa*·bree·ka
factory worker operário/operária ⓜ/ⓕ o·pe·*raa*·ryoo/o·pe·*raa*·rya

fall cair ka·*eer*
family família ⓕ fa·*mee*·lya
family name apelido ⓜ a·pe·*lee*·doo
famous famoso/famosa ⓜ/ⓕ fa·*mo*·zoo/fa·*mo*·za
fan (machine) ventoínha ⓕ veng·too·*ee*·nya
fan (sport, etc) adepto/adepta ⓜ/ⓕ a·*de*·pe·too/a·*de*·pe·ta
fanbelt correia da ventoinha ⓕ koo·*rray*·a da veng·too·*ee*·nya
far longe *long*·zhe
fare preço da passagem ⓜ *pre*·soo da pa·*saa*·zheng
farm quinta ⓕ *keeng*·ta
farmer agricultor ⓜ&ⓕ a·gree·kool·*tor*
fashion moda ⓕ *mo*·da
fast a rápido/rápida ⓜ/ⓕ *rraa*·pee·doo/*rraa*·pee·da
fast adv depressa de·*pre*·sa
fat gordo/gorda ⓜ/ⓕ *gor*·doo/*gor*·da
father pai ⓜ pai
father-in-law sogro ⓜ *so*·groo
faucet torneira ⓕ toor·*nay*·ra
fault (someone's) culpa ⓕ *kool*·pa
faulty defeituoso/defeituosa ⓜ/ⓕ de·fay·too·*o*·zoo/de·fay·too·*o*·za
fax fax ⓜ faaks
feed alimentar a·lee·meng·*taar*
feel (touch) tocar too·*kaar*
feeling (physical) sensação ⓕ seng·sa·*sowng*
feelings sentimentos ⓜ pl seng·tee·*meng*·toosh
female a feminino/feminina ⓜ/ⓕ fe·mee·*nee*·noo/fe·mee·*nee*·na
fence cerca ⓕ *ser*·ka
ferry ferryboat ⓜ *fe*·rree·boht
festival festival ⓜ fesh·tee·*vaal*
fever febre ⓕ *fe*·bre
few alguns/algumas ⓜ/ⓕ pl aal·*goongsh*/aal·*goo*·mash
fiancé/fiancée noivo/noiva ⓜ/ⓕ *noy*·voo/*noy*·va
fiction ficção ⓕ feek·*sowng*
fight luta ⓕ *loo*·ta
fill encher eng·*sher*
film filme ⓜ *feel*·me
film speed velocidade do filme ⓕ ve·loo·see·*daa*·de doo *feel*·me
filtered filtrado/filtrada ⓜ/ⓕ feel·*traa*·doo/feel·*traa*·da
find encontrar eng·kong·*traar*
fine (payment) multa ⓕ *mool*·ta
fine bom/boa ⓜ/ⓕ bong/*bo*·a
finger dedo ⓜ *de*·doo
finish terminar ter·mee·*naar*
fire fogo ⓜ *fo*·goo
firewood lenha ⓕ *le*·nya
first primeiro/primeira ⓜ/ⓕ pree·*may*·roo/pree·*may*·ra
first-aid kit estojo de primeiros socorros ⓜ *shto*·zhoo de pree·*may*·roosh so·*ko*·rroosh
first class primeira classe ⓕ pree·*may*·ra *klaa*·se
fish peixe ⓜ *pay*·she
fishing pesca ⓕ *pesh*·ka
fishmonger peixeiro/peixeira ⓜ/ⓕ pay·*shay*·roo/pay·*shay*·ra
fish shop peixaria ⓕ pay·sha·*ree*·a
flag bandeira ⓕ bang·*day*·ra
flannel (face cloth) toalha de rosto ⓜ *twaa*·lya de *rrosh*·too
flash (camera) flash ⓜ flaash
flashlight (torch) luz do flash ⓕ loosh doo flaash
flat (apartment) apartamento ⓜ a·par·ta·*meng*·too
flat a plano/plana ⓜ/ⓕ *pla*·noo/*pla*·na
flea pulga ⓕ *pool*·ga
fleamarket feira da ladra ⓕ *fay*·ra da *laa*·dra
flight voo ⓜ *vo*·oo
flood inundação ⓕ ee·noong·da·*sowng*
floor chão ⓜ showng
floor (storey) andar ⓜ ang·*daar*
florist (shop) florista ⓕ floo·*reesh*·ta
flower flor ⓕ flor
flu gripe ⓕ *gree*·pe
fly voar voo·*aar*

foggy enevoado/enevoada ⓜ/ⓕ
e·ne·voo·*aa*·doo/e·ne·voo·*aa*·da
folk music música popular ⓕ
moo·zee·ka poo·poo·*laar*
follow seguir se·*geer*
food comida ⓕ koo·*mee*·da
foot pé ⓜ pe
footpath caminho ⓜ ka·*mee*·nyoo
foreign estrangeiro/estrangeira ⓜ/ⓕ
shtrang·*zhay*·roo/shtrang·*zhay*·ra
forest floresta ⓕ floo·*resh*·ta
forever para sempre *pa*·ra *seng*·pre
forget esquecer shke·*ser*
forgive perdoar per·doo·*aar*
fork garfo ⓜ *gaar*·foo
fortnight quinzena ⓕ keeng·*ze*·na
fortune teller vidente ⓜ&ⓕ
vee·*deng*·te
foyer sala de estar ⓕ *saa*·la de shtaar
fragile frágil *fraa*·zheel
free (available) a disponível
deesh·po·*nee*·vel
free (gratis) a grátis *graa*·teesh
free (not bound) a livre *lee*·vre
freeze congelar kong·zhe·*laar*
fresh fresco/fresca ⓜ/ⓕ *fresh*·koo/
fresh·ka
fridge frigorífico ⓜ
free·goo·*ree*·fee·koo
friend amigo/amiga ⓜ/ⓕ
a·*mee*·goo/a·*mee*·ga
from de de
frost geada ⓕ zhee·*aa*·da
frozen gelado/gelada ⓜ/ⓕ
zhe·*laa*·doo/zhe·*laa*·da
fruit-picking colheita de frutas ⓕ
koo·*lyay*·ta de *froo*·tash
full cheio/cheia ⓜ/ⓕ *shay*·oo/*shay*·a
full-time tempo inteiro *teng*·poo
eeng·*tay*·roo
fun divertido/divertida ⓜ/ⓕ
dee·ver·*tee*·doo/dee·ver·*tee*·da
funeral funeral ⓜ foo·ne·*raal*
funny engraçado/engraçada ⓜ/ⓕ
eng·gra·*saa*·doo/eng·gra·*saa*·da
furniture móveis ⓜ pl *mo*·vaysh
future futuro ⓜ foo·*too*·roo

G

game (sport) jogo ⓜ *zho*·goo
garage garagem ⓕ ga·*raa*·zheng
garbage lixo ⓜ *lee*·shoo
garbage can caixote do lixo ⓜ
kai·*sho*·te doo *lee*·shoo
garden jardim ⓜ zhar·*deeng*
gardening jardinagem ⓕ
zhar·dee·*naa*·zheng
gas (cooking) gás ⓜ gaash
gas (petrol) gasolina ⓕ
ga·zoo·*lee*·na
gas cartridge botija de gás ⓜ
boo·*tee*·zha de gaash
gastroenteritis gastrenterite ⓕ
gash·treng·te·*ree*·te
gate (airport) portão/porta ⓜ/ⓕ
por·*towng*/*por*·ta
gauze gaze ⓕ *gaa*·ze
gearbox caixa de velocidades ⓕ
kai·sha de ve·loo·see·*daa*·desh
get agarrar a·ga·*rraar*
get off (bus, train) descer
desh·*ser*
gift presente ⓜ pre·*zeng*·te
girl menina ⓕ me·*nee*·na
girlfriend namorada ⓕ
na·moo·*raa*·da
give dar daar
glandular fever febre glandular ⓕ
fe·bre glang·doo·*laar*
glass (drinking) copo ⓜ *ko*·poo
glasses (spectacles) óculos ⓜ pl
o·koo·loosh
gloves luvas ⓕ pl *loo*·vash
gloves (latex) luvas de borracha ⓕ pl
loo·vash de boo·*rraa*·sha
glue cola ⓕ *ko*·la
go ir eer
goal (sport) golo ⓜ *go*·loo
goalkeeper guarda-redes
gwaar·da·*rre*·desh
goat cabra ⓕ *kaa*·bra
God (general) Deus ⓜ *de*·oosh
goggles (skiing) óculos de
esqui ⓜ pl *o*·koo·loosh de shkee

goggles (swimming) óculos de natação ⓜ pl o·koo·loosh de na·ta·*sowng*
gold ouro ⓜ *oh*·roo
golf ball bola de golfe ⓕ *bo*·la de *gol*·fe
golf course campo de golfe ⓜ *kang*·poo de *gol*·fe
good bom/boa ⓜ/ⓕ bong/*bo*·a
go out (with) sair (com) sa·*eer* (kong)
go shopping fazer compras fa·*zer* *kong*·prash
government governo ⓜ goo·*ver*·noo
gram grama ⓜ *graa*·ma
grandchild neto/neta ⓜ/ⓕ *ne*·too/*ne*·ta
grandfather avô ⓜ a·*voh*
grandmother avó ⓕ a·*vo*
grass (lawn) relva ⓕ *rrel*·va
grateful grato/grata ⓜ/ⓕ *graa*·too/*graa*·ta
grave túmulo ⓜ *too*·moo·loo
great óptimo/óptima ⓜ/ⓕ *o*·tee·moo/*o*·tee·ma
green verde *ver*·de
greengrocer vendedor de hortaliças ⓜ veng·de·*dor* de or·ta·*lee*·sash
grey a cinzento/cinzenta ⓜ/ⓕ seeng·*zeng*·too/seeng·*zeng*·ta
grocery mercearia ⓕ mer·see·a·*ree*·a
grow crescer kresh·*ser*
guaranteed garantido/garantida ⓜ/ⓕ ga·rang·*tee*·doo/ga·rang·*tee*·da
guess adivinhar a·dee·vee·*nyaar*
guesthouse casa de hóspedes ⓕ *kaa*·za de *osh*·pe·desh
guide (audio) guia auditivo ⓜ *gee*·a ow·dee·*tee*·voo
guide (person) guia ⓜ *gee*·a
guidebook guia de viagem ⓜ *gee*·a de vee·*aa*·zheng
guide dog cão-guia ⓜ kowng·*gee*·a
guided tour excursão guiada ⓕ shkoor·*sowng* gee·*aa*·da
guilty culpado/culpada ⓜ/ⓕ kool·*paa*·doo/kool·*paa*·da
guitar guitarra ⓕ gee·*taa*·rra
gun pistola ⓕ peesh·*to*·la
gym (place) ginásio ⓜ zhee·*naa*·zyoo
gynaecologist ginecologista ⓜ&ⓕ zhee·ne·koo·loo·*zheesh*·ta

H

hair cabelo ⓜ ka·*be*·loo
hairbrush escova ⓕ *shko*·va
haircut corte de cabelo ⓜ *kor*·te de ka·*be*·loo
hairdresser cabeleireiro/cabeleireira ⓜ/ⓕ ka·be·lay·*ray*·roo/ka·be·lay·*ray*·ra
half a metade ⓕ a me·*taa*·de
hallucination alucinação ⓕ a·loo·see·na·*sowng*
hammer martelo ⓜ mar·*te*·loo
hammock cama de rede ⓕ *ka*·ma de *rre*·de
hand mão ⓕ mowng
handbag mala de mão ⓕ *maa*·la de mowng
handicrafts artesanato ⓜ ar·te·za·*naa*·too
handkerchief lenço de mão ⓜ *leng*·soo de mowng
handlebars guiador ⓜ gee·a·*dor*
handmade feito/feita à mão ⓜ/ⓕ *fay*·too/*fay*·ta aa mowng
handsome bonito/bonita ⓜ/ⓕ bo·*nee*·too/bo·*nee*·ta
happy feliz fe·*leesh*
harassment assédio ⓜ a·*se*·dyoo
harbour porto ⓜ *por*·too
hard (not soft) duro/dura ⓜ/ⓕ *doo*·roo/*doo*·ra
hardware store loja de ferramentas ⓕ *lo*·zha de fe·rra·*meng*·tash
hat chapéu ⓜ sha·*pe*·oo
have ter ter
have fun divertir-se dee·ver·*teer*·se
hay fever febre dos fenos ⓕ *fe*·bre doosh *fe*·noosh

he ele *e*·le
head cabeça ⓕ ka·*be*·sa
headache dor de cabeça ⓕ dor de ka·*be*·sa
headlights faróis ⓜ pl fa·*roysh*
health saúde ⓕ sa·*oo*·de
hear escutar shkoo·*taar*
hearing aid aparelho auditivo ⓜ a·pa·*re*·lyoo ow·dee·*tee*·voo
heart coração ⓜ koo·ra·*sowng*
heart attack ataque de coração ⓜ a·*taa*·ke de koo·ra·*sowng*
heart condition problema de coração ⓜ proo·*ble*·ma de koo·ra·*sowng*
heat calor ⓜ ka·*lor*
heated aquecido/aquecida ⓜ/ⓕ a·ke·*see*·doo/a·ke·*see*·da
heater aquecedor ⓜ a·ke·se·*dor*
heating aquecimento ⓜ a·ke·see·*meng*·too
heavy pesado/pesada ⓜ/ⓕ pe·*zaa*·doo/pe·*zaa*·da
helmet capacete ⓜ ka·pa·*se*·te
help ajuda ⓕ a·*zhoo*·da
help ajudar a·zhoo·*daar*
hepatitis hepatite ⓕ e·pa·*tee*·te
her (possessive) dela *de*·la
herb erva ⓕ *er*·va
here aqui a·*kee*
high alto/alta ⓜ/ⓕ *aal*·too/*aal*·ta
highchair cadeira de refeição para bebé ⓕ ka·*day*·ra de rre·fay·*sowng* pa·ra be·*be*
high school escola secundária ⓕ *shko*·la se·koong·*daa*·ree·a
highway autoestrada ⓕ ow·to·*shtraa*·da
hike caminhar ka·mee·*nyaar*
hiking caminhada ⓕ ka·mee·*nyaa*·da
hiking boots botas para caminhadas ⓕ pl *bo*·tash *pa*·ra ka·mee·*nyaa*·dash
hiking route rota de caminhada ⓕ *ro*·ta de ka·mee·*nyaa*·da
hill colina ⓕ koo·*lee*·na
Hindu n&a hindu ⓜ&ⓕ eeng·*doo*
hire alugar a·loo·*gaar*
his (possessive) dele *de*·le
historical histórico/histórica ⓜ/ⓕ *shto*·ree·koo/*shto*·ree·ka
history história ⓕ *shto*·rya
hitchhike apanhar boleia a·pa·*nyaar* boo·*lay*·a
HIV VIH ⓜ ve ee a·*gaa*
hockey hóquei ⓜ *o*·kay
holiday feriado ⓜ fe·ree·*aa*·doo
holidays férias ⓕ pl *fe*·ryash
home casa ⓕ *kaa*·za
homeless sem abrigo seng a·*bree*·goo
homemaker dona de casa ⓕ *do*·na de *kaa*·za
homesick com saudades kong sow·*da*·desh
homosexual n&a homosexual ⓜ&ⓕ o·mo·sek·soo·*aal*
honeymoon lua de mel ⓕ *loo*·a de mel
horoscope horóscopo ⓜ o·*rosh*·koo·poo
horse cavalo ⓜ ka·*vaa*·loo
horseriding hipismo ⓜ ee·*peezh*·moo
hospital hospital ⓜ osh·pee·*taal*
hospitality hospitalidade ⓕ osh·pee·ta·lee·*daa*·de
hot quente *keng*·te
hotel hotel ⓜ o·*tel*
hour hora ⓕ *o*·ra
house casa ⓕ *kaa*·za
housework trabalho doméstico ⓜ tra·*baa*·lyoo doo·*mesh*·tee·koo
how como *ko*·moo
hug abraçar a·bra·*saar*
huge enorme ⓜ&ⓕ ee·*nor*·me
human resources recursos humanos ⓜ pl rre·*koor*·soosh oo·*ma*·noosh
human rights direitos humanos ⓜ pl dee·*ray*·toosh oo·*ma*·noosh
hungry faminto/faminta ⓜ/ⓕ fa·*meeng*·too/fa·*meeng*·ta
hurt aleijar a·lay·*zhaar*
husband marido ⓜ ma·*ree*·doo

I

I eu *e*·oo
ice gelo ⓜ *zhe*·loo
ice axe machado de gelo ⓜ ma·*shaa*·doo de *zhe*·loo
ice hockey hóquei sobre o gelo ⓜ *o*·kay *so*·bre oo *zhe*·loo
identification identificação ⓕ ee·deng·tee·fee·ka·*sowng*
identification card (ID) bilhete de identidade ⓜ bee·*lye*·te de ee·deng·tee·*daa*·de
idiot idiota ⓜ&ⓕ ee·dee·*o*·ta
if se se
ill doente doo·*eng*·te
immigration imigração ⓕ ee·mee·gra·*sowng*
important importante eeng·por·*tang*·te
impossible impossível eeng·po·*see*·vel
in em eng
in a hurry com pressa kong *pre*·sa
included incluído/incluída ⓜ/ⓕ eeng·kloo·*ee*·doo/eeng·kloo·*ee*·da
income tax imposto de rendimentos ⓜ eeng·*posh*·too de rreng·dee·*meng*·toosh
indigestion indigestão ⓕ eeng·dee·zhesh·*towng*
indoors no interior noo eeng·te·ree·*or*
industry indústria ⓕ eeng·*doosh*·trya
infection infecção ⓕ eeng·fe·*sowng*
inflammation inflamação ⓕ eeng·fla·ma·*sowng*
influenza gripe ⓕ *gree*·pe
information informação ⓕ eeng·for·ma·*sowng*
in front of na frente de na *freng*·te de
ingredient ingrediente ⓜ eeng·gre·dee·*eng*·te
inhaler inalador ⓜ ee·na·la·*dor*
inject injectar eeng·zhe·*taar*
injection injecção ⓕ eeng·zhe·*sowng*
injured ferido/ferida ⓜ/ⓕ fe·*ree*·doo/fe·*ree*·da
injury ferimento ⓜ fe·ree·*meng*·too
inner tube câmara de ar ⓕ *ka*·ma·ra de aar
innocent inocente ee·noo·*seng*·te
insect repellant repelente ⓜ rre·pe·*leng*·te
inside dentro *deng*·troo
instructor instrutor/instrutora ⓜ/ⓕ eeng·shtroo·*tor*/eeng·shtroo·*to*·ra
insurance seguro ⓜ se·*goo*·roo
interesting interessante eeng·te·re·*sang*·te
intermission intervalo ⓜ eeng·ter·*vaa*·loo
international internacional eeng·ter·naa·syoo·*naal*
internet cafe café da internet ⓜ ka·*fe* da eeng·ter·*net*
interpreter intérprete ⓜ&ⓕ eeng·*ter*·pre·te
interview entrevista ⓕ eng·tre·*veesh*·ta
invite convidar kong·vee·*daar*
Ireland Irlanda ⓕ eer·*lang*·da
iron (clothes) ferro de engomar ⓜ *fe*·rroo de eng·goo·*maar*
island ilha ⓕ *ee*·lya
it ele/ela ⓜ/ⓕ *e*·le/*e*·la
IT informática ⓕ eeng·for·*maa*·tee·ka
itch comichão ⓕ koo·mee·*showng*
itinerary itinerário ⓜ ee·tee·ne·*raa*·ryoo
IUD DIU ⓜ de·ee·*oo*

J

jacket casaco ⓜ ka·*zaa*·koo
jail prisão ⓕ pree·*zowng*
jam compota ⓕ kong·*po*·ta
jar frasco ⓜ *fraash*·koo
jaw (human) maxilar ⓜ maak·see·*laar*
jealous ciumento/ciumenta ⓜ/ⓕ see·oo·*meng*·too/see·oo·*meng*·ta
jeep jipe ⓜ *zhee*·pe
jewellery ourivesaria ⓕ oh·ree·ve·za·*ree*·a
Jewish Judeu/Judia ⓜ/ⓕ zhoo·*de*·oo/zhoo·*dee*·a

ob emprego ⓜ eng·*pre*·goo
ogging corrida ⓕ koo·*rree*·da
oke piada ⓕ pee·*aa*·da
ournalist jornalista ⓜ&ⓕ
:hor·na·*leesh*·ta
ourney viagem ⓕ vee·*aa*·zheng
udge juiz/juiza ⓜ/ⓕ zhoo·*eesh*/
:hoo·*ee*·za
ump saltar saal·*taar*
umper (sweater) camisola ⓕ
ka·mee·*zo*·la
umper leads recarregador de
bateria ⓜ rre·ka·rre·ga·*dor* de
ba·te·*ree*·a

K

key chave ⓕ *shaa*·ve
keyboard teclado ⓜ te·*klaa*·doo
kick chutar shoo·*taar*
kidney rim ⓜ rreeng
kill matar ma·*taar*
kilogram quilograma ⓜ
kee·loo·*graa*·ma
kilometre quilómetro ⓜ
kee·*lo*·me·troo
kind (nice) amável ⓜ&ⓕ a·*maa*·vel
kindergarten jardim de infância ⓜ
zhar·*deeng* de eeng·*fang*·sya
king rei ⓜ rray
kiosk quiosque ⓜ kee·*osh*·ke
kiss beijo ⓜ *bay*·zhoo
kiss beijar bay·*zhaar*
kitchen cozinha ⓕ koo·*zee*·nya
knee joelho ⓜ zhoo·*e*·lyoo
knife faca ⓕ *faa*·ka
know saber sa·*ber*

L

labourer trabalhador/
trabalhadora ⓜ/ⓕ tra·ba·lya·*dor*/
tra·ba·lya·*do*·ra
lace renda ⓕ *reng*·da
lake lago ⓜ *laa*·goo
lamb (animal) cordeiro ⓜ
koor·*day*·roo
land terra ⓕ *te*·rra
landlady senhoria se·nyoo·*ree*·a
landlord senhorio se·nyoo·*ree*·oo
language língua ⓕ *leeng*·gwa
laptop computador portátil ⓜ
kong·poo·ta·*dor* por·*taa*·teel
large grande *grang*·de
last (final) último/última ⓜ/ⓕ
ool·tee·moo/*ool*·tee·ma
last (previous) passado/
passada ⓜ/ⓕ pa·*saa*·doo/pa·*saa*·da
late atrasado/atrasada ⓜ/ⓕ
a·tra·*zaa*·doo/a·tra·*zaa*·da
later mais tarde maish *tar*·de
laugh rir rreer
laundry lavandaria ⓕ la·vang·da·*ree*·a
law lei ⓕ lay
law (study/profession) Direito ⓜ
dee·*ray*·too
lawyer advogado/advogada ⓜ/ⓕ
a·de·voo·*gaa*·doo/a·de·voo·*gaa*·da
laxative laxante ⓜ la·*shang*·te
lazy preguiçoso/preguiçosa ⓜ/ⓕ
pre·gee·*so*·zoo/pre·gee·*so*·za
leader líder ⓜ&ⓕ *lee*·der
leaf folha ⓕ *fo*·lya
learn aprender a·preng·*der*
leather couro ⓜ *koh*·roo
lecturer professor/professora ⓜ/ⓕ
proo·fe·*sor*/proo·fe·*so*·ra
ledge parapeito ⓜ pa·ra·*pay*·too
left (direction) esquerda ⓕ *shker*·da
left luggage perdidos e achados ⓜ pl
per·*dee*·doosh ee aa·*shaa*·doosh
leg (body) perna ⓕ *per*·na
legal legal le·*gaal*
lens (camera) lente ⓕ *leng*·te
lesbian n&a lésbica ⓕ *lezh*·bee·ka
less menos *me*·noosh
letter (mail) carta ⓕ *kaar*·ta
liar mentiroso/mentirosa ⓜ/ⓕ
meng·tee·*ro*·zoo/meng·tee·*ro*·za
library biblioteca ⓕ bee·blee·oo·*te*·ka
lice piolhos ⓜ pl pee·o·lyoosh
licence licença ⓕ lee·*seng*·sa
license plate number número da
matrícula ⓜ *noo*·me·roo da
ma·*tree*·koo·la

lie (not stand) deitar-se day·*taar*·se
lie (not tell the truth) mentir meng·*teer*
life vida ⓕ *vee*·da
lifeboat barco salva-vidas ⓜ *baar*·koo *saal*·va·*vee*·dash
life jacket colete salva-vidas ⓜ koo·*le*·te *saal*·va·*vee*·dash
lift (elevator) elevador ⓜ ee·le·va·*dor*
light luz ⓕ loosh
light (colour) claro/clara ⓜ/ⓕ *klaa*·roo/*klaa*·ra
light (weight) leve *le*·ve
light bulb lâmpada ⓕ *lang*·pa·da
lighter (cigarette) isqueiro ⓜ eesh·*kay*·roo
light meter fotómetro ⓜ foo·*to*·me·troo
like gostar goosh·*taar*
linen (material) linho ⓜ *lee*·nyoo
lip balm bálsamo para os lábios ⓜ *baal*·sa·moo *pa*·ra oosh *laa*·byoosh
lips lábios ⓜ pl *laa*·byoosh
lipstick batom ⓜ ba·*tong*
liquor store loja de bebidas ⓕ *lo*·zha de be·*bee*·dash
listen escutar shkoo·*taar*
little (quantity) pouco/pouca ⓜ/ⓕ *poh*·koo/*poh*·ka
little (size) pequeno/pequena ⓜ/ⓕ pe·*ke*·noo/pe·*ke*·na
live (somewhere) morar moo·*raar*
liver fígado ⓜ *fee*·ga·doo
lizard lagarto ⓜ la·*gaar*·too
local a local loo·*kaal*
lock tranca ⓕ *trang*·ka
lock trancar trang·*kaar*
locked trancado/trancada ⓜ/ⓕ trang·*kaa*·doo/trang·*kaa*·da
long longo/longa ⓜ/ⓕ *long*·goo/*long*·ga
look olhar oo·*lyaar*
look after cuidar kwee·*daar*
look for procurar pro·koo·*raar*
lookout miradouro ⓜ mee·ra·*doh*·roo
loose solto/solta ⓜ/ⓕ *sol*·too/*sol*·ta
loose change trocos ⓜ pl *tro*·koosh
lose perder per·*der*
lost perdido/perdida ⓜ/ⓕ per·*dee*·doo/per·*dee*·da
lost-property office gabinete de perdidos e achados ⓜ gaa·bee·*ne*·te de per·*dee*·doosh ee a·*shaa*·doosh
(a) lot muito/muita ⓜ/ⓕ *mweeng*·too/*mweeng*·ta
loud alto/alta ⓜ/ⓕ *aal*·too/*aal*·ta
love amor ⓜ a·*mor*
love amar a·*maar*
lover amante ⓜ&ⓕ a·*maang*·te
low baixo/baixa ⓜ/ⓕ *bai*·shoo/*bai*·sha
lubricant lubrificante ⓜ loo·bree·fee·*kang*·te
luck sorte ⓕ *sor*·te
lucky afortunado/afortunada ⓜ/ⓕ a·foor·too·*naa*·doo/a·foor·too·*naa*·da
luggage bagagem ⓕ ba·*gaa*·zheng
luggage locker depósito de bagagens ⓜ de·*po*·zee·too de ba·*gaa*·zhengsh
luggage tag etiqueta de bagagem ⓕ e·tee·*ke*·ta de ba·*gaa*·zheng
lump nódulo ⓜ *no*·doo·loo
lunch almoço ⓜ aal·*mo*·soo
lung pulmão ⓜ pool·*mowng*
luxury luxo ⓜ *loo*·shoo

M

machine máquina ⓕ *maa*·kee·na
magazine revista ⓕ rre·*veesh*·ta
mail enviar eng·vee·*aar*
mail correio ⓜ koo·*rray*·oo
mailbox caixa do correio ⓕ *kai*·sha doo koo·*rray*·oo
main principal preeng·see·*paal*
main road rua principal ⓕ *rroo*·a preeng·see·*paal*
make fazer fa·*zer*
make-up maquilhagem ⓕ ma·kee·*lyaa*·zheng
mammogram mamograma ⓜ ma·moo·*graa*·ma
man homem ⓜ *o*·meng

ıanager (business) gerente
he·*reng*·te
ıanager (sport) treinador/
ʳeinadora Ⓜ/Ⓕ tray·na·*dor*/
ʳay·na·*do*·ra
ıanual worker trabalhador/
ʳabalhadora Ⓜ/Ⓕ tra·ba·lya·*dor*/
ʳa·ba·lya·*do*·ra
ıany vários/várias Ⓜ/Ⓕ
aa·ryoosh/*vaa*·ryash
nap mapa Ⓜ *maa*·pa
ıarital status estado civil Ⓜ
htaa·doo see·*veel*
narket mercado Ⓜ mer·*kaa*·doo
narriage casamento Ⓜ
a·za·*meng*·too
ıarried casado/casada Ⓜ/Ⓕ
a·*zaa*·doo/ka·*zaa*·da
ıarry casar ka·*zaar*
ıartial arts artes marciais Ⓕ pl
ʳ·tesh mar·see·*aish*
ıass (Catholic) missa Ⓕ *mee*·sa
ıassage massagem Ⓕ ma·*saa*·zheng
ıasseur/masseuse
ıassagista Ⓜ&Ⓕ ma·sa·*zheesh*·ta
ıat capacho Ⓜ ka·*paa*·shoo
ıatch (sport) partida Ⓕ par·*tee*·da
ıatches (for lighting) fósforos Ⓜ pl
ɔsh·foo·roosh
ıattress colchão Ⓜ kol·*showng*
ıaybe talvez tal·*vesh*
nayor presidente da câmara Ⓜ&Ⓕ
re·zee·*deng*·te da *ka*·ma·ra
ıe mim Ⓜ&Ⓕ meeng
neal refeição Ⓕ rre·fay·*sowng*
ıeasles sarampo Ⓜ sa·*rang*·poo
ıechanic mecânico/mecânica Ⓜ/Ⓕ
ıe·*ka*·nee·koo/me·*ka*·nee·ka
ıedia os meios de
ɔmunicação Ⓜ pl oosh *may*·oosh
e koo·moo·nee·ka·*sowng*
ıedicine medicamentos Ⓜ pl
ıe·dee·ka·*meng*·toosh
ıedicine (study/profession)
ıedicina Ⓕ me·dee·*see*·na
neditation meditação Ⓕ
ıe·dee·ta·*sowng*

meet encontrar eng·kong·*traar*
meet (first time) conhecer
koo·nye·*ser*
member membro Ⓜ&Ⓕ *meng*·broo
memory card memória Ⓕ
me·*mo*·ree·a
menstruation menstruação Ⓕ
meng·shtroo·a·*sowng*
menu ementa Ⓕ ee·*meng*·ta
message mensagem Ⓕ
meng·*saa*·zheng
metal metal Ⓜ me·*taal*
metre metro Ⓜ *me*·troo
metro (train) metropolitano Ⓜ
me·troo·poo·lee·*ta*·noo
metro station estacão de
metropolitano Ⓕ shta·*sowng* de
me·troo·poo·lee·*ta*·noo
microwave oven microondas Ⓜ pl
mee·kro·*ong*·dash
midday meio-dia Ⓜ *may*·oo·*dee*·a
midnight meia-noite Ⓕ *may*·a·*noy*·te
migraine enxaqueca Ⓕ eng·sha·*ke*·ka
military forças armadas Ⓕ pl
for·sash ar·*maa*·dash
milk leite Ⓜ *lay*·te
millimetre milímetro Ⓜ
mee·*lee*·me·troo
minute minuto Ⓜ mee·*noo*·too
mirror espelho Ⓜ *shpe*·lyoo
miscarriage aborto espontâneo Ⓜ
a·*bor*·too shpong·*ta*·nee·oo
miss (feel absence of) ter saudades
ter sow·*daa*·desh
mistake erro Ⓜ e·rroo
mix misturar meesh·too·*raar*
mobile phone telemóvel Ⓜ
te·le·*mo*·vel
modem modem Ⓜ *mo*·deng
modern moderno/moderna Ⓜ/Ⓕ
moo·*der*·noo/moo·*der*·na
moisturiser hidratante Ⓜ
ee·dra·*tang*·te
monastery mosteiro Ⓜ
moosh·*tay*·roo
money dinheiro Ⓜ dee·*nyay*·roo
month mês Ⓜ mesh

monument monumento ⓜ moo·noo·*meng*·too
moon lua ⓕ *loo*·a
more mais maish
morning manhã ⓕ ma·*nyang*
morning sickness enjoo matinal ⓜ eng·*zho*·oo ma·tee·*naal*
mosque mesquita ⓕ mesh·*kee*·ta
mosquito coil repelente em espiral ⓜ rre·pe·*leng*·te eng shpee·*raal*
mosquito net mosquiteiro ⓜ moosh·kee·*tay*·roo
motel motel ⓜ mo·*tel*
mother mãe ⓕ maing
mother-in-law sogra ⓕ *so*·gra
motorbike mota ⓕ *mo*·ta
motorboat barco a motor ⓜ *baar*·koo a moo·*tor*
motorway (tollway) autoestrada ⓕ ow·to·*shtraa*·da
mountain montanha ⓕ mong·*ta*·nya
mountain bike bicicleta de montanha ⓕ bee·see·*kle*·ta de mong·*ta*·nya
mountaineering montanhismo ⓜ mong·ta·*nyeezh*·moo
mountain path trilho de montanha ⓜ *tree*·lyoo de mong·*ta*·nya
mountain range cordilheira ⓕ koor·dee·*lyay*·ra
mouse rato ⓜ *rraa*·too
mouth boca ⓕ *bo*·ka
movie filme ⓜ *feel*·me
mud lama ⓕ *la*·ma
mumps papeira ⓕ pa·*pay*·ra
murder assassinato ⓜ a·sa·see·*naa*·too
murder assassinar a·sa·see·*naar*
muscle músculo ⓜ *moosh*·koo·loo
museum museu ⓜ moo·*ze*·oo
music música ⓕ *moo*·zee·ka
music group tuna ⓜ *too*·na
musician músico/música ⓜ/ⓕ *moo*·zee·koo/*moo*·zee·ka
music shop loja de música ⓕ *lo*·zha de *moo*·zee·ka
Muslim n&a muçulmano/muçulmana ⓜ/ⓕ moo·sool·*ma*·noo moo·sool·*ma*·na
mute mudo/muda ⓜ/ⓕ *moo*·doo/*moo*·da
my meu/minha ⓜ/ⓕ *me*·oo/*mee*·ny

N

nail clippers corta-unhas ⓜ *kor*·ta·*oong*·nyash
name nome ⓜ *no*·me
napkin guardanapo ⓜ gwar·da·*naa*·poo
nappy (diaper) fralda ⓕ *fraal*·da
nappy rash irritação por causa da fralda ⓕ ee·rree·ta·*sowng* poor *kow*·sa da *fraal*·da
nationality nacionalidade ⓕ na·syoo·na·lee·*daa*·de
national park parque nacional ⓜ *paar*·ke na·syoo·*naal*
nature natureza ⓕ na·too·*re*·za
nausea náusea ⓕ *now*·zee·a
near perto *per*·too
nearby próximo/próxima ⓜ/ⓕ *pro*·see·moo/*pro*·see·ma
nearby por perto poor *per*·too
nearest o/a mais perto ⓜ/ⓕ oo/a maish *per*·too
necessary necessário/necessária ⓜ/ⓕ ne·se·*saa*·ryoo/ne·se·*saa*·rya
neck pescoço ⓜ pesh·*ko*·soo
necklace colar ⓜ koo·*laar*
need precisar pre·see·*zaar*
needle (sewing) agulha ⓕ a·*goo*·ly
needle (syringe) seringa ⓕ se·*reeng*·ga
negatives (film) negativos ⓜ pl ne·ga·*tee*·voosh
neither nenhum/nenhuma ⓜ/ⓕ neng·*yoong*/neng·*yoo*·ma
net/network rede ⓕ *rre*·de
never nunca *noong*·ka
new novo/nova ⓜ/ⓕ *no*·voo/*no*·va
news notícias ⓕ pl noo·*tee*·syash
newspaper jornal ⓜ zhor·*naal*

ewsstand quiosque ⓜ kee·*osh*·ke
New Year Ano Novo ⓜ *a*·noo *no*·voo
New Zealand Nova Zelândia ⓕ
o·va ze·*lang*·dya
next próximo/próxima ⓜ/ⓕ
ro·see·moo/*pro*·see·ma
next to ao lado de ow *laa*·doo de
nice simpático/simpática ⓜ/ⓕ
eeng·*paa*·tee·koo/seeng·*paa*·tee·ka
nickname alcunha ⓕ aal·*koo*·nya
night noite ⓕ *noy*·te
nightclub discoteca ⓕ
eesh·koo·*te*·ka
night out saída à noite ⓕ saa·*ee*·da
a *noy*·te
no não nowng
noisy barulhento/barulhenta ⓜ/ⓕ
a·roo·*lyeng*·too/ba·roo·*lyeng*·ta
none nenhum/nenhuma ⓜ/ⓕ
eng·*yoong*/neng·*yoo*·ma
nonsmoking não-fumador
owng·foo·ma·*dor*
noon meio-dia ⓜ *may*·oo·*dee*·a
nose nariz ⓜ na·*reesh*
notebook bloco-notas ⓜ
lo·koo·*no*·tash
nothing nada ⓜ *naa*·da
now agora a·*go*·ra
nuclear energy energia nuclear ⓕ
e·ner·*zhee*·a noo·klee·*aar*
nuclear testing teste nuclear ⓜ
esh·te noo·klee·*aar*
nuclear waste resíduos
nucleares ⓜ pl rre·*zee*·doo·oosh
noo·klee·*aar*·esh
number número ⓜ *noo*·me·roo
numberplate número de matrícula ⓕ
oo·me·roo de ma·*tree*·koo·la
nurse enfermeiro/enfermeira ⓜ/ⓕ
eng·fer·*may*·roo/eng·fer·*may*·ra

O

oats aveia ⓕ sg a·*vay*·a
ocean oceano ⓜ o·see·*a*·noo
off (spoiled) estragado/
estragada ⓜ/ⓕ shtra·*gaa*·doo/
shtra·*gaa*·da
off (power) desligado/
desligada ⓜ/ⓕ desh·lee·*gaa*·doo/
desh·lee·*gaa*·da
office escritório ⓜ shkree·*to*·ryoo
office worker empregado/
empregada de escritório ⓜ/ⓕ
eng·pre·*gaa*·doo/eng·pre·*gaa*·da de
shkree·*to*·ryoo
often frequentemente
fre·kweng·te·*meng*·te
oil (food) óleo ⓜ *o*·lyoo
oil (petrol) petróleo ⓜ pe·*tro*·lyoo
old (age) velho/velha ⓜ/ⓕ *ve*·lyoo/
ve·lya
old (former) antigo/antiga ⓜ/ⓕ
ang·*tee*·goo/ang·*tee*·ga
on sobre *so*·bre
on (power) ligado/ligada ⓜ/ⓕ
lee·*gaa*·doo/lee·*gaa*·da
once uma vez *oo*·ma vezh
one-way (ticket) só de ida so de *ee*·da
only somente so·*meng*·te
on time a horas a *o*·rash
open a aberto/aberta ⓜ/ⓕ
a·*ber*·too/a·*ber*·ta
open abrir a·*breer*
opening hours horário de
expediente ⓜ o·*raa*·ryoo de
shpe·dee·*eng*·te
operation (medical) cirurgia ⓕ
see·roor·*zhee*·a
operator (phone) telefonista ⓜ&ⓕ
te·le·foo·*neesh*·ta
opinion opinião ⓕ o·pee·nee·*owng*
opposite oposto/oposta ⓜ/ⓕ
o·*posh*·too/o·*posh*·ta
optometrist optometrista ⓜ&ⓕ
o·to·me·*treesh*·ta
or ou oh
orange (colour) cor de laranja kor de
la·*rang*·zha
orchestra orquestra ⓕ or·*kesh*·tra
order pedido ⓜ pe·*dee*·doo
order pedir pe·*deer*
ordinary comum koo·*moong*
orgasm orgasmo ⓜ or·*gaazh*·moo
original a original o·ree·zhee·*naal*

other n&a outro/outra ⓜ/ⓕ *oh*·troo/*oh*·tra
our (one thing) nosso/nossa ⓜ/ⓕ *no*·soo/*no*·sa
our (more than one thing) nossos/nossas ⓜ/ⓕ *no*·soosh/*no*·sash
out of order avariado/avariada ⓜ/ⓕ a·va·ree·*aa*·doo/a·va·ree·*aa*·da
outside fora *fo*·ra
ovarian cyst cisto no ovário ⓜ *seesh*·too noo o·*vaa*·ryoo
ovary ovário ⓜ o·*vaa*·ryoo
oven forno ⓜ *for*·noo
overcoat sobretudo ⓜ soo·bre·*too*·doo
overdose dose excessiva ⓕ *do*·ze she·*see*·va
overnight de noite de *noy*·te
overseas no estrangeiro noo shtrang·*zhay*·roo
owe dever de·*ver*
owner dono/dona ⓜ/ⓕ *do*·noo/*do*·na
oxygen oxigénio ⓜ ok·see·*zhe*·nyoo
ozone layer camada de ozono ⓕ ka·*maa*·da de o·*zo*·noo

P

package embrulho ⓜ eng·*broo*·lyoo
packet pacote ⓜ pa·*ko*·te
padlock cadeado ⓜ ka·dee·*aa*·doo
page página ⓕ *paa*·zhee·na
pain dor ⓕ dor
painkiller analgésico ⓜ a·nal·*zhe*·zee·koo
painter pintor/pintora ⓜ/ⓕ peeng·*tor*/peeng·*to*·ra
painting pintura ⓕ peeng·*too*·ra
pair (couple) casal ⓜ ka·*zaal*
palace palácio ⓜ pa·*laa*·syoo
pan panela ⓕ pa·*ne*·la
pants (trousers) calças ⓕ pl *kaal*·sash
pantyhose collants ⓜ pl ko·*langsh*
panty liner penso higiénico ⓜ *peng*·soo ee·zhee·*e*·nee·koo
paper papel ⓜ pa·*pel*
paperwork papelada ⓕ pa·pe·*laa*·da
pap smear exame papa nicolau ⓜ e·*za*·me *paa*·pa nee·koo·*low*
parcel encomenda ⓕ eng·koo·*meng*·da
parents pais ⓜ pl paish
park parque ⓜ *paar*·ke
park (a car) estacionar shta·syoo·*naa*
parliament parlamento ⓜ par·la·*meng*·too
part (component) parte ⓕ *paar*·te
part-time meio tempo *may*·oo *teng*·poo
party (night out) festa ⓕ *fesh*·ta
party (politics) partido ⓜ par·*tee*·do
passenger passageiro/passageira pa·sa·*zhay*·roo/pa·sa·*zhay*·ra
passport passaporte ⓜ paa·sa·*por*·t
past passado ⓜ pa·*saa*·doo
pastry shop pastelaria ⓕ pash·te·la·*ree*·a
path caminho ⓜ ka·*mee*·nyoo
pay pagar pa·*gaar*
payment pagamento ⓜ pa·ga·*meng*·too
peace paz ⓕ pash
peak (mountain) pico ⓜ *pee*·koo
pedal pedal ⓜ pe·*daal*
pedestrian peão ⓜ pee·*owng*
pen caneta ⓕ ka·*ne*·ta
pencil lápis ⓜ *laa*·peesh
penis pénis ⓜ *pe*·neesh
penknife canivete ⓜ ka·nee·*ve*·te
pensioner pensionista ⓜ&ⓕ peng·syoo·*neesh*·ta
people pessoas ⓕ pl pe·*so*·ash
per (day) por poor
per cent por cento poor *seng*·too
perfect perfeito/perfeita ⓜ/ⓕ per·*fay*·too/per·*fay*·ta
performance actuação ⓕ a·too·a·*sowng*
perfume perfume ⓜ per·*foo*·me
period pain dor menstrual ⓕ dor meng·shtroo·*aal*
permission licença ⓕ lee·*seng*·sa
permit licença ⓕ lee·*seng*·sa
person pessoa ⓕ pe·*so*·a

etition petição ⓕ pe·tee·*sowng*
etrol gasolina ⓕ ga·zoo·*lee*·na
etrol station posto de gasolina ⓜ
osh·too de ga·zoo·*lee*·na
harmacist farmacêutico/farma-
êutica ⓜ/ⓕ far·ma·se·*oo*·tee·koo/
ar·ma·se·*oo*·tee·ka
harmacy farmácia ⓕ far·*maa*·sya
hone book lista telefónica ⓕ
eesh·ta te·le·*fo*·nee·ka
hone box telefone público ⓜ
e·le·*fo*·ne *poo*·blee·koo
honecard cartão telefónico ⓜ
ar·*towng* te·le·*fo*·nee·koo
hoto fotografar foo·too·gra·*faar*
hotographer fotógrafo/
otógrafa ⓜ/ⓕ foo·*to*·gra·foo/
oo·*to*·gra·fa
hotography fotografia ⓕ
oo·too·gra·*fee*·a
hrasebook livro de frases ⓜ
ee·vroo de *fraa*·zesh
ickaxe picareta ⓕ pee·ka·*re*·ta
icnic piquenique ⓜ pee·ke·*nee*·ke
iece pedaço ⓜ pe·*daa*·soo
ig porco/porca ⓜ/ⓕ *por*·koo/*por*·ka
ill comprimido ⓜ
ong·pree·*mee*·doo
the) pill pílula ⓕ *pee*·loo·la
illory (column) pilar ⓜ pee·*laar*
illow almofada ⓕ al·moo·*faa*·da
illowcase fronha ⓕ *fro*·nya
ink cor-de-rosa kor·de·*rro*·za
lace lugar ⓜ loo·*gaar*
lace of birth local de nascimento ⓜ
oo·*kaal* de nash·see·*meng*·too
lane avião ⓜ a·vee·*owng*
lant planta ⓕ *plang*·ta
late prato ⓜ *praa*·too
lateau planalto ⓜ pla·*naal*·too
latform plataforma ⓕ pla·ta·*for*·ma
lay (theatre) peça ⓕ *pe*·sa
lay (cards, etc) jogar zhoo·*gaar*
lay (guitar, etc) tocar too·*kaar*
lug (bath) tampão ⓜ tang·*powng*
lug (electricity) tomada ⓕ
oo·*maa*·da

pocket bolso ⓜ *bol*·soo
pocketknife canivete ⓜ ka·nee·*ve*·te
poetry poesia ⓕ po·ee·*zee*·a
point ponto ⓜ *pong*·too
point apontar a·pong·*taar*
poisonous venenoso/venenosa ⓜ/ⓕ
ve·ne·*no*·zoo/ve·ne·*no*·za
police polícia ⓕ poo·*lee*·sya
police officer polícia poo·*lee*·sya
police station esquadra da polícia ⓕ
shkwaa·dra da poo·*lee*·sya
policy política ⓕ poo·*lee*·tee·ka
politician político/política ⓜ/ⓕ
poo·*lee*·tee·koo/poo·*lee*·tee·ka
politics política ⓕ poo·*lee*·tee·ka
pollen pólen ⓜ *po*·leng
pollution poluição ⓕ
poo·loo·ee·*sowng*
pool (game) bilhar ⓜ bee·*lyaar*
pool (swimming) piscina ⓕ
pesh·*see*·na
poor pobre *po*·bre
popular popular poo·poo·*laar*
port (river/sea) porto ⓜ *por*·too
Portugal Portugal ⓜ poor·too·*gaal*
Portuguese português ⓜ
poor·too·*gesh*
positive positivo/positiva ⓜ/ⓕ
poo·zee·*tee*·voo/poo·zee·*tee*·vaa
possible possível poo·*see*·vel
post enviar eng·vee·*aar*
postage tarifa postal ⓕ ta·*ree*·fa
poosh·*taal*
postcode código postal ⓜ
ko·dee·goo poosh·*taal*
poster cartaz ⓜ kar·*taash*
post office correio ⓜ koo·*rray*·oo
pot (cooking) panela ⓕ pa·*ne*·la
pottery cerâmica ⓕ se·*raa*·mee·ka
pound (weight) libra ⓕ *lee*·bra
poverty pobreza ⓕ poo·*bre*·za
powder pó ⓜ po
power poder ⓜ poo·*der*
prayer oração ⓕ o·ra·*sowng*
prefer preferir pre·fe·*reer*
pregnancy test kit teste de
gravidez ⓜ *tesh*·te de gra·vee·*desh*

pregnant grávida *graa*·vee·da
premenstrual tension tensão pré-menstrual ⓕ teng·*sowng* pre·meng·shtroo·*aal*
prepare preparar pre·pa·*raar*
prescription receita médica ⓕ rre·*say*·ta *me*·dee·ka
present (gift/time) presente ⓜ pre·*zeng*·te
president presidente ⓜ&ⓕ pre·zee·*deng*·te
pressure (tyre) pressão ⓕ pre·*sowng*
pretty bonito/bonita ⓜ/ⓕ boo·*nee*·too/boo·*nee*·ta
price preço ⓜ *pre*·soo
priest padre ⓜ *paa*·dre
prime minister primeiro ministro/primeira ministra ⓜ/ⓕ pree·*may*·roo mee·*nee*·shtroo/pree·*may*·ra mee·*nee*·shtra
printer (computer) impressora ⓕ eeng·pre·*so*·ra
prison prisão ⓕ pree·*zowng*
private privado/privada pree·*vaa*·doo/pree·*vaa*·da
produce produzir proo·doo·*zeer*
profit lucro ⓜ *loo*·kroo
program programa ⓜ proo·*gra*·ma
projector projector ⓜ proo·zhe·*tor*
promise prometer proo·me·*ter*
prostitute prostituto/prostituta ⓜ/ⓕ proosh·tee·*too*·too/proosh·tee·*too*·ta
protect proteger proo·te·*zher*
protected (species) protegido/protegida ⓜ/ⓕ proo·te·*zhee*·doo/proo·te·*zhee*·da
protest manifestação ⓕ ma·nee·fesh·ta·*sowng*
protest protestar proo·tesh·*taar*
provisions provisões ⓕ pl proo·vee·*zoyngsh*
pub (bar) bar ⓜ baar
public gardens jardins públicos ⓜ pl zhar·*deengzh* *poo*·blee·koosh
public relations relações públicas ⓕ pl rre·la·*soyngsh* *poo*·blee·kash
public telephone telefone público ⓜ te·le·*fo*·ne *poo*·blee·koo
public toilet casa de banho pública ⓕ *kaa*·za de *ba*·nyoo *poo*·blee·ka
pull puxar poo·*shaar*
pump bomba ⓕ *bong*·ba
puncture furo ⓜ *foo*·roo
pure puro/pura ⓜ/ⓕ *poo*·roo/*poo*·ra
purple roxo/roxa ⓜ/ⓕ *rro*·shoo/*rro*·sha
purse bolsa ⓕ *bol*·sa
push empurrar eng·poo·*rraar*
put colocar koo·loo·*kaar*

Q

qualifications qualificações ⓕ pl kwa·lee·fee·ka·*soyngsh*
quality qualidade ⓕ kwa·lee·*daa*·de
quarantine quarentena ⓕ kwa·reng·*te*·na
queen rainha ⓕ rra·*ee*·nya
question pergunta ⓕ per·*goong*·ta
queue fila ⓕ *fee*·la
quick rápido/rápida ⓜ/ⓕ *rraa*·pee·doo/*rraa*·pee·da
quiet calado/calada ⓜ/ⓕ ka·*laa*·doo/ka·*laa*·da
quit desistir de·zeesh·*teer*

R

rabbit coelho ⓜ koo·*e*·lyoo
race (sport) corrida ⓕ koo·*rree*·da
racetrack pista de corridas ⓕ *peesh*·ta de koo·*rree*·dash
racing bike bicicleta de corrida ⓕ bee·see·*kle*·ta de koo·*rree*·da
racism racismo ⓜ rra·*seezh*·moo
racquet raquete ⓕ rra·*ke*·te
radiator radiador ⓜ rra·dee·a·*dor*
radio rádio *rraa*·dyoo
railway station estação de caminhos de ferro ⓕ shta·*sowng* de ka·*mee*·nyoosh de *fe*·rroo
rain chuva ⓕ *shoo*·va
raincoat gabardina ⓕ gaa·baar·*dee*·na

ape violação ⓕ vee·oo·la·*sowng*
are (uncommon) raro/rara ⓜ/ⓕ
raa·roo/*rraa*·ra
ash irritação da pele ⓕ
e·rree·ta·*sowng* da *pe*·le
at ratazana ⓜ&ⓕ rra·ta·*za*·na
aw cru/crua ⓜ/ⓕ kroo/*kroo*·a
azor gilete ⓕ zhee·*le*·te
azor blade lâmina de barbear ⓕ
a·mee·na de bar·bee·*aar*
ead ler ler
eading leitura ⓕ lay·*too*·ra
eady pronto/pronta ⓜ/ⓕ
rong·too/*prong*·ta
eal estate agent agente
nobiliário ⓜ&ⓕ a·*zheng*·te
e·moo·bee·*lyaa*·ryoo
ealistic realista rree·a·*leesh*·ta
eason razão ⓕ rra·*zowng*
eceipt recibo ⓜ rre·*see*·boo
ecently recentemente
re·seng·te·*meng*·te
ecommend recomendar
re·koo·meng·*daar*
ecord gravar gra·*vaar*
ecording gravação ⓕ gra·va·*sowng*
ecyclable reciclável rre·see·*klaa*·vel
ecycle reciclar rre·see·*klaar*
ed vermelho/vermelha ⓜ/ⓕ
er·*me*·lyoo/ver·*me*·lya
referee juiz/juiza ⓜ/ⓕ zhoo·*eesh*/
hoo·*ee*·za
eference referência ⓕ rre·fe·*reng*·sya
efrigerator frigorífico ⓜ
ree·goo·*ree*·fee·koo
efugee refugiado/refugiada ⓜ/ⓕ
re·foo·zhee·*aa*·doo/rre·foo·zhee·*aa*·da
efund reembolso ⓜ rre·eng·*bol*·soo
efuse recusar rre·koo·*zaar*
egional regional rre·zhyoo·*naal*
egistered mail correio registado ⓜ
oo·*rray*·oo re·zhee·*shtaa*·doo
ehydration salts sais de
idratação ⓜ pl saish de
e·dra·ta·*sowng*
relationship relacionamento ⓜ
re·la·syoo·na·*meng*·too

relax relaxar rre·laa·*shaar*
relic relíquia ⓕ rre·*lee*·kya
religion religião ⓕ rre·lee·zhee·*owng*
religious religioso/religiosa ⓜ/ⓕ
rre·lee·zhee·*o*·zoo/rre·lee·zhee·*o*·za
remote remoto/remota ⓜ/ⓕ
rre·*mo*·too/rre·*mo*·ta
remote control telecomando ⓜ
te·le·koo·*mang*·doo
rent alugar a·loo·*gaar*
repair consertar kong·ser·*taar*
reservation reserva ⓕ rre·*zer*·va
rest descansar desh·kang·*saar*
restaurant restaurante ⓜ
rresh·tow·*rang*·te
résumé currículo ⓜ koo·*rree*·koo·loo
retired aposentado/aposentada ⓜ/ⓕ
a·poo·zeng·*taa*·doo/a·poo·zeng·*taa*·da
return (ticket) a ida e volta *ee*·da
ee *vol*·ta
return voltar vol·*taar*
review revisão ⓕ rre·vee·*zowng*
rhythm ritmo ⓜ *rreet*·moo
rib costela ⓕ koosh·*te*·la
rich (wealthy) rico/rica ⓜ/ⓕ
rree·koo/*rree*·ka
ride (car) boleia ⓕ boo·*lay*·a
ride andar
ride a bike andar de bicicleta
ang·*daar* de bee·see·*kle*·ta
ride a horse andar a cavalo ang·*daar*
a ka·*vaa*·loo
right (correct) a correcto/
correcta ⓜ/ⓕ koo·*rre*·too/koo·*rre*·ta
right (direction) (à) direita (aa)
dee·*ray*·ta
ring (jewellery) anel ⓜ a·*nel*
rip-off roubo ⓜ *rroh*·boo
risk risco ⓜ *rreesh*·koo
river rio ⓜ *rree*·oo
road estrada ⓕ *shtraa*·da
road map mapa de estradas ⓜ
maa·pa de *shtraa*·dash
rob roubar rroh·*baar*
rock pedra ⓕ *pe*·dra
rock climbing alpinismo ⓜ
aal·pee·*neezh*·moo

rock group banda de rock ⓕ *baang*·da de *rro*·ke
rollerblading patins em linha ⓜ pl pa·*teengzh* eng *lee*·nya
romantic romântico/romântica ⓜ/ⓕ rroo·*maang*·tee·koo/rroo·*maang*·tee·ka
room quarto ⓜ *kwaar*·too
room number número do quarto ⓜ *noo*·me·roo doo *kwaar*·too
rope corda ⓕ *kor*·da
round redondo/redonda ⓜ/ⓕ rre·*dong*·doo/rre·*dong*·da
roundabout rotunda ⓕ rroo·*toong*·da
route rota ⓕ *rro*·ta
rubbish lixo ⓜ *lee*·shoo
rubella rubéola ⓕ rroo·*be*·o·la
rug tapete ⓜ ta·*pe*·te
ruins ruínas ⓕ pl rroo·*ee*·nash
rule regra ⓕ *rre*·gra
run correr koo·*rrer*
running corrida ⓕ koo·*rree*·da
runny nose nariz a pingar ⓜ na·*reesh* a peeng·*gaar*

S

sad triste *treesh*·te
safe cofre ⓜ *ko*·fre
safe seguro/segura ⓜ/ⓕ se·*goo*·roo/se·*goo*·ra
safe sex sexo protegido ⓜ *sek*·soo proo·te·*zhee*·doo
sailboarding windsurf ⓕ *weend*·sarf
saint n santo/santa ⓜ/ⓕ *sang*·too/*sang*·ta
salary salário ⓜ sa·*laa*·ryoo
sale liquidação ⓕ lee·kee·da·*sowng*
sales tax IVA ⓜ *ee*·va
same mesmo/mesma ⓜ/ⓕ *mezh*·moo/*mezh*·ma
sand areia ⓕ a·*ray*·a
sandal sandália ⓕ sang·*daa*·lya
sanitary napkin penso higiénico ⓜ *peng*·soo ee·zhee·e·nee·koo
sauna sauna ⓕ *sow*·na
say dizer dee·*zer*
scalp couro cabeludo ⓜ *koh*·roo ka·be·*loo*·doo
scarf lenço ⓜ *leng*·soo
school escola ⓕ *shko*·la
science ciências ⓕ pl see·*eng*·syash
scientist cientista ⓜ&ⓕ see·eng·*teesh*·ta
scissors tesoura ⓕ sg te·*zoh*·ra
score (a goal) marcar mar·*kaar*
scoreboard placar ⓜ pla·*kaar*
Scotland Escócia ⓕ *shko*·sya
sculpture escultura ⓕ shkool·*too*·ra
sea mar ⓜ maar
seasick enjoado/enjoada ⓜ/ⓕ eng·zhoo·*aa*·doo/eng·zhoo·*aa*·da
seaside beira mar ⓕ *bay*·ra maar
season estação ⓕ shta·*sowng*
seat assento ⓜ a·*seng*·too
seatbelt cinto de segurança ⓜ *seeng*·too de se·goo·*raang*·sa
second (time) segundo ⓜ se·*goong*·doo
second segundo/segunda ⓜ/ⓕ se·*goong*·doo/se·*goong*·da
second class segunda classe ⓕ se·*goong*·da *klaa*·se
second-hand em segunda mão eng se·*goong*·da mowng
second-hand shop loja de segunda mão ⓕ *lo*·zha de se·*goon*·da mowng
secretary secretário/secretária ⓜ/ⓕ se·kre·*taa*·ryoo/se·kre·*taa*·rya
see ver ver
self-employed person empregado/empregada por conta própria ⓜ/ⓕ eng·pre·*gaa*·doo/eng·pre·*gaa*·da poor *kong*·ta *pro*·pree·a
selfish egoísta e·goo·*eesh*·ta
sell vender veng·*der*
send enviar eng·vee·*aar*
sensible razoável rra·zoo·*aa*·vel
sensual sensual seng·soo·*aal*
separate separado/separada ⓜ/ⓕ se·pa·*raa*·doo/se·pa·*raa*·da
serious sério/séria ⓜ/ⓕ *se*·ryoo/*se*·rya
service serviço ⓜ ser·*vee*·soo
service charge taxa de serviço ⓕ *taa*·sha de ser·*vee*·soo

serviette guardanapo ⓜ *gwar·da·naa·poo*
several vários/várias ⓜ/ⓕ pl *vaa·ryoosh/vaa·ryash*
sew coser *koo·zer*
sex sexo ⓜ *sek·soo*
sexism machismo ⓜ *ma·sheezh·moo*
sexy sexy *sek·see*
shadow sombra ⓕ *song·bra*
shampoo champô ⓜ *shang·poo*
shape forma ⓕ *for·ma*
share (a room) partilhar *par·tee·lyaar*
shave fazer a barba *fa·zer a baar·ba*
shaving cream creme de barbear ⓜ *kre·me de bar·bee·aar*
she ela *e·la*
sheep ovelha ⓕ *oo·ve·lya*
sheet (bed) lençol ⓜ *leng·sol*
shingles (illness) zona ⓕ *zo·na*
ship navio ⓜ *na·vee·oo*
shirt camisa ⓕ *ka·mee·za*
shoe sapato ⓜ *sa·paa·too*
shoe shop sapataria ⓕ *sa·pa·ta·ree·a*
shoot atirar *a·tee·raar*
shop loja ⓕ *lo·zha*
shop fazer compras *fa·zer kong·prash*
shopping compras ⓕ pl *kong·prash*
shopping centre centro comercial ⓜ *seng·troo koo·mer·see·aal*
short (length) curto/curta ⓜ/ⓕ *koor·too/koor·ta*
shorts calções ⓜ pl *kaal·soyngsh*
shoulder ombro ⓜ *ong·broo*
shout gritar *gree·taar*
show espectáculo ⓜ *shpe·taa·koo·loo*
show mostrar *moosh·traar*
shower chuveiro ⓜ *shoo·vay·roo*
shrine santuário ⓜ *sang·too·aa·ryoo*
shut fechado/fechada ⓜ/ⓕ *fe·shaa·doo/fe·shaa·da*
shy tímido/tímida ⓜ/ⓕ *tee·mee·doo/tee·mee·da*
sick doente *doo·eng·te*
side lado ⓜ *laa·doo*
sign sinal ⓜ *see·naal*
signature assinatura ⓕ *a·see·na·too·ra*
silk seda ⓕ *se·da*
silver prata ⓕ *praa·ta*
SIM card cartão SIM ⓜ *kar·towng seeng*
similar parecido/parecida ⓜ/ⓕ *pa·re·see·doo/pa·re·see·da*
simple simples *seeng·plesh*
since (time) desde *dezh·de*
singer cantor/cantora ⓜ/ⓕ *kang·tor/kang·to·ra*
single (person) a solteiro/solteira ⓜ/ⓕ *sol·tay·roo/sol·tay·ra*
single room quarto de solteiro ⓜ *kwaar·too de sol·tay·roo*
sister irmã ⓕ *eer·mang*
sit sentar *seng·taar*
size tamanho ⓜ *ta·ma·nyoo*
skate patinar *pa·tee·naar*
skateboarding skate ⓜ *skay·te*
ski esquiar *shkee·aar*
skiing esqui ⓜ *shkee*
skim milk leite magro ⓜ *lay·te maa·groo*
skin pele ⓕ *pe·le*
skirt saia ⓕ *sai·a*
skull crânio ⓜ *kra·nyoo*
sky céu ⓜ *se·oo*
sleep dormir *door·meer*
sleeping bag saco de dormir ⓜ *saa·koo de dor·meer*
sleeping car vagão cama ⓜ *va·gowng ka·ma*
sleeping pills pílula para dormir ⓕ *pee·loo·laa pa·ra door·meer*
sleepy sonolento/sonolenta ⓜ/ⓕ *soo·noo·leng·too/soo·noo·leng·ta*
slice fatia ⓕ *fa·tee·a*
slide (transparency) diapositivo ⓜ *dee·a·po·zee·tee·voo*
slide film filme de diapositivos ⓜ *feel·me de dee·a·po·zee·tee·voosh*
slow (down) devagar *de·va·gaar*
slowly vagarosamente *va·ga·ro·za·meng·te*
small pequeno/pequena ⓜ/ⓕ *pe·ke·noo/pe·ke·na*
smell cheiro ⓜ *shay·roo*

S

smile sorrir so·*rreer*
smoke fumar foo·*maar*
snack refeição ligeira ⓕ rre·fay·*sowng* lee·*zhay*·ra
snake cobra ⓕ *ko*·bra
snorkelling snorkel ⓜ *snor*·kel
snow neve ⓕ *ne*·ve
soap sabonete ⓜ sa·boo·*ne*·te
soap opera telenovela ⓕ te·le·noo·*ve*·la
soccer futebol ⓜ foo·te·*bol*
socialist n&a socialista ⓜ&ⓕ soo·see·a·*leesh*·ta
sock meia ⓕ *may*·a
soft drink refrigerante ⓜ rre·free·zhe·*rang*·te
soldier soldado ⓜ&ⓕ sol·*daa*·doo
some uns/umas ⓜ/ⓕ pl oongsh/ *oo*·mash
someone alguém ⓜ&ⓕ aal·*geng*
something alguma coisa ⓕ aal·*goo*·ma *koy*·za
sometimes às vezes aash *ve*·zesh
son filho ⓜ *fee*·lyoo
song canção ⓕ kang·*sowng*
soon em breve eng *bre*·ve
sore a dorido/dorida ⓜ/ⓕ doo·*ree*·doo/doo·*ree*·da
souvenir lembrança ⓕ leng·*brang*·sa
souvenir shop loja de lembranças ⓕ *lo*·zha de leng·*brang*·sash
soy milk leite de soja ⓜ *lay*·te de *so*·zha
space (room) espaço ⓜ *shpaa*·soo
Spain Espanha ⓕ *shpa*·nya
speak falar fa·*laar*
special especial shpe·see·*aal*
specialist especialista ⓜ&ⓕ shpe·see·a·*leesh*·ta
speed (velocity) velocidade ⓕ ve·loo·see·*daa*·de
speed limit limite de velocidade ⓜ lee·*mee*·te de ve·loo·see·*daa*·de
speedometer mostrador de velocidade ⓜ moosh·tra·*dor* de ve·loo·see·*daa*·de
spider aranha ⓕ a·*ra*·nya
spoilt (person) mimado/ mimada ⓜ/ⓕ mee·*maa*·doo/ mee·*maa*·da
spoke raio de roda ⓜ *rraa*·yoo de *rro*·da
spoon colher ⓕ koo·*lyer*
sport desporto ⓜ desh·*por*·too
sportsperson desportista ⓜ&ⓕ desh·poor·*teesh*·ta
sports store loja de desporto ⓕ *lo*·zha de desh·*por*·too
sprain entorse ⓕ eng·*tor*·se
spring (coil) molas ⓕ pl *mo*·lash
square (town) praça ⓕ *praa*·sa
stadium estádio ⓜ *shtaa*·dyoo
stairway escadaria ⓕ shka·da·*ree*·a
stale seco/seca ⓜ/ⓕ *se*·koo/*se*·ka
stamp (postage) selo ⓜ *se*·loo
stand-by ticket bilhete sem garantia ⓜ bee·*lye*·te seng ga·rang·*tee*·a
star estrela ⓕ *shtre*·la
(four-)star (quatro) estrelas ⓕ pl (*kwaa*·troo) *shtre*·lash
start começo ⓜ koo·*me*·soo
start começar koo·me·*saar*
station estação ⓕ shta·*sowng*
stationery shop papelaria ⓕ pa·pe·la·*ree*·a
statue estátua ⓕ *shtaa*·too·a
stay ficar fee·*kaar*
steal roubar rroh·*baar*
steep íngreme *eeng*·gre·me
step passo ⓜ *paa*·soo
stereo estéreo ⓜ *shte*·ree·oo
stockings meias de vidro ⓕ pl *may*·ash de *vee*·droo
stolen roubado/roubada ⓜ/ⓕ rroh·*baa*·doo/rroh·*baa*·da
stomach estômago ⓜ *shto*·ma·goo
stomachache dor de estômago ⓕ dor de *shto*·ma·goo
stone pedra ⓕ *pe*·dra
stoned (drugged) drogado/ drogada ⓜ/ⓕ droo·*gaa*·doo/ droo·*gaa*·da
stop parar pa·*raar*

storm tempestade ⓕ
teng·pesh·*taa*·de
story história ⓕ *shto*·rya
stove fogão ⓜ foo·*gowng*
straight directo/directa ⓜ/ⓕ
dee·*re*·too/dee·*re*·ta
strange estranho/estranha ⓜ/ⓕ
shtra·nyoo/*shtra*·nya
stranger estranho/estranha ⓜ/ⓕ
shtra·nyoo/*shtra*·nya
stream ribeiro ⓜ rree·*bay*·roo
street rua ⓕ *rroo*·a
street market feira ⓕ *fay*·ra
street party festa na rua ⓕ *fesh*·ta
na *rroo*·a
strike greve ⓕ *gre*·ve
string cordel ⓜ koor·*del*
stroke (health) trombose ⓕ
trong·*bo*·ze
strong forte *for*·te
stubborn teimoso/teimosa ⓜ/ⓕ
tay·*mo*·zoo/tay·*mo*·za
student estudante ⓜ&ⓕ
shtoo·*dang*·te
studio estúdio ⓜ *shtoo*·dyoo
stupid burro/burra ⓜ/ⓕ *boo*·rroo/
boo·rra
style estilo ⓜ *shtee*·loo
subtitles legendas ⓕ pl
le·*zheng*·dash
suburb bairro ⓜ *bai*·rroo
subway (train) metropolitano ⓜ
me·troo·poo·lee·*ta*·no
suit bag saco de fatos ⓜ *saa*·koo de
faa·toosh
suitcase mala de viagem ⓕ *maa*·la
de vee·*aa*·zheng
sun sol ⓜ sol
sunblock protecção anti-solar ⓕ
proo·te·*sowng* ang·tee·soo·*laar*
sunburnt queimado/queimada do
sol ⓜ/ⓕ kay·*maa*·doo/kay·*maa*·da
doo sol
sunglasses óculos de sol ⓜ pl
o·koo·loosh de sol
sunny ensolarado/ensolarada ⓜ/ⓕ
eng·soo·la·*raa*·doo/eng·soo·la·*raa*·da

sunrise nascer do sol ⓜ *nash*·ser
doo sol
sunset pôr do sol ⓜ por doo sol
sunstroke insolação ⓕ
eeng·soo·la·*sowng*
supermarket supermercado ⓜ
soo·per·mer·*kaa*·doo
superstition superstição ⓕ
soo·persh·tee·*sowng*
supporter (politics) partidário/
partidária ⓜ/ⓕ par·tee·*daa*·ryoo/
par·tee·*daa*·rya
supporter (sport) adepto/
adepta ⓜ/ⓕ a·*de*·pe·too/a·*de*·pe·ta
surf fazer surf fa·*zer* sarf
surfboard prancha de surf ⓕ
prang·sha de sarf
surfing surf ⓜ sarf
surname apelido ⓜ a·pe·*lee*·doo
surprise surpresa ⓕ soor·*pre*·za
sweater camisola ⓕ ka·mee·*zo*·la
sweet a doce *do*·se
swelling inchaço ⓜ eeng·*shaa*·soo
swim nadar na·*daar*
swimming natação ⓕ na·ta·*sowng*
swimming pool piscina ⓕ
pesh·*see*·na
swimsuit fato de banho ⓜ *faa*·too
de *ba*·nyoo
synagogue sinagoga ⓕ see·na·*go*·ga
synthetic sintético/sintética ⓜ/ⓕ
seeng·*te*·tee·koo/seeng·*te*·tee·ka
syringe seringa ⓕ se·*reeng*·ga

T

table mesa ⓕ *me*·za
tablecloth toalha de mesa ⓕ
twaa·lya de *me*·za
table tennis ténis de mesa ⓜ
te·neesh de *me*·za
tail cauda ⓕ *kow*·da
tailor alfaiate ⓜ aal·fai·*aa*·te
take levar le·*vaar*
take a photo tirar uma foto tee·*raar*
oo·ma *fo*·too
talk falar fa·*laar*
tall alto/alta ⓜ/ⓕ *aal*·too/*aal*·ta

T

tampon tampão Ⓜ tang·*powng*
tap torneira Ⓕ toor·*nay*·ra
tasty gostoso/gostosa Ⓜ/Ⓕ goosh·*to*·zoo/goosh·*to*·za
tax imposto Ⓜ eeng·*posh*·too
taxi rank praça de táxis Ⓕ *praa*·sa de *taak*·seesh
tea chá Ⓜ shaa
teacher professor/professora Ⓜ/Ⓕ proo·fe·*sor*/proo·fe·*so*·ra
tea house casa de chá Ⓕ *kaa*·za de shaa
team equipa Ⓕ e·*kee*·pa
teaspoon colher de chá Ⓕ koo·*lyer* de shaa
technique técnica Ⓕ *tek*·nee·ka
teeth dentes Ⓜ pl *deng*·tesh
telephone telefone Ⓜ te·le·*fo*·ne
telephone telefonar te·le·foo·*naar*
telescope telescópio Ⓜ te·lesh·*ko*·pyoo
television televisão Ⓕ te·le·vee·*zowng*
tell dizer dee·*zer*
temperature (fever) febre Ⓕ *fe*·bre
temperature (weather) temperatura Ⓕ teng·pe·ra·*too*·ra
tennis ténis Ⓜ *te*·neesh
tennis court campo de ténis Ⓜ *kang*·poo de *te*·neesh
tent tenda Ⓕ *teng*·da
tent peg estaca Ⓕ *shtaa*·ka
terrible terrível te·*rree*·vel
terrorism terrorismo Ⓜ te·rroo·*reezh*·moo
test teste Ⓜ *tesh*·te
thank agradecer a·gra·de·*ser*
that aquele/aquela Ⓜ/Ⓕ a·*ke*·le/a·*ke*·la
theatre teatro Ⓜ te·*aa*·troo
their deles *de*·lesh
there (where neither of us is) lá laa
there (where you are) aí a·*ee*
thermometer termómetro Ⓜ ter·*mo*·me·troo
they eles/elas Ⓜ/Ⓕ e·lesh/e·lash
thick grosso/grossa Ⓜ/Ⓕ *gro*·soo/*gro*·sa
thief ladrão/ladra Ⓜ/Ⓕ la·*drowng*/*laa*·dra
thin fino/fina Ⓜ/Ⓕ *fee*·noo/*fee*·na
think pensar peng·*saar*
thirsty sedento/sedenta Ⓜ/Ⓕ se·*deng*·too/se·*deng*·ta
this este/esta Ⓜ/Ⓕ *esh*·te/*esh*·ta
thread linha de coser Ⓕ *lee*·nya de koo·*zer*
throat garganta Ⓕ gar·*gang*·ta
thrush (health) corrimento Ⓜ koo·rree·*meng*·too
thunderstorm trovoada Ⓕ troo·voo·*aa*·da
ticket bilhete Ⓜ bee·*lye*·te
ticket collector cobrador Ⓜ koo·bra·*dor*
ticket machine máquina de vender bilhetes Ⓕ *maa*·kee·na de veng·*der* bee·*lye*·tesh
ticket office bilheteira Ⓕ bee·lye·*tay*·ra
tide maré Ⓕ ma·*re*
tight apertado/apertada Ⓜ/Ⓕ a·per·*taa*·doo/a·per·*taa*·da
time tempo Ⓜ *teng*·poo
time difference diferença horária Ⓕ dee·fe·*reng*·sa o·*raa*·rya
timetable horário Ⓜ o·*raa*·ryoo
tin (can) lata Ⓕ *laa*·ta
tin opener abre latas Ⓜ *aa*·bre *laa*·tash
tiny minúsculo/minúscula Ⓜ/Ⓕ mee·*noosh*·koo·loo/mee·*noosh*·koo·la
tip (gratuity) gorjeta Ⓕ gor·*zhe*·ta
tire pneu Ⓜ pe·*ne*·oo
tired cansado/cansada Ⓜ/Ⓕ kang·*saa*·doo/kang·*saa*·da
tissue lenço de papel Ⓜ *leng*·soo de pa·*pel*
to a a
toaster torradeira Ⓕ too·rra·*day*·ra
tobacco tabaco Ⓜ ta·*baa*·koo
tobacconist tabacaria Ⓕ ta·ba·ka·*ree*·a
tobogganing tobogã Ⓜ to·bo·*gang*
today hoje *o*·zhe

toe dedo do pé ⓜ *de*·doo doo pe
together junto/junta ⓜ/ⓕ
zhoong·too/*zhoong*·ta
toilet casa de banho ⓕ *kaa*·za de
ba·nyoo
toilet paper papel higiénico ⓜ
pa·*pel* ee·zhee·e·nee·koo
toiletry bag necessaire ⓜ ne·se·*ser*
tomorrow amanhã aa·ma·*nyang*
tonight hoje à noite o·zhe aa *noy*·te
too (also) também tang·*beng*
too (much) demais de·*maish*
tooth dente ⓜ *deng*·te
toothache dor de dentes ⓕ dor de
deng·tesh
toothbrush escova de dentes ⓕ
shko·va de *deng*·tesh
toothpaste pasta de dentes ⓕ
paash·ta de *deng*·tesh
toothpick palito ⓜ pa·*lee*·too
torch (flashlight) lanterna
eléctrica ⓕ lang·*ter*·na ee·*le*·tree·ka
touch tocar too·*kaar*
tour excursão ⓕ shkoor·*sowng*
tourist turista ⓜ&ⓕ too·*reesh*·ta
tourist office escritório de turismo ⓜ
shkree·*to*·ryoo de too·*reezh*·moo
towel toalha ⓕ *twaa*·lya
tower torre ⓕ *to*·rre
toy shop loja de brinquedos ⓕ
lo·zha de breeng·*ke*·doosh
track (path) caminho ⓜ ka·*mee*·nyoo
track (sport) pista ⓕ *peesh*·ta
tradesperson comerciante ⓜ&ⓕ
koo·mer·see·*aang*·te
traffic tráfico ⓜ *traa*·fee·koo
traffic light semáforo ⓜ
se·*maa*·foo·roo
trail atalho ⓜ a·*taa*·lyoo
train comboio ⓜ kong·*boy*·oo
train station estação de caminhos
de ferro ⓕ shta·*sowng* de
ka·*mee*·nyoosh de *fe*·rroo
tram eléctrico ⓜ ee·*le*·tree·koo
transit lounge sala de trânsito ⓕ
saa·la de *trang*·zee·too
translate traduzir tra·doo·*zeer*
transport transporte ⓜ
trangsh·*por*·te
travel viajar vee·a·*zhaar*
travel agency agência de viagens ⓕ
a·*zheng*·sya de vee·*aa*·zhengsh
travellers cheques travellers
cheques ⓜ pl *tra*·ve·ler *she*·kesh
travel sickness enjoo de viagem ⓜ
eng·*zho*·oo de vee·*aa*·zheng
tree árvore ⓕ *aar*·vo·re
trip viagem ⓕ vee·*aa*·zheng
trolley carrinho ⓜ ka·*rree*·nyoo
trousers calças ⓕ pl *kaal*·sash
truck camião ⓜ ka·mee·*yowng*
trust confiar kong·fee·*aar*
try (attempt) tentar teng·*taar*
tube (tyre) câmara ⓕ *ka*·ma·ra
tumour tumor ⓜ too·*mor*
tune melodia ⓕ me·loo·*dee*·a
turn virar vee·*raar*
TV televisão ⓕ te·le·vee·*zowng*
tweezers pinça ⓕ *peeng*·sa
twice duas vezes *doo*·ash *ve*·zesh
twin beds camas gémeas ⓕ pl
ka·mash *zhe*·me·ash
twins gémeos/gémeas ⓜ/ⓕ
zhe·mee·oosh/*zhe*·mee·ash
type tipo ⓜ *tee*·poo
typical típico/típica ⓜ/ⓕ
tee·pee·koo/*tee*·pee·ka
tyre pneu ⓜ pe·*ne*·oo

U

ultrasound ultrasom ⓜ ool·tra·*song*
umbrella guarda-chuva ⓜ
gwaar·da·*shoo*·va
uncomfortable desconfortável
desh·kong·foor·*taa*·vel
understand compreender
kong·pree·eng·*der*
underwear roupa interior ⓕ *rroh*·pa
eeng·te·ree·*or*
unemployed desempregado/desem-
pregada ⓜ/ⓕ de·zeng·pre·*gaa*·doo/
de·zeng·pre·*gaa*·da
unfair injusto/injusta ⓜ/ⓕ
eeng·*zhoosh*·too/eeng·*zhoosh*·ta

uniform farda ⓕ *faar*·da
universe universo ⓜ oo·nee·*ver*·soo
university universidade ⓕ oo·nee·ver·see·*daa*·de
unsafe inseguro/insegura ⓜ/ⓕ eeng·se·*goo*·roo/eeng·se·*goo*·ra
until até a·*te*
unusual invulgar eeng·vool·*gaar*
up para cima *pa*·ra *see*·ma
urgent urgente oor·*zheng*·te
urinary infection infecção urinária ⓕ eeng·fek·*sowng* oo·ree·*naa*·rya
USA EUA ⓜ pl e·oo·*aa*
useful útil *oo*·teel

V

vacancy vaga ⓕ *vaa*·ga
vacant vago/vaga ⓜ/ⓕ *vaa*·goo/*vaa*·ga
vacation férias ⓕ pl *fe*·ree·ash
vaccination vacina ⓕ va·*see*·na
validate validar va·lee·*daar*
valley vale ⓜ *vaa*·le
valuable valioso/valiosa ⓜ/ⓕ va·lee·*o*·zoo/va·lee·*o*·za
value valor ⓜ va·*lor*
van carrinha ⓕ ka·*rree*·nya
vegetarian n&a vegetariano/vegetariana ⓜ/ⓕ ve·zhe·ta·ree·*a*·noo/ve·zhe·ta·ree·*a*·na
vein veia ⓕ *vey*·a
venereal disease doença venérea ⓕ do·*eng*·sa ve·*ne*·ree·a
venue local ⓜ loo·*kaal*
very muito *mweeng*·too
video camera câmara de vídeo ⓕ *ka*·ma·ra de *vee*·dee·oo
video recorder gravador de vídeo ⓜ gra·va·*dor* de *vee*·dee·oo
video tape cassete de vídeo ⓕ ka·*se*·te de *vee*·dee·oo
view vista ⓕ *veesh*·ta
village aldeia ⓕ aal·*day*·a
vineyard vinha ⓕ *vee*·nya
virus vírus ⓜ *vee*·roosh
visa visto ⓜ *veesh*·too
visit visitar vee·zee·*taar*
vitamin vitamina ⓕ vee·ta·*mee*·na
voice voz ⓕ vosh
volleyball (sport) vóleibol ⓜ *vo*·lay·bol
volume volume ⓜ voo·*loo*·me
vote votar voo·*taar*

W

wage salário ⓜ sa·*laa*·ryoo
wait (for) esperar shpe·*raar*
waiter criado/criada de mesa ⓜ/ⓕ kree·*aa*·doo/kree·*aa*·da de *me*·za
waiting room sala de espera ⓕ *saa*·la de *shpe*·ra
wake (someone) up acordar a·koor·*daar*
Wales País de Gales ⓜ pa·*eesh* de *gaa*·lesh
walk caminhar ka·mee·*nyaar*
wall (outer) parede ⓕ pa·*re*·de
want querer ke·*rer*
war guerra ⓕ *ge*·rra
wardrobe guarda-roupa ⓜ gwaar·da·*rroh*·pa
warm morno/morna ⓜ/ⓕ *mor*·noo/*mor*·na
warn avisar a·vee·*zaar*
wash lavar la·*vaar*
wash (oneself) lavar-se la·*vaar*·se
washing machine máquina de lavar roupa ⓕ *maa*·kee·na de la·*vaar* *rroh*·pa
watch relógio ⓜ rre·*lo*·zhyoo
watch (look after) vigiar vee·zhee·*aar*
watch (television, etc) ver ver
water água ⓕ *aa*·gwa
water bottle garrafa de água ⓕ ga·*rraa*·fa de *aa*·gwa
waterfall cascata ⓕ kash·*kaa*·ta
waterproof à prova d'água aa *pro*·va *daa*·gwa
water-skiing esqui aquático ⓜ shkee a·*kwaa*·tee·koo
wave (ocean) onda ⓕ *ong*·da
way caminho ⓜ ka·*mee*·nyoo
we nós nosh
weak fraco/fraca ⓜ/ⓕ *fraa*·koo/*fraa*·ka

wealthy rico/rica ⓜ/ⓕ *rree*·koo/ *rree*·ka
wear usar oo·*zaar*
weather tempo ⓜ *teng*·poo
wedding casamento ⓜ ka·za·*meng*·too
week semana ⓕ se·*ma*·na
weekend fim-de-semana ⓜ feeng·de·se·*ma*·na
weigh pesar pe·*zaar*
weight peso ⓜ pe·*zoo*
welcome receber rre·se·*ber*
welfare seguro social ⓜ se·*goo*·roo soo·see·*aal*
well bem beng
wet molhado/molhada ⓜ/ⓕ moo·*lyaa*·doo/moo·*lyaa*·da
what que ke
wheel roda ⓕ *rro*·da
wheelchair cadeira de rodas ⓕ ka·*day*·ra de *rro*·dash
when quando *kwang*·doo
where onde *ong*·de
which qual kwaal
white branco/branca ⓜ/ⓕ *brang*·koo/*brang*·ka
who quem keng
why porquê poor·*ke*
wide largo/larga ⓜ/ⓕ *laar*·goo/ *laar*·ga
wife esposa ⓕ *shpo*·za
win ganhar ga·*nyaar*
wind vento ⓜ *veng*·too
window janela ⓕ zha·*ne*·la
windscreen (windshield) pára-brisas ⓜ pl *pa*·ra·*bree*·zash
wine vinho ⓜ *vee*·nyoo
winner vencedor/vencedora ⓜ/ⓕ veng·se·*dor*/veng·se·*do*·ra
wish desejar de·ze·*zhaar*
with com kong
within (time) dentro de *deng*·troo de
without sem seng
woman mulher ⓕ moo·*lyer*
wonderful maravilhoso/ maravilhosa ⓜ/ⓕ ma·ra·vee·*lyo*·zoo/ ma·ra·vee·*lyo*·za
wood madeira ⓕ ma·*day*·ra
wool lã ⓕ lang
word palavra ⓕ pa·*laa*·vra
work trabalho ⓜ tra·*baa*·lyoo
work trabalhar tra·ba·*lyaar*
work experience experiência de trabalho ⓕ shpe·ree·*eng*·sya de tra·*baa*·lyoo
workout treinamento ⓜ tre·na·*meng*·too
work permit licença de trabalho ⓕ lee·*seng*·sa de tra·*baa*·lyoo
workshop oficina ⓕ o·fe·*see*·na
world mundo ⓕ *moong*·doo
worms (intestinal) lombrigas ⓕ pl long·*bree*·gash
worried preocupado/preocupada ⓜ/ⓕ pree·o·koo·*paa*·doo/ pree·o·koo·*paa*·da
worship reverenciar rre·ve·reng·see·*aar*
wrist pulso ⓜ *pool*·soo
write escrever shkre·*ver*
writer escritor/escritora ⓜ/ⓕ shkree·*tor*/shkree·*to*·ra
wrong errado/errada ⓜ/ⓕ e·*rraa*·doo/e·*rraa*·da

Y

yacht iate ⓜ ee·*aat*
year ano ⓜ *a*·noo
yellow amarelo/amarela ⓜ/ⓕ a·ma·*re*·loo/a·ma·*re*·la
yes sim seeng
yesterday ontem *ong*·teng
you inf sg/pl tu/vocês too/vo·*sesh*
you pol sg/pl você/vós vo·*se*/vosh
young jovem *zho*·veng
youth hostel pousada de juventude ⓕ poh·*zaa*·da de zhoo·veng·*too*·de

Z

zipper fecho écler ⓜ *fe*·shoo e·*kler*
zoo jardim zoológico ⓜ zhar·*deeng* zoo·oo·*lo*·zhee·koo

A

Dictionary

PORTUGUESE *to* ENGLISH

português – inglês

Portuguese nouns have their gender indicated with ⓜ (masculine) and ⓕ (feminine). Where adjectives or nouns have separate masculine and feminine forms, these are divided by a slash and marked ⓜ/ⓕ. You'll also see words marked as v (verb), n (noun), a (adjective), pl (plural), sg (singular), inf (informal) and pol (polite) where necessary. Verbs are given in the infinitive – for details on how to change verbs for use in a sentence, see **grammar** (p25). For food and drink terms, see the **menu decoder** (p194).

A

a a to
à a at
abaixo a·*bai*·shoo below
abalo cerebral ⓜ a·*baa*·loo se·re·*braal* concussion
abelha ⓕ a·*be*·lya bee
aberto/aberta ⓜ/ⓕ a·*ber*·too/ a·*ber*·ta open a
a bordo a *bor*·doo aboard
aborrecido/aborrecida ⓜ/ⓕ a·boo·rre·*see*·doo/a·boo·rre·*see*·da bored
aborto ⓜ a·*bor*·too abortion
— espontâneo shpong·*ta*·nee·oo miscarriage
abraçar a·bra·*saar* hug
abrir a·*breer* open
acampamento ⓜ a·kang·pa·*meng*·too campsite
acampar a·kang·*paar* camp
acidente ⓜ a·see·*deng*·te accident
acordar a·koor·*daar* wake up
actor/actriz ⓜ/ⓕ aa·*tor*/aa·*treesh* actor
actuação ⓕ a·too·a·*sowng* performance
adepto/adepta ⓜ/ⓕ a·*de*·pe·too/ a·*de*·pe·ta supporter (sport)
adivinhar a·dee·vee·*nyaar* guess
admitir a·de·mee·*teer* acknowledge • let in
adulto/adulta ⓜ/ⓕ a·*dool*·too/ a·*dool*·ta adult n&a
advogado/advogada a·de·voo·*gaa*·doo/a·de·voo·*gaa*·da lawyer
aeroporto ⓜ a·e·ro·*por*·too airport
afortunado/afortunada ⓜ/ⓕ a·foor·too·*naa*·doo/a·foor·too·*naa*·da lucky
agarrar a·ga·*rraar* get
agência ⓕ a·*zheng*·sya agency
— de imobiliário de ee·mo·bee·*lyaa*·ryoo real estate agency

- de viagens de vee·*aa*·zhengsh
ravel agency
- noticiosa noo·tee·see·*o*·za
ewsagency
gora a·*go*·ra now
gradecer a·gra·de·*ser* thank
gricultor ⓜ&ⓕ a·gree·kool·*tor*
armer
gricultura ⓕ a·gree·kool·*too*·ra
griculture
gua ⓕ *aa*·gwa water
gulha ⓕ a·*goo*·lya needle (sewing)
horas a *o*·rash on time
í a·*ee* there (where you are)
juda ⓕ a·*zhoo*·da help
judar a·zhoo·*daar* help
lcunha ⓕ aal·*koo*·nya nickname
ldeia ⓕ aal·*day*·a village
leijar a·lay·*zhaar* hurt
lfândega ⓕ aal·*fang*·de·ga customs
lgodão ⓜ aal·goo·*downg* cotton
lguém ⓜ&ⓕ aal·*geng* someone
lguma coisa ⓕ aal·*goo*·ma *koy*·za
omething
lguns/algumas ⓜ/ⓕ pl
al·*goongsh*/aal·*goo*·mash few • some
limentar a·lee·meng·*taar* feed
lmoço ⓜ aal·*mo*·soo lunch
lmofada ⓕ al·moo·*faa*·da pillow
lto/alta ⓜ/ⓕ *aal*·too/*aal*·ta high •
oud • tall
lugar a·loo·*gaar* hire (rent)
luguer de automóvel ⓜ a·loo·*ger*
e ow·too·*mo*·vel car hire
ma ⓕ *a*·ma babysitter • childminding
maciador ⓜ a·ma·see·a·*dor* hair
onditioner
manhã aa·ma·*nyang* tomorrow
mante ⓜ&ⓕ a·*maang*·te lover
mar a·*maar* love
marelo/amarela ⓜ/ⓕ a·ma·*re*·loo/
·ma·*re*·la yellow
mável ⓜ&ⓕ a·*maa*·vel kind (nice)
mbiente ⓜ ang·bee·*eng*·te
nvironment
mbos/ambas ⓜ/ⓕ *ang*·boosh/
ng·bash both

ambulância ⓕ ang·boo·*lang*·sya
ambulance
amigo/amiga ⓜ/ⓕ a·*mee*·goo/
a·*mee*·ga friend
amor ⓜ a·*mor* love
analgésico ⓜ a·nal·*zhe*·zee·koo
painkiller
análise de sangue ⓕ a·*naa*·lee·ze
de *sang*·ge blood test
andar ⓜ ang·*daar* floor (storey)
andar ang·*daar* ride
— a cavalo a ka·*vaa*·loo ride a
horse
— de bicicleta de bee·see·*kle*·ta ride
a bicycle
anel ⓜ a·*nel* ring (jewellery)
anemia ⓕ a·ne·*mee*·a anaemia
aniversário ⓜ a·nee·ver·*saa*·ryoo
birthday
ano ⓜ *a*·noo year
anteontem ang·tee·*ong*·teng day
before yesterday
antes *ang*·tesh before
antibióticos ⓜ pl
ang·tee·bee·o·tee·koosh antibiotics
antigo/antiga ⓜ/ⓕ ang·*tee*·goo/
ang·*tee*·ga ancient • antique • old
antiguidade ⓕ ang·tee·gwee·*daa*·de
antique
antiséptico ⓜ ang·tee·*se*·tee·koo
antiseptic
anúncio ⓜ a·*noong*·syoo
advertisement
ao ow at
ao lado de ow *laa*·doo de next to
apanhar boleia a·pa·*nyaar* boo·*lay*·a
hitchhike
aparelho auditivo ⓜ a·pa·*re*·lyoo
ow·dee·*tee*·voo hearing aid
apelido ⓜ a·pe·*lee*·doo
family name
apertado/apertada ⓜ/ⓕ
a·per·*taa*·doo/a·per·*taa*·da tight
apontar a·pong·*taar* point
aposentado/aposentada ⓜ/ⓕ
a·poo·zeng·*taa*·doo/
a·poo·zeng·*taa*·da retired

aposta ⓕ a·*posh*·ta bet
aprender a·preng·*der* learn
à prova d'água aa *pro*·va *daa*·gwa waterproof
aquecedor ⓜ a·ke·se·*dor* heater
aquecido/aquecida ⓜ/ⓕ a·ke·*see*·doo/a·ke·*see*·da heated
aquecimento ⓜ a·ke·see·*meng*·too heating
aquele/aquela ⓜ/ⓕ a·*ke*·le/a·*ke*·la that
aqui a·*kee* here
ar ⓜ aar air
— condicionado kong·dee·syoo·*naa*·doo air-con
aranha ⓕ a·*ra*·nya spider
areia ⓕ a·*ray*·a sand
arquitectura ⓕ ar·kee·te·*too*·ra architecture
arte ⓕ *aar*·te art
artesanato ⓜ ar·te·za·*naa*·too crafts
artes marciais ⓕ pl *ar*·tesh mar·see·*aish* martial arts
árvore ⓕ *aar*·vo·re tree
asma ⓕ *ash*·ma asthma
aspirina ⓕ ash·pee·*ree*·na aspirin
assassinato ⓜ a·sa·see·*naa*·too murder
assédio ⓜ a·se·dyoo harassment
assento ⓜ a·*seng*·too seat
assinar a·see·*naar* sign
assinatura ⓕ a·see·na·*too*·ra signature
assistência social ⓕ a·seesh·*teng*·sya soo·see·*aal* welfare
às vezes aash *ve*·zesh sometimes
atalho ⓜ a·*taa*·lyoo trail
ataque de coração ⓜ a·*taa*·ke de koo·ra·*sowng* heart attack
até a·*te* until
atirar a·tee·*raar* shoot
atmosfera ⓕ at·moosh·*fe*·ra atmosphere
atrás a·*traash* back (position) • behind
atrasado/atrasada ⓜ/ⓕ a·tra·*zaa*·doo/a·tra·*zaa*·da late
atraso ⓜ a·*traa*·zoo delay
através a·tra·*vesh* across
autocarro ⓜ ow·to·*kaa*·roo bus
autoestrada ⓕ ow·to·*shtraa*·da highway • motorway (tollway)
avariado/avariada ⓜ/ⓕ a·va·ree·*aa*·doo/a·va·ree·*aa*·da broken down (car) • out of order
avariar a·va·ree·*aar* break down (car
avenida ⓕ a·ve·*nee*·da avenue
avião ⓜ a·vee·*owng* airplane
avisar a·vee·*zaar* warn
avó ⓕ a·*vo* grandmother
avô ⓜ a·*voh* grandfather
azul a·*zool* blue
azulejo ⓜ a·zoo·*le*·zhoo painted tile

B

bagagem ⓕ ba·*gaa*·zheng baggage
baixo *bai*·shoo down
baixo/baixa ⓜ/ⓕ *bai*·shoo/*bai*·sha low
balcão ⓜ bal·*kowng* counter (at bar
— de bagagens de ba·*gaa*·zhengsh baggage claim
balde ⓜ *baal*·de bucket
banco ⓜ *bang*·koo bank
bandeira ⓕ bang·*day*·ra flag
banho ⓜ *ba*·nyoo bath
baptismo ⓜ ba·*teezh*·moo baptism
barata ⓕ ba·*raa*·ta cockroach
barato/barata ⓜ/ⓕ ba·*raa*·too/ba·*raa*·ta cheap
barbeiro ⓜ bar·*bay*·roo barber
barco ⓜ *baar*·koo boat
— a motor a moo·*tor* motorboat
barulhento/barulhenta ⓜ/ⓕ ba·roo·*lyeng*·too/ba·roo·*lyeng*·ta nois
basquetebol ⓜ bash·ke·te·*bol* basketball
batom ⓜ ba·*tong* lipstick
bêbado/bêbada ⓜ/ⓕ *be*·ba·doo/*be*·ba·da drunk
bebé ⓜ&ⓕ be·*be* baby
beber be·*ber* drink
bechigas ⓕ pl be·*shee*·gash chicke pox
beijo ⓜ *bay*·zhoo kiss

eira mar ⓕ *bay*·ra maar seaside
em beng well
engaleiro ⓜ beng·ga·*lay*·roo loakroom
exiga ⓕ be·*shee*·ga bladder
iblioteca ⓕ bee·blee·oo·*te*·ka library
icho ⓜ *bee*·shoo bug
icicleta ⓕ bee·see·*kle*·ta bicycle
– de corrida de koo·*rree*·da racing ike
– de montanha de mong·*ta*·nya nountain bike
ilhar ⓜ bee·*lyaar* pool (game)
ilhete ⓜ bee·*lye*·te ticket
– de identidade de e·deng·tee·*daa*·de ID card
– sem garantia seng ga·rang·*tee*·a tand-by ticket
ilheteira ⓕ bee·lye·*tay*·ra ticket ffice
inóculos ⓜ pl bee·*no*·koo·loosh inoculars
loco-notas ⓜ *blo*·koo·*no*·tash otebook
loqueado/bloqueada ⓜ/ⓕ lo·kee·*aa*·doo/blo·kee·*aa*·da blocked
oca ⓕ *bo*·ka mouth
ola ⓕ *bo*·la ball (sport)
olas de algodão ⓕ pl *bo*·lash de al·goo·*downg* cotton balls
oleia ⓕ boo·*lay*·a ride (car, etc)
olha ⓕ *bo*·lya blister
olo ⓜ *bo*·loo cake
olsa ⓕ *bol*·sa purse
olso ⓜ *bol*·soo pocket
om/boa ⓜ/ⓕ bong/*bo*·a fine • good
omba ⓕ *bong*·ba pump
oneco/boneca ⓜ/ⓕ boo·*ne*·koo/ oo·*ne*·ka doll
onito/bonita ⓜ/ⓕ boo·*nee*·too/ oo·*nee*·ta beautiful • handsome
otão ⓜ boo·*towng* button
otas ⓕ *bo*·tash boots
– para caminhadas *pa*·ra a·mee·*nyaa*·dash hiking boots
otija de gás ⓜ boo·*tee*·zha de aash gas cartridge

boxe ⓜ *bok*·se boxing
braço ⓜ *braa*·soo arm (body)
branco/branca ⓜ/ⓕ *brang*·koo/ *brang*·ka white
brincos ⓜ pl *breeng*·koosh earrings
brochura ⓕ broo·*shoo*·ra brochure
bronquite ⓕ brong·*kee*·te bronchitis
budista ⓜ&ⓕ boo·*deesh*·ta Buddhist
bufete ⓜ boo·*fe*·te buffet
burro/burra ⓜ/ⓕ *boo*·rroo/*boo*·rra stupid
bússola ⓕ *boo*·soo·la compass

C

cabeça ⓕ ka·*be*·sa head
cabeleireiro/cabeleireira ⓜ/ⓕ ka·be·lay·*ray*·roo/ka·be·lay·*ray*·ra hairdresser
cabelo ⓜ ka·*be*·loo hair
cabra ⓕ *kaa*·bra goat
caça ⓕ *kaa*·sa hunting
cada *ka*·da each
cadeado ⓜ ka·dee·*aa*·doo padlock
cadeira ⓕ ka·*day*·ra chair
— de criança de kree·*ang*·sa child seat
— de rodas de *rro*·dash wheelchair
cair ka·*eer* fall
caixa ⓕ *kai*·sha box
— automático ow·too·*maa*·tee·koo automated teller machine (ATM)
— de papelão de pa·pe·*lowng* carton
— de velocidades de ve·loo·see·*daa*·desh gearbox
— do correio doo koo·*rray*·oo mailbox
— registadora rre·zheesh·ta·*do*·ra cash register
caixote do lixo ⓜ kai·*sho*·te doo *lee*·shoo garbage can • rubbish bin
calado/calada ⓜ/ⓕ ka·*laa*·doo/ ka·*laa*·da quiet
calças ⓕ pl *kaal*·sash trousers
calções ⓜ pl kaal·*soyngsh* shorts
calculadora ⓕ kaal·koo·la·*do*·ra calculator
calendário ⓜ ka·leng·*daa*·ryoo calendar

C

calor ⓜ ka·*lor* heat
cama ⓕ *ka*·ma bed
— de casal de ka·*zaal* double bed
— de rede de *rre*·de hammock
câmara ⓕ *ka*·ma·ra tube (tyre)
câmara de vídeo ⓕ *ka*·ma·ra de *vee*·dee·oo video camera
camas gémeas ⓕ pl *ka*·mash *zhe*·me·ash twin beds
câmbio ⓜ *kang*·byoo currency exchange
camião ⓜ ka·mee·*yowng* truck
caminhada ⓕ ka·mee·*nyaa*·da hiking
caminhar ka·mee·*nyaar* hike • walk
caminho ⓜ ka·*mee*·nyoo path • way
camisa ⓕ ka·*mee*·za shirt
camisola ⓕ ka·mee·*zo*·la sweater
campeonatos ⓜ pl kang·pe·oo·*naa*·toosh championships
campo de golfe ⓜ *kang*·poo de *gol*·fe golf course
campo de ténis ⓜ *kang*·poo de *te*·neesh tennis court
canção ⓕ kang·*sowng* song
cancelar kang·se·*laar* cancel
cancro ⓜ *kang*·kroo cancer
caneta ⓕ ka·*ne*·ta pen
canivete ⓜ ka·nee·*ve*·te pocketknife
cansado/cansada ⓜ/ⓕ kang·*saa*·doo/kang·*saa*·da tired
cantor/cantora ⓜ/ⓕ kang·*tor*/kang·*to*·ra singer
cão ⓜ kowng dog
cão-guia ⓜ kowng·*gee*·a guide dog
capacete ⓜ ka·pa·*se*·te helmet
capacho ⓜ ka·*paa*·shoo mat
caro/cara ⓜ/ⓕ *kaa*·roo/*kaa*·ra expensive
carregar ka·rre·*gaar* carry
carrinha ⓕ ka·*rree*·nya van
carrinho ⓜ ka·*rree*·nyoo trolley
— de bebé de be·*be* stroller
carro ⓜ *kaa*·rroo car
carta ⓕ *kaar*·ta letter (mail)
carta de condução ⓕ *kaar*·ta de kong·doo·*sowng* drivers licence
cartão ⓜ kar·*towng* card
— de crédito de *kre*·dee·too credit card
— de embarque de eng·*baar*·ke boarding pass
— telefónico te·le·*fo*·nee·koo phonecard
cartas ⓕ pl *kaar*·tash playing cards
cartaz ⓜ kar·*taash* poster
casa ⓕ *kaa*·za home • house
— de banho de *ba*·nyoo bathroom • toilet
— de chá de shaa tea house
— de fados de *faa*·doosh fado house
— de hóspedes de *osh*·pe·desh guesthouse
casaco ⓜ ka·*zaa*·koo coat • jacket
casado/casada ⓜ/ⓕ ka·*zaa*·doo/ka·*zaa*·da married
casal ⓜ ka·*zaal* pair (couple)
casamento ⓜ ka·za·*meng*·too marriage • wedding
casar ka·*zaar* marry
cascata ⓕ kash·*kaa*·ta waterfall
cassete ⓕ kaa·*se*·te cassette
— de vídeo de *vee*·dee·oo video tape
castanho/castanha ⓜ/ⓕ kash·*ta*·nyoo/kash·*ta*·nya brown
castelo ⓜ kash·*te*·loo castle
catedral ⓕ ka·te·*draal* cathedral
católico/católica ⓜ/ⓕ ka·*to*·lee·koo/ka·*to*·lee·ka Catholic
cauda ⓕ *kow*·da tail
cavaleiro ⓜ ka·va·*lay*·roo bullfighter
cavalo ⓜ ka·*vaa*·loo horse
caverna ⓕ ka·*ver*·na cave
cedo *se*·doo early
cego/cega ⓜ/ⓕ *se*·goo/*se*·ga blind
cemitério ⓜ se·mee·*te*·ryoo cemetery
centímetro ⓜ seng·*tee*·me·troo centimetre
cêntimo ⓜ *seng*·tee·moo cent
centro ⓜ *seng*·troo centre
— comercial koo·mer·see·*aal* shopping centre
— da cidade da see·*daa*·de city centre
cerâmica ⓕ se·*raa*·mee·ka pottery

cerca ⓕ *ser*·ka fence
cerca de *ser*·ka de about
certidão de nascimento ⓕ ser·tee·*downg* de nash·see·*meng*·too birth certificate
cesto ⓕ *sesh*·too basket
céu ⓜ *se*·oo sky
champô ⓜ shang·*poo* shampoo
chão ⓜ showng floor
chapéu ⓜ sha·*pe*·oo hat
charcutaria ⓕ shar·koo·ta·*ree*·a delicatessen
charmoso/charmosa ⓜ/ⓕ shar·*mo*·zoo/shar·*mo*·za charming
charuto ⓜ sha·*roo*·too cigar
chato/chata ⓜ/ⓕ *shaa*·too/*shaa*·ta boring
chave ⓕ *shaa*·ve key
chávena ⓕ *shaa*·ve·na cup
chegada ⓕ she·*gaa*·da arrival
chegar she·*gaar* arrive
cheio/cheia ⓜ/ⓕ *shay*·oo/*shay*·a crowded • full
cheiro ⓜ *shay*·roo smell
chupeta ⓕ shoo·*pe*·ta dummy (pacifier)
chutar shoo·*taar* kick
chuva ⓕ *shoo*·va rain
chuveiro ⓜ shoo·*vay*·roo shower
ciclismo ⓜ see·*kleesh*·moo cycling
cidadania ⓕ see·da·da·*nee*·a citizenship
cidade ⓕ see·*daa*·de city
ciências ⓕ pl see·*eng*·syash science
cigarro ⓜ see·*gaa*·rroo cigarette
cinema ⓜ see·*ne*·ma cinema
cinto de segurança ⓜ *seeng*·too de se·goo·*raang*·sa seatbelt
cinzeiro ⓜ seeng·*zay*·roo ashtray
cinzento/cinzenta ⓜ/ⓕ seeng·*zeng*·too/seeng·*zeng*·ta grey
circo ⓜ *seer*·koo circus
cirurgia ⓕ see·roor·*zhee*·a operation (medical)
ciumento/ciumenta ⓜ/ⓕ see·oo·*meng*·too/see·oo·*meng*·ta jealous

claro/clara ⓜ/ⓕ *klaa*·roo/*klaa*·ra light (colour)
classe ⓕ *klaa*·se class (category)
— económica ee·koo·*no*·mee·ka economy class
— executiva ee·zhe·koo·*tee*·va business class
— primeira pree·*may*·ra first class
— segunda se·*goong*·da second class
cliente ⓜ&ⓕ klee·*eng*·te client
cobertor ⓜ koo·ber·*tor* blanket
cobra ⓕ *ko*·bra snake
cobrador ⓜ koo·bra·*dor* ticket collector
código postal ⓜ *ko*·dee·goo poosh·*taal* postcode
coelho ⓜ koo·*e*·lyoo rabbit
cofre ⓜ *ko*·fre safe
cola ⓕ *ko*·la glue
colar ⓜ koo·*laar* necklace
colchão ⓜ kol·*showng* mattress
colega ⓜ&ⓕ koo·*le*·ga colleague
colete salva-vidas ⓜ koo·*le*·te *saal*·va·*vee*·dash life jacket
colher ⓕ koo·*lyer* spoon
— de chá de shaa teaspoon
colina ⓕ koo·*lee*·na hill
colírio ⓜ koo·*lee*·ree·oo eye drops
collants ⓜ pl ko·*langsh* pantyhose
colocar koo·loo·*kaar* put
colóquio ⓜ koo·*lo*·kyoo small conference
com kong with
— pressa *pre*·sa in a hurry
— saudades sow·*da*·desh homesick
comboio ⓜ kong·*boy*·oo train
começar koo·me·*saar* start
começo ⓜ koo·*me*·soo start
comédia ⓕ koo·*me*·dya comedy
comemoração ⓕ koo·me·moo·ra·*sowng* celebration
comer koo·*mer* eat
comerciante ⓜ&ⓕ koo·mer·see·*aang*·te tradesperson
comércio ⓜ koo·*mer*·syoo trade
comichão ⓕ koo·mee·*showng* itch

comida ⓕ koo·*mee*·da food
— de bebé de be·*be* baby food
comissão ⓕ koo·mee·*sowng* commission
como *ko*·moo how
companheiro/companheira ⓜ/ⓕ kong·pa·*nyay*·roo/kong·pa·*nyay*·ra companion
companhia aérea ⓕ kong·pa·*nyee*·a a·e·ree·a airline
compota ⓕ kong·*po*·ta jam
comprar kong·*praar* buy
compras ⓕ pl *kong*·prash shopping
compreender kong·pree·eng·*der* understand
comprimido ⓜ kong·pree·*mee*·doo pill
computador ⓜ kong·poo·ta·*dor* computer
— portátil por·*taa*·teel laptop
comum koo·*moong* ordinary
comunhão ⓕ koo·moo·*nyowng* communion
concerto ⓜ kong·*ser*·too concert
concordar kong·koor·*daar* agree
conduzir kong·doo·*zeer* drive
conferência ⓕ kong·fe·*reng*·sya big conference
confiar kong·fee·*aar* trust
confirmar kong·feer·*maar* confirm
confissão ⓕ kong·fee·*sowng* confession
confortável kong·for·*taa*·vel comfortable
congelar kong·zhe·*laar* freeze
conhecer koo·nye·*ser* meet (first time)
conjuntivite ⓕ kong·zhoong·tee·*vee*·te conjunctivitis
conselho ⓜ kong·*se*·lyoo advice
consertar kong·ser·*taar* repair
conservador/conservadora ⓜ/ⓕ kong·ser·va·*dor*/kong·ser·va·*do*·ra conservative n&a
constipação ⓕ kong·shtee·pa·*sowng* cold (illness)
construir kong·shtroo·*eer* build
construtor ⓜ kong·shtroo·*tor* builder
consulado ⓜ kong·soo·*laa*·doo consulate
consulta ⓕ kong·*sool*·ta appointment
consumo obrigatório ⓜ kon·soo·moo o·bree·ga·*to*·ree·oo cover charge
conta ⓕ *kong*·ta bill • account
— bancária bang·*kaa*·rya bank account
contar kong·*taar* count
contraceptivo ⓜ kong·tra·se·*tee*·voo contraceptives
contrato ⓜ kong·*traa*·too contract
convidar kong·vee·*daar* invite
copo ⓜ *ko*·poo glass (drinking)
cor ⓕ kor colour
— de laranja de la·*rang*·zha orange (colour)
coração ⓜ koo·ra·*sowng* heart
corajoso/corajosa ⓜ/ⓕ koo·ra·*zho*·zoo/koo·ra·*zho*·za brave
corda ⓕ *kor*·da rope
cordeiro ⓜ koor·*day*·roo lamb
cordel ⓜ koor·*del* string
cor-de-rosa kor·de·*rro*·za pink
cordilheira ⓕ koor·dee·*lyay*·ra mountain range
corpo ⓜ *kor*·poo body
correcto/correcta ⓜ/ⓕ koo·*rre*·too/koo·*rre*·ta right (correct)
correia da ventoinha ⓕ koo·*rray*·a da veng·too·ee·nya fanbelt
correio ⓜ koo·*rray*·oo mail • post office
— azul a·*zool* express mail
— registado re·zhee·*shtaa*·doo registered mail
corrente ⓕ koo·*rreng*·te current (electricity)
corrente de bicicleta ⓕ koo·*rreng*·te de bee·see·*kle*·ta bike chain
correr koo·*rrer* run
correspondência ⓕ koo·rresh·pong·*deng*·sya mail (letters)
— por via marítima poor *vee*·a ma·*ree*·tee·ma surface mail (sea)

— por via terrestre poor *vee*·a te·*rresh*·tre surface mail (land)
corrida ⓕ koo·*rree*·da jogging • race (sport)
corrimento ⓜ koo·rree·*meng*·too thrush (health)
corrupto/corrupta ⓜ/ⓕ koo·*rroop*·too/koo·*rroop*·ta corrupt
cortar koor·*taar* cut
corta-unhas ⓜ *kor*·ta·*oong*·nyash nail clippers
corte de cabelo ⓜ *kor*·te de ka·*be*·loo haircut
coser koo·*zer* sew
costas ⓕ pl *kosh*·tash back (body)
costela ⓕ koosh·*te*·la rib (body)
costume ⓜ koosh·*too*·me custom
cotonete ⓜ ko·to·*ne*·te cotton buds
couro cabeludo ⓜ *koh*·roo ka·be·*loo*·doo scalp
couro ⓜ *koh*·roo leather
coxia ⓜ koo·*shee*·a aisle
cozinha ⓕ koo·*zee*·nya cooking • kitchen
cozinhar koo·zee·*nyaar* cook
cozinheiro/cozinheira ⓜ/ⓕ koo·zee·*nyay*·roo/koo·zee·*nyay*·ra cook
crânio ⓜ *kra*·nyoo skull
crédito ⓜ *kre*·dee·too credit
creme ⓜ *kre*·me cream
— de barbear de bar·bee·*aar* shaving cream
crescer kresh·*ser* grow
criado/criada de mesa ⓜ/ⓕ kree·*aa*·doo/kree·*aa*·da de *me*·za waiter/waitress
criança ⓜ&ⓕ kree·*ang*·sa child
Cristão/Cristã ⓜ/ⓕ kreesh·*towng*/kreesh·*tang* Christian
cru/crua ⓜ/ⓕ kroo/*kroo*·a raw
cruz ⓕ kroosh cross (religious)
cuidar kwee·*daar* look after
culpa ⓕ *kool*·pa fault (someone's)
culpado/culpada ⓜ/ⓕ kool·*paa*·doo/kool·*paa*·da guilty
cupão ⓜ koo·*powng* coupon
currículo ⓜ koo·*rree*·koo·loo résumé
curto/curta ⓜ/ⓕ *koor*·too/*koor*·ta short (length)
custar koosh·*taar* cost

D

dança ⓕ *dang*·sa dance • dancing
dançar dang·*saar* dance
da noite ⓜ da *noy*·te evening
dar daar give • deal (cards)
dar conversa daar kong·*ver*·sa chat up (flirt)
data ⓕ *daa*·ta date (day)
— de nascimento de nash·see·*meng*·too date of birth
de de from
decidir de·see·*deer* decide
dedo ⓜ *de*·doo finger
— do pé doo pe toe
defeituoso/defeituosa ⓜ/ⓕ de·fay·too·*o*·zoo/de·fay·too·*o*·za faulty
deficiente de·fee·see·*eng*·te disabled
deitar-se day·*taar*·se lie (not stand)
demais de·*maish* too (much)
democracia ⓕ de·moo·kra·*see*·a democracy
de noite de *noy*·te overnight
dente ⓜ *deng*·te tooth
dentes ⓜ pl *deng*·tesh teeth
dentista ⓜ&ⓕ deng·*teesh*·ta dentist
dentro *deng*·troo inside
dentro de *deng*·troo de within (time)
depois de·*poysh* after
— de amanhã de aa·ma·*nyang* day after tomorrow
depósito ⓜ de·*po*·zee·too deposit (bank)
— de bagagens de·*po*·zee·too de ba·*gaa*·zhengsh luggage locker
depressa de·*pre*·sa fast adv
descansar desh·kang·*saar* rest
descer desh·*ser* get off (bus, train)
desconfortável desh·kong·foor·*taa*·vel uncomfortable
desconto ⓜ desh·*kong*·too discount
desde *dezh*·de since (time)
desejar de·ze·*zhaar* wish

D

desempregado/desempregada ⓜ/ⓕ de·zeng·pre·*gaa*·doo/ de·zeng·pre·*gaa*·da unemployed
deserto ⓜ de·*zer*·too desert
desistir de·zeesh·*teer* quit
desligado/desligada ⓜ/ⓕ desh·lee·*gaa*·doo/desh·lee·*gaa*·da off (power)
desodorizante ⓜ de·zo·doo·ree·*zang*·te deodorant
despertador ⓜ desh·per·ta·*dor* alarm clock
desportista ⓜ&ⓕ desh·poor·*teesh*·ta sportsperson
desporto ⓜ desh·*por*·too sport
destino ⓜ desh·*tee*·noo destination
detalhes ⓜ pl de·*taa*·lyesh details
Deus ⓜ *de*·oosh God (general)
devagar de·va·*gaar* slow (down) v
dever de·*ver* owe
dia ⓜ *dee*·a day
diafragma ⓜ dee·a·*fraa*·ge·ma diaphragm
diapositivo ⓜ dee·a·po·zee·*tee*·voo slide (transparency)
diário ⓜ dee·*aa*·ryoo diary
diário/diária ⓜ/ⓕ dee·*aa*·ryoo/ dee·*aa*·rya daily
dicionário ⓜ dee·syoo·*naa*·ryoo dictionary
dieta ⓕ dee·*e*·ta diet
diferença horária ⓕ dee·fe·*reng*·sa o·*raa*·rya time difference
diferente dee·fe·*reng*·te different
difícil dee·*fee*·seel difficult
dinheiro ⓜ dee·*nyay*·roo money
direcção ⓕ dee·re·*sowng* direction
directo/directa ⓜ/ⓕ dee·*re*·too/ dee·*re*·ta direct • straight
director/directora ⓜ/ⓕ dee·re·*tor*/ dee·re·*to*·ra director
direita dee·*ray*·ta right (direction)
Direito ⓜ dee·*ray*·too law (profession)
direitos ⓜ pl dee·*ray*·toosh rights
— civis *see*·veesh civil rights
— humanos oo·*ma*·noosh human rights

discoteca ⓕ deesh·koo·*te*·ka nightclub
discutir deesh·koo·*teer* argue
disponível deesh·po·*nee*·vel available
DIU ⓜ de·ee·*oo* IUD
divertido/divertida ⓜ/ⓕ dee·ver·*tee*·doo/dee·ver·*tee*·da fun
divertir-se dee·ver·*teer*·se enjoy (oneself)
divorciado/divorciada ⓜ/ⓕ dee·vor·see·*aa*·doo/ dee·vor·see·*aa*·da divorced
dizer dee·*zer* say • tell
doce *do*·se sweet
documentário ⓜ doo·koo·meng·*taa*·ryoo documentary
doença ⓕ doo·*eng*·sa disease
— venérea ve·*ne*·ree·a venereal disease
doente doo·*eng*·te sick
doloroso/dolorosa ⓜ/ⓕ doo·loo·*ro*·zoo/doo·loo·*ro*·za painful
dona de casa ⓕ *do*·na de *kaa*·za homemaker
dono/dona ⓜ/ⓕ *do*·noo/*do*·na owner
dor ⓕ dor pain
— de cabeça de ka·*be*·sa headache
— de dentes de *deng*·tesh toothache
— de estômago de *shto*·ma·goo stomachache
— menstrual meng·shtroo·*aal* period pain
dorido/dorida ⓜ/ⓕ doo·*ree*·doo/ doo·*ree*·da sore
dormir door·*meer* sleep
dose excessiva ⓕ *do*·ze she·*see*·va overdose
droga ⓕ *dro*·ga drug
drogado/drogada ⓜ/ⓕ droo·*gaa*·doo/droo·*gaa*·da stoned (drugged)
duas vezes *doo*·ash *ve*·zesh twice
duplo/dupla ⓜ/ⓕ *doo*·ploo/*doo*·pla double
duro/dura ⓜ/ⓕ *doo*·roo/*doo*·ra hard (not soft)

E

e e and
educação ⓕ e·doo·ka·*sowng* education
egoísta e·goo·*eesh*·ta selfish
ela *e*·la she
ele *e*·le he
electricidade ⓕ ee·le·tree·see·*daa*·de electricity
eléctrico ⓜ ee·*le*·tree·koo tram
eleição ⓕ e·lay·*sowng* election
eles/elas *e*·lesh/*e*·lash they
elevador ⓜ ee·le·va·*dor* lift (elevator)
em eng at • in
— breve *bre*·ve soon
— frente *freng*·te ahead
— segunda mão se·*goong*·da mowng second-hand
embaixada ⓕ eng·bai·*shaa*·da embassy
embaixador/embaixatriz ⓜ/ⓕ eng·bai·sha·*dor*/eng·bai·sha·*treesh* ambassador
embraiagem ⓕ eng·brai·*aa*·zheng clutch (car)
embrulho ⓜ eng·*broo*·lyoo package
ementa ⓕ ee·*meng*·ta menu
emergência ⓕ ee·mer·*zheng*·sya emergency
empregado/empregada ⓜ/ⓕ eng·pre·*gaa*·doo/eng·pre·*gaa*·da employee
—de escritório de shkree·*to*·ryoo office worker
— por conta própria poor *kong*·ta *pro*·pree·a self-employed person
emprego ⓜ eng·*pre*·goo job
empresa ⓕ eng·*pre*·za company (firm)
empurrar eng·poo·*rraar* push
encher eng·*sher* fill
encomenda ⓕ eng·koo·*meng*·da parcel
encontrar eng·kong·*traar* find • meet
encontro ⓜ eng·*kong*·troo date (appointment)
endereço ⓜ eng·de·*re*·soo address
enevoado/enevoada ⓜ/ⓕ e·ne·voo·*aa*·doo/e·ne·voo·*aa*·da foggy
enfermeiro/enfermeira ⓜ/ⓕ eng·fer·*may*·roo/eng·fer·*may*·ra nurse
engenharia ⓕ eng·zhe·nya·*ree*·a engineering
engraçado/engraçada ⓜ/ⓕ eng·gra·*saa*·doo/eng·gra·*saa*·da funny
enjoado/enjoada ⓜ/ⓕ eng·zhoo·*aa*·doo/eng·zhoo·*aa*·da seasick
enjoo ⓜ eng·*zho*·oo nausea
— de viagem de vee·*aa*·zheng travel sickness
— matinal ma·tee·*naal* morning sickness
enorme ee·*nor*·me huge
ensolarado/ensolarada ⓜ/ⓕ eng·soo·la·*raa*·doo/eng·soo·la·*raa*·da sunny
entorse ⓕ eng·*tor*·se sprain
entrada ⓕ eng·*traa*·da entry
entrar eng·*traar* enter
entre *eng*·tre between
entregar eng·tre·*gaar* deliver
entrevista ⓕ eng·tre·*veesh*·ta interview
envergonhado/envergonhada ⓜ/ⓕ en·ver·goo·*nyaa*·doo/en·ver·goo·*nyaa*·da embarrassed
enviar eng·vee·*aar* post • send
enxaqueca ⓕ eng·sha·*ke*·ka migraine
equipa ⓕ e·*kee*·pa team
equipamento ⓜ e·kee·pa·*meng*·too equipment
— de mergulho de mer·*goo*·lyoo diving equipment
errado/errada ⓜ/ⓕ e·*rraa*·doo/e·*rraa*·da wrong
erro ⓜ *e*·rroo mistake
escadaria ⓕ shka·da·*ree*·a stairway
escada rolante ⓕ *shkaa*·da rroo·*lang*·te escalator
escola ⓕ *shko*·la school
— secundária se·koong·*daa*·ree·a high school

escolher shkoo·*lyer* choose
escova ⓕ *shko*·va hairbrush
— de dentes de *deng*·tesh toothbrush
escrever shkre·*ver* write
escritor/escritora ⓜ/ⓕ shkree·*tor*/shkree·*to*·ra writer
escritório ⓜ shkree·*to*·ryoo office
— de turismo de too·*reezh*·moo tourist office
escultura ⓕ shkool·*too*·ra sculpture
escuro/escura ⓜ/ⓕ *shkoo*·roo/*shkoo*·ra dark (colour/night)
escutar shkoo·*taar* hear • listen
esgotado/esgotada ⓜ/ⓕ shgoo·*taa*·doo/shgoo·*taa*·da booked out
espaço ⓜ *shpaa*·soo space (room)
Espanha ⓕ *shpa*·nya Spain
espanhol ⓜ shpa·*nyol* Spanish
especial shpe·see·*aal* special
especialista ⓜ&ⓕ shpe·see·a·*leesh*·ta specialist
espectáculo ⓜ shpe·*taa*·koo·loo show
espelho ⓜ *shpe*·lyoo mirror
esperar shpe·*raar* wait (for)
esposa ⓕ *shpo*·za wife
esquadra da polícia ⓕ *shkwaa*·dra da poo·*lee*·sya police station
esquecer shke·*ser* forget
esquerda ⓕ *shker*·da left (direction)
esqui ⓜ shkee ski • skiing
— aquático a·*kwaa*·tee·koo waterskiing
esquiar shkee·*aar* ski
esquina ⓕ *shkee*·na corner
estaca ⓕ *shtaa*·ka tent peg
estação ⓕ shta·*sowng* season • station
— de caminhos de ferro de ka·*mee*·nyoosh de *fe*·rroo train station
— de metropolitano de me·troo·poo·lee·*ta*·noo metro station
estacionar shta·syoo·*naar* park (a car)
estádio ⓜ *shtaa*·dyoo stadium
estado civil ⓜ *shtaa*·doo see·*veel* marital status
estar shtaar be (temporary)
— constipado/constipada ⓜ/ⓕ kong·shtee·*paa*·doo/kong·shtee·*paa*·da have a cold
estátua ⓕ *shtaa*·too·a statue
este/esta ⓜ/ⓕ *esh*·te/*esh*·ta this
estendal da roupa ⓕ shteng·*daal* da *rroh*·pa clothesline
estéreo ⓜ *shte*·ree·oo stereo
estilo ⓜ *shtee*·loo style
estojo de primeiros socorros ⓜ *shto*·zhoo de pree·*may*·roosh so·*ko*·rroosh first-aid kit
estômago ⓜ *shto*·ma·goo stomach
estrada ⓕ *shtraa*·da road
estrangeiro/estrangeira ⓜ/ⓕ shtrang·*zhay*·roo/shtrang·*zhay*·ra foreign
estranho/estranha ⓜ/ⓕ *shtra*·nyoo/*shtra*·nya strange • stranger
estrela ⓕ *shtre*·la star
estudante ⓜ&ⓕ shtoo·*dang*·te student
estúdio ⓜ *shtoo*·dyoo studio
etiqueta de bagagem ⓕ e·tee·*ke*·ta de ba·*gaa*·zheng luggage tag
eu e·oo I
EUA ⓜ pl e·oo·*aa* USA
euro ⓜ *e*·oo·roo euro
exactamente e·za·ta·*meng*·te exactly
exame papa nicolau ⓜ e·*za*·me *paa*·pa nee·koo·*low* pap smear
exaustor ⓜ ee·zowsh·*tor* exhaust (car)
excelente ay·she·*leng*·te excellent
excluído/excluída ⓜ/ⓕ aysh·kloo·*ee*·doo/aysh·kloo·*ee*·da excluded
excursão ⓕ shkoor·*sowng* tour
— guiada gee·*aa*·da guided tour
exemplo ⓜ e·*zeng*·ploo example
experiência ⓕ shpe·ree·*eng*·sya experience
— de trabalho ⓕ de tra·*baa*·lyoo work experience
exploração ⓕ shplo·ra·*sowng* exploitation

exposição ⓕ shpoo·zee·*sowng* exhibition
expresso/expressa ⓜ/ⓕ *shpre*·soo/esh·*pre*·sa express
extensão ⓕ shteng·*sowng* extension (visa)

F

fábrica ⓕ *faa*·bree·ka factory
faca ⓕ *faa*·ka knife
fácil *faa*·seel easy
fado ⓜ *faa*·doo fado (music)
falar fa·*laar* speak • talk
falta ⓕ *faal*·ta foul (soccer)
família ⓕ fa·*mee*·lya family
faminto/faminta ⓜ/ⓕ fa·*meeng*·too/fa·*meeng*·ta hungry
famoso/famosa ⓜ/ⓕ fa·*mo*·zoo/fa·*mo*·za famous
farda ⓕ *faar*·da uniform
farinha ⓕ fa·*ree*·nya flour
farmacêutico/farmacêutica ⓜ/ⓕ far·ma·se·*oo*·tee·koo/far·ma·se·*oo*·tee·ka pharmacist
farmácia ⓕ far·*maa*·sya pharmacy
faróis ⓜ pl fa·*roysh* headlights
fatia ⓕ fa·*tee*·a slice
fato de banho ⓜ *faa*·too de *ba*·nyoo swimsuit
fazer fa·*zer* do • make
— a barba a *baar*·ba shave
— a contagem a kong·*taa*·zheng score (keep)
— compras *kong*·prash go shopping
— surf sarf surf
febre ⓕ *fe*·bre fever
— dos fenos doosh *fe*·noosh hay fever
— glandular glang·doo·*laar* glandular fever
fechado/fechada ⓜ/ⓕ fe·*shaa*·doo/fe·*shaa*·da closed
fechar fe·*shaar* close
fecho écler ⓜ fe·shoo e·*kler* zipper
feira ⓕ *fay*·ra fair • street market
— da ladra da *laa*·dra fleamarket
feito/feita à mão ⓜ/ⓕ *fay*·too/*fay*·ta aa mowng handmade
feliz fe·*leesh* happy
feminino/feminina ⓜ/ⓕ fe·mee·*nee*·noo/fe·mee·*nee*·na female
feriado ⓜ fe·ree·*aa*·doo holiday
férias ⓕ pl *fe*·ryash vacation
ferido/ferida ⓜ/ⓕ fe·*ree*·doo/fe·*ree*·da injured
ferimento ⓜ fe·ree·*meng*·too injury
ferro de engomar ⓜ *fe*·rroo de eng·goo·*maar* iron (clothes)
festa ⓕ *fesh*·ta party (night out)
— na rua na *rroo*·a street party
festival ⓜ fesh·tee·*vaal* festival
ficar fee·*kaar* stay
ficção ⓕ feek·*sowng* fiction
fígado ⓜ *fee*·ga·doo liver
fila ⓕ *fee*·la queue
filha ⓕ *fee*·lya daughter
filho ⓜ *fee*·lyoo son
filme ⓜ *feel*·me film
— de diapositivos de dee·a·po·zee·*tee*·voosh slide film
filtrado/filtrada ⓜ/ⓕ feel·*traa*·doo/feel·*traa*·da filtered
fim ⓜ feeng end
fim-de-semana ⓜ feeng·de·se·*ma*·na weekend
fino/fina ⓜ/ⓕ *fee*·noo/*fee*·na thin
fio dental ⓜ *fee*·oo deng·*taal* dental floss
fixe *fee*·she cool (exciting)
flor ⓕ flor flower
floresta ⓕ floo·*resh*·ta forest
florista ⓕ floo·*reesh*·ta florist (shop)
fogão ⓜ foo·*gowng* stove
fogo ⓜ *fo*·goo fire
folha ⓕ *fo*·lya leaf
fora *fo*·ra outside
forças armadas ⓕ pl *for*·sash ar·*maa*·dash military
forma ⓕ *for*·ma shape
forno ⓜ *for*·noo oven
forte *for*·te strong
fósforos ⓜ pl *fosh*·foo·roosh matches (for lighting)
fotografar foo·too·gra·*faar* photograph

fotografia ⓕ foo·too·gra·*fee*·a photography
fotógrafo/fotógrafa ⓜ/ⓕ foo·*to*·gra·foo/foo·*to*·gra·fa photographer
fotómetro ⓜ foo·*to*·me·troo light meter
fraco/fraca ⓜ/ⓕ *fraa*·koo/*fraa*·ka weak
frágil *fraa*·zheel fragile
fralda ⓕ *fraal*·da nappy (diaper)
frequentemente fre·kweng·te·*meng*·te often
fresco/fresca ⓜ/ⓕ *fresh*·koo/*fresh*·ka cool (cold) • fresh
frigorífico ⓜ free·goo·*ree*·fee·koo refrigerator
frio/fria ⓜ/ⓕ *free*·oo/*free*·a cold
fronha ⓕ *fro*·nya pillowcase
fronteira ⓕ frong·*tay*·ra border
fumar foo·*maar* smoke
fundo ⓕ *foong*·doo bottom (position)
funeral ⓜ foo·ne·*raal* funeral
furo ⓜ *foo*·roo puncture
futuro ⓜ foo·*too*·roo future

G

gabardina ⓕ gaa·baar·*dee*·na raincoat
gabinete de perdidos e achados ⓜ gaa·bee·*ne*·te de per·*dee*·doosh ee a·*shaa*·doosh lost property office
galeria de arte ⓕ ga·le·*ree*·a de *aar*·te art gallery
galinha ⓕ ga·*lee*·nya chicken
ganhar ga·*nyaar* earn • win
garagem ⓕ ga·*raa*·zheng garage
garantido/garantida ⓜ/ⓕ ga·rang·*tee*·doo/ga·rang·*tee*·da guaranteed
garfo ⓜ *gaar*·foo fork
garganta ⓕ gar·*gang*·ta throat
garrafa ⓕ ga·*rraa*·fa bottle
gás ⓜ gaash gas (cooking)
gasolina ⓕ ga·zoo·*lee*·na gas (petrol)
gastrenterite ⓕ gash·treng·te·*ree*·te gastroenteritis
gato/gata ⓜ/ⓕ *gaa*·too/*gaa*·ta cat
gaze ⓕ *gaa*·ze gauze
geada ⓕ zhee·*aa*·da frost
gelado/gelada ⓜ/ⓕ zhe·*laa*·doo/zhe·*laa*·da frozen
gelo ⓜ *zhe*·loo ice
gémeos/gémeas ⓜ/ⓕ *zhe*·mee·oosh/*zhe*·mee·ash twins
gerente zhe·*reng*·te manager
gilete ⓕ zhee·*le*·te razor
ginásio ⓜ zhee·*naa*·zyoo gym (place)
golo ⓜ *go*·loo goal (sport)
gordo/gorda ⓜ/ⓕ *gor*·doo/*gor*·da fat
gorjeta ⓕ gor·*zhe*·ta tip (gratuity)
gostar goosh·*taar* care for • like
gostoso/gostosa ⓜ/ⓕ goosh·*to*·zoo/goosh·*to*·za tasty
governo ⓜ goo·*ver*·noo government
grama ⓜ *graa*·ma gram
grande *grang*·de big
grátis *graa*·teesh complimentary
grato/grata ⓜ/ⓕ *graa*·too/*graa*·ta grateful
graus ⓜ pl growsh degrees (temperature)
gravação ⓕ gra·va·*sowng* recording
gravador de vídeo ⓜ gra·va·*dor* de *vee*·dee·oo video recorder
gravar gra·*vaar* record
grávida *graa*·vee·da pregnant
greve ⓕ *gre*·ve strike
gripe ⓕ *gree*·pe influenza
gritar gree·*taar* shout
grosso/grossa ⓜ/ⓕ *gro*·soo/*gro*·sa thick
grupo ⓜ *groo*·poo band • group
— sanguíneo sang·*gwee*·nee·oo blood type
guarda-chuva ⓜ *gwaar*·da·*shoo*·va umbrella
guardanapo ⓜ gwar·da·*naa*·poo napkin
guarda-redes *gwaar*·da·*rre*·desh goalkeeper
guarda-roupa ⓜ gwaar·da·*rroh*·pa wardrobe

uerra ⓕ ge·rra war
uia ⓜ gee·a guide (person)
- auditivo ow·dee·tee·voo audio uide
- de espectáculos de hpe·taa·koo·loosh entertainment uide
- de viagem de vee·aa·zheng uidebook

H

epatite ⓕ e·pa·tee·te hepatitis
idratante ⓜ ee·dra·tang·te noisturiser
indu ⓜ&ⓕ eeng·doo Hindu
ipismo ⓜ ee·peezh·moo orseriding
istória ⓕ shto·rya history • story
oje o·zhe today
- à noite aa noy·te tonight
omem ⓜ o·meng man
- de negócios de ne·go·syoosh usinessman
omosexual ⓜ&ⓕ o·mo·sek·soo·aal omosexual n&a
óquei ⓜ o·kay hockey
- sobre o gelo so·bre oo zhe·loo e hockey
ora ⓕ o·ra hour
orário ⓜ o·raa·ryoo timetable
- de expediente de shpe·dee·eng·te pening hours
oróscopo ⓜ o·rosh·koo·poo oroscope
orrível o·rree·vel awful
ospedagem ⓕ osh·pe·daa·zheng ccommodation
ospital ⓜ osh·pee·taal hospital
ospitalidade ⓕ sh·pee·ta·lee·daa·de hospitality
otel ⓜ o·tel hotel

I

dade ⓕ ee·daa·de age
da e volta ee·da ee vol·ta return ticket)

identificação ⓕ ee·deng·tee·fee·ka·sowng identification
igreja ⓕ ee·gre·zha church
igualdade ⓕ ee·gwal·daa·de equality
— de oportunidades de o·poor·too·nee·daa·desh equal opportunity
ilha ⓕ ee·lya island
imigração ⓕ ee·mee·gra·sowng immigration
importante eeng·por·tang·te important
impossível eeng·po·see·vel impossible
imposto ⓜ eeng·posh·too tax
— de rendimentos de rreng·dee·meng·toosh income tax
impressora ⓕ eeng·pre·so·ra printer (computer)
inchaço ⓜ eeng·shaa·soo swelling
incluído/incluída ⓜ/ⓕ eeng·kloo·ee·doo/eeng·kloo·ee·da included
indigestão ⓕ eeng·dee·zhesh·towng indigestion
indústria ⓕ eeng·doosh·trya industry
infantário ⓜ eeng·fang·taa·ree·oo crèche
infecção ⓕ eeng·fe·sowng infection
— urinária oo·ree·naa·rya urinary infection
inflamação ⓕ eeng·fla·ma·sowng inflammation
informação ⓕ eeng·for·ma·sowng information
informática ⓕ eeng·for·maa·tee·ka IT
Inglaterra ⓕ eeng·gla·te·rra England
inglês ⓜ eeng·glesh English
ingrediente ⓜ eeng·gre·dee·eng·te ingredient
íngreme eeng·gre·me steep
injecção ⓕ eeng·zhe·sowng injection
injectar eeng·zhe·taar inject
injusto/injusta ⓜ/ⓕ eeng·zhoosh·too/eeng·zhoosh·ta unfair
inocente ee·noo·seng·te innocent

inseguro/insegura ⓜ/ⓕ eeng·se·*goo*·roo/eeng·se·*goo*·ra unsafe
insolação ⓕ eeng·soo·la·*sowng* sunstroke
instrutor/instrutora ⓜ/ⓕ eeng·shtroo·*tor*/eeng·shtroo·*to*·ra instructor
interessante eeng·te·re·*sang*·te interesting
interior do país ⓜ eeng·te·ree·*or* doo pa·*eesh* countryside
internacional eeng·ter·naa·syoo·*naal* international
intervalo ⓜ eeng·ter·*vaa*·loo intermission
inundação ⓕ ee·noong·da·*sowng* flood
inverno ⓜ eeng·*ver*·noo winter
invulgar eeng·vool·*gaar* unusual
ir eer go
irmã ⓕ eer·*mang* sister
irmão ⓜ eer·*mowng* brother
irritação da pele ⓕ ee·rree·ta·*sowng* da *pe*·le rash
irritação por causa da fralda ⓕ ee·rree·ta·*sowng* poor *kow*·sa da *fraal*·da nappy rash
isqueiro ⓜ eesh·*kay*·roo cigarette lighter
itinerário ⓜ ee·tee·ne·*raa*·ryoo itinerary
IVA ⓜ *ee*·va sales tax

J

já zhaa already
janela ⓕ zha·*ne*·la window
jantar ⓜ zhang·*taar* dinner
jardim ⓜ zhar·*deeng* garden
— botânico boo·*ta*·nee·koo botanic garden
— de infância de eeng·*fang*·sya kindergarten
— zoológico zoo·oo·*lo*·zhee·koo zoo
jardinagem ⓕ zhar·dee·*naa*·zheng gardening
jardins públicos ⓜ pl zhar·*deengzh* *poo*·blee·koosh public gardens
jipe ⓜ *zhee*·pe jeep
joelho ⓜ zhoo·e·lyoo knee
jogar zhoo·*gaar* play (cards, etc)
jogo ⓜ *zho*·goo game (sport)
— de computador de kong·poo·ta·*dor* computer game
jornal ⓜ zhor·*naal* newspaper
jornalista ⓜ&ⓕ zhor·na·*leesh*·ta journalist
jovem *zho*·veng young
Judeu/Judia ⓜ/ⓕ zhoo·*de*·oo/zhoo·*dee*·a Jewish
juiz/juiza ⓜ/ⓕ zhoo·*eesh*/zhoo·ee·za judge • referee
junto/junta ⓜ/ⓕ *zhoong*·too/*zhoong*·ta together

L

lá laa there (where neither of us is)
lã ⓕ lang wool
lábios ⓜ pl *laa*·byoosh lips
lado ⓜ *laa*·doo side
ladrão/ladra ⓜ/ⓕ la·*drowng*/*laa*·dra thief
lagarto ⓜ la·*gaar*·too lizard
lago ⓜ *laa*·goo lake
lama ⓕ *la*·ma mud
lâmina de barbear ⓕ *la*·mee·na de bar·bee·*aar* razor blade
lâmpada ⓕ *lang*·pa·da light bulb
lanterna eléctrica ⓕ lang·*ter*·na ee·*le*·tree·ka torch (flashlight)
lápis ⓜ *laa*·peesh pencil
largo/larga ⓜ/ⓕ *laar*·goo/*laar*·ga wide
lata ⓕ *laa*·ta tin (can)
lavandaria ⓕ la·vang·da·*ree*·a laundry (clothes/place)
lavar la·*vaar* wash
lavar-se la·*vaar*·se wash (oneself)
laxante ⓜ la·*shang*·te laxative
legal le·*gaal* legal
legendas ⓕ pl le·*zheng*·dash subtitles
legislação ⓕ le·zheezh·la·*sowng* legislation
lei ⓕ lay law (legislation)
leitura ⓕ lay·*too*·ra reading

lembrança ⓕ leng·*brang*·sa souvenir
lenço ⓜ *leng*·soo scarf
— de mão de mowng handkerchief
— de papel de pa·*pel* tissue
lençóis e mantas ⓕ pl leng·*soysh* ee *mang*·tash bedding
lençol ⓜ leng·*sol* sheet (bed)
lenha ⓕ *le*·nya firewood
lente ⓕ *leng*·te lens (camera)
lentes de contacto ⓜ pl *leng*·tesh de kong·*taak*·too contact lenses
ler ler read
lésbica ⓕ *lezh*·bee·ka lesbian
levantar (um cheque) le·vang·*taar* (oong *she*·ke) cash (a cheque)
levar le·*vaar* take
leve *le*·ve light (weight)
libra ⓕ *lee*·bra pound (weight)
licença ⓕ lee·*seng*·sa licence • permit
— de trabalho de tra·*baa*·lyoo work permit
ligação ⓕ lee·ga·*sowng* connection
— a cobrar a koo·*braar* collect call
— directa dee·*re*·ta direct-dial
ligado/ligada ⓜ/ⓕ lee·*gaa*·doo/ lee·*gaa*·da on (power)
ligadura ⓕ lee·ga·*doo*·ra bandage
limite de peso ⓜ lee·*mee*·te de pe·zoo baggage allowance
limite de velocidade ⓜ lee·*mee*·te de ve·loo·see·*daa*·de speed limit
limpar leeng·*paar* clean
limpeza ⓕ leeng·*pe*·za cleaning
limpo/limpa ⓜ/ⓕ *leeng*·poo/ *leeng*·pa clean
língua ⓕ *leeng*·gwa language
liquidação ⓕ lee·kee·da·*sowng* sale
lista telefónica ⓕ *leesh*·ta te·le·*fo*·nee·ka phone book
livraria ⓕ lee·vra·*ree*·a book shop
livre *lee*·vre free (not bound)
livro ⓜ *lee*·vroo book
— de frases de *fraa*·zesh phrasebook
lixo ⓜ *lee*·shoo garbage • rubbish
local ⓜ loo·*kaal* venue
— de nascimento de nash·see·*meng*·too place of birth

local ⓜ&ⓕ loo·*kaal* local
loja ⓕ *lo*·zha shop
— de aparelhos eléctricos de a·pa·*re*·lyoosh ee·*le*·tree·koosh electrical store
— de bebidas de be·*bee*·dash liquor store
— de brinquedos de breeng·*ke*·doosh toy shop
— de campismo de kang·*peezh*·moo camping store
— de ciclismo de see·*kleesh*·moo bike shop
— de conveniência de kong·ve·*nyeng*·sya convenience store
— de desporto de desh·*por*·too sports store
— de equipamentos fotográficos de e·kee·pa·*meng*·toosh foo·too·*graa*·fee·koosh camera shop
— de ferramentas de fe·rra·*meng*·tash hardware store
— de lembranças de leng·*brang*·sash souvenir shop
— de música de *moo*·zee·ka music shop
— de roupas de *rroh*·pash clothing store
— de segunda mão de se·*goon*·da mowng second-hand shop
lombrigas ⓕ pl long·*bree*·gash worms (intestinal)
longe *long*·zhe far
longo/longa ⓜ/ⓕ *long*·goo/*long*·ga long
louco/louca ⓜ/ⓕ *loh*·koo/*loh*·ka crazy
lua ⓕ *loo*·a moon
— de mel de mel honeymoon
lubrificante ⓜ loo·bree·fee·*kang*·te lubricant
lucro ⓜ *loo*·kroo profit
lugar ⓜ loo·*gaar* place
luta ⓕ *loo*·ta fight
luvas ⓕ pl *loo*·vash gloves
— de borracha de boo·*rraa*·sha gloves (latex)

luxo ⓜ *loo*·shoo luxury
luz ⓕ loosh light
— do flash doo flaash flashlight (torch)

M

machado de gelo ⓜ ma·*shaa*·doo de *zhe*·loo ice axe
machismo ⓜ ma·*sheezh*·moo sexism
madeira ⓕ ma·*day*·ra wood
madrugada ⓕ ma·droo·*gaa*·da dawn
mãe ⓕ maing mother
maior may·*or* bigger
mais maish more
— tarde *tar*·de later
mala de mão ⓕ *maa*·la de mowng handbag
mala de viagem ⓕ *maa*·la de vee·*aa*·zheng suitcase
manhã ⓕ ma·*nyang* morning
manifestação ⓕ ma·nee·fesh·ta·*sowng* demonstration
Manuelino/Manuelina ⓜ/ⓕ man·wel·*ee*·noo/man·wel·*ee*·na Manueline (art)
mão ⓕ mowng hand
mapa ⓜ *maa*·pa map
— de estradas de *shtraa*·dash road map
maquilhagem ⓕ ma·kee·*lyaa*·zheng make-up
máquina ⓕ *maa*·kee·na machine
— de lavar roupa de la·*vaar rroh*·pa washing machine
— de vender bilhetes de veng·*der* bee·*lye*·tesh ticket machine
— fotográfica foo·too·*graa*·fee·ka camera
mar ⓜ maar sea
maravilhoso/maravilhosa ⓜ/ⓕ ma·ra·vee·*lyo*·zoo/ma·ra·vee·*lyo*·za wonderful
marcar mar·*kaar* score (a goal)
maré ⓕ ma·*re* tide
marido ⓜ ma·*ree*·doo husband
martelo ⓜ mar·*te*·loo hammer
mas mash but
massagem ⓕ ma·*saa*·zheng massage
matar ma·*taar* kill
mau/má ⓜ/ⓕ *ma*·oo/maa bad
maxilar ⓜ maak·see·*laar* jaw (human)
mecânico/mecânica ⓜ/ⓕ me·*ka*·nee·koo/me·*ka*·nee·ka mechanic
medicamentos ⓜ pl me·dee·ka·*meng*·toosh medication
medicina ⓕ me·dee·*see*·na medicine (profession)
médico/médica ⓜ/ⓕ *me*·dee·koo/*me*·dee·ka doctor
meditação ⓕ me·dee·ta·*sowng* meditation
meia ⓕ *may*·a sock
meia-noite ⓕ *may*·a·*noy*·te midnight
meias de vidro ⓕ pl *may*·ash de *vee*·droo stockings
meio-dia ⓜ *may*·oo·*dee*·a midday
meio tempo *may*·oo *teng*·poo part-time
melhor me·*lyor* better
melodia ⓕ me·loo·*dee*·a tune
membro ⓜ&ⓕ *meng*·broo member
memória ⓕ me·*mo*·ree·a memory card
menina ⓕ me·*nee*·na girl
Menina me·*nee*·na Miss (title)
menino ⓜ me·*nee*·noo boy
menor me·*nor* smaller
menos *me*·noosh less
mensagem ⓕ meng·*saa*·zheng message
menstruação ⓕ meng·shtroo·a·*sowng* menstruation
mentir meng·*teer* lie (not tell the truth)
mentiroso/mentirosa ⓜ/ⓕ meng·tee·*ro*·zoo/meng·tee·*ro*·za liar
mercado ⓜ mer·*kaa*·doo market
mercearia ⓕ mer·see·a·*ree*·a grocery
mergulho ⓜ mer·*goo*·lyoo diving
mês ⓜ mesh month
mesa ⓕ *me*·za table
mesmo/mesma ⓜ/ⓕ *mezh*·moo/*mezh*·ma same
mesquita ⓕ mesh·*kee*·ta mosque

metro ⓜ *me*·troo metre
metropolitano ⓜ me·troo·poo·lee·*ta*·no subway (train)
meu/minha ⓜ/ⓕ *me*·oo/*mee*·nya my
microondas ⓜ pl mee·kro·*ong*·dash microwave oven
milímetro ⓜ mee·*lee*·me·troo millimetre
mim ⓜ&ⓕ meeng me
mimado/mimada ⓜ/ⓕ mee·*maa*·doo/mee·*maa*·da spoiled (person)
minúsculo/minúscula ⓜ/ⓕ mee·*noosh*·koo·loo/mee·*noosh*·koo·la tiny
minuto ⓜ mee·*noo*·too minute
miradouro ⓜ mee·ra·*doh*·roo lookout
missa ⓕ *mee*·sa mass (Catholic)
misturar meesh·too·*raar* mix
mochila ⓕ moo·*shee*·la backpack
moda ⓕ *mo*·da fashion
moderno/moderna ⓜ/ⓕ moo·*der*·noo/moo·*der*·na modern
moedas ⓕ pl moo·*e*·dash coins
molas ⓕ pl *mo*·lash spring (coil)
molhado/molhada ⓜ/ⓕ moo·*lyaa*·doo/moo·*lyaa*·da wet
montanha ⓕ mong·*ta*·nya mountain
montanhismo ⓜ mong·ta·*nyeezh*·moo mountaineering
monumento ⓜ moo·noo·*meng*·too monument
morar moo·*raar* live (somewhere)
mordedura ⓕ moor·de·*doo*·ra bite (dog)
mordida ⓕ mor·*dee*·da bite (insect)
morno/morna ⓜ/ⓕ *mor*·noo/*mor*·na warm
morrer moo·*rrer* die
morto/morta ⓜ/ⓕ *mor*·too/*mor*·ta dead
mosquiteiro ⓜ moosh·kee·*tay*·roo mosquito net
mosquito ⓜ moosh·*kee*·too mosquito
mosteiro ⓜ moosh·*tay*·roo monastery
mostrador de velocidade ⓜ moosh·tra·*dor* de ve·loo·see·*daa*·de speedometer
mostrar moosh·*traar* show
mota ⓕ *mo*·ta motorbike
motor ⓜ moo·*tor* engine
mourisco/mourisca ⓜ/ⓕ moh·*reesh*·koo/moh·*reesh*·ka Moorish
móveis ⓜ pl *mo*·vaysh furniture
muçulmano/muçulmana ⓜ/ⓕ moo·sool·*ma*·noo/moo·sool·*ma*·na Muslim
mudança ⓕ moo·*dang*·sa change
mudo/muda ⓜ/ⓕ *moo*·doo/*moo*·da mute
muito *mweeng*·too very
muito/muita ⓜ/ⓕ *mweeng*·too/*mweeng*·ta (a) lot
mulher ⓕ moo·*lyer* woman
— de negócios de ne·*go*·syoosh businesswoman
multa ⓕ *mool*·ta fine (payment)
mundo ⓕ *moong*·doo world
músculo ⓜ *moosh*·koo·loo muscle
museu ⓜ moo·*ze*·oo museum
música ⓕ *moo*·zee·ka music
— popular poo·poo·*laar* folk music
músico/música ⓜ/ⓕ *moo*·zee·koo/*moo*·zee·ka musician

N

na frente de na *freng*·te de in front of
nacionalidade ⓕ na·syoo·na·lee·*daa*·de nationality
nada ⓜ *naa*·da nothing
nadar na·*daar* swim
nádegas ⓕ pl *naa*·de·gash bottom (body)
namorada ⓕ na·moo·*raa*·da girlfriend
namorado ⓜ na·moo·*raa*·doo boyfriend
namorar na·moo·*raar* date (a person)
não nowng no • not
não-fumador nowng·foo·ma·*dor* nonsmoking

nariz (m) na·*reesh* nose
— a pingar a peeng·*gaar* runny nose
nascer do sol (m) *nash*·ser doo sol sunrise
natação (f) na·ta·*sowng* swimming
Natal (m) na·*taal* Christmas
natureza (f) na·too·*re*·za nature
navio (m) na·*vee*·oo ship
necessário/necessária (m)/(f) ne·se·*saa*·ryoo/ne·se·*saa*·rya necessary
negativos (m) pl ne·ga·*tee*·voosh negatives (photos)
negócios (m) pl ne·*go*·syoosh business
nenhum/nenhuma (m)/(f) neng·*yoong*/neng·*yoo*·ma neither • none
neto/neta (m)/(f) *ne*·too/*ne*·ta grandchild
neve (f) *ne*·ve snow
nódoa negra (f) *no*·doo·a *ne*·gra bruise
nódulo (m) *no*·doo·loo lump
no estrangeiro noo shtrang·*zhay*·roo abroad • overseas
no interior noo eeng·te·ree·*or* indoors
noite (f) *noy*·te night
noivado (m) noy·*vaa*·doo engagement
noivo/noiva (m)/(f) *noy*·voo/*noy*·va fiancé/fiancée
nome (m) *no*·me name
nós nosh we
nosso/nossa (m)/(f) *no*·soo/*no*·sa our (one thing)
nossos/nossas (m)/(f) *no*·soosh/*no*·sash our (more than one thing)
nota bancária (f) *no*·ta bang·*kaa*·rya banknote
notícias (f) pl noo·*tee*·syash news
novamente no·va·*meng*·te again
novo/nova (m)/(f) *no*·voo/*no*·va new
nublado/nublada (m)/(f) noo·*blaa*·doo/noo·*blaa*·da cloudy
número (m) *noo*·me·roo number
— da matrícula da ma·*tree*·koo·la license plate number (car)
— do passaporte doo paa·sa·*por*·te passport number
— do quarto doo *kwaar*·too room number
nunca *noong*·ka never
nuvem (f) noo·*veng* cloud

oceano (m) o·see·*a*·noo ocean
óculos (m) pl *o*·koo·loosh glasses (eye)
— de esqui de shkee goggles (skiing)
— de natação de na·ta·*sowng* goggles (swimming)
— de sol de sol sunglasses
ocupado (m) o·koo·*paa*·doo engaged (phone)
ocupado/ocupada (m)/(f) o·koo·*paa*·doo/o·koo·*paa*·da busy
oficina (f) o·fe·*see*·na workshop
olhar oo·*lyaar* look
olho (m) *o*·lyoo eye
ombro (m) *ong*·broo shoulder
onda (f) *ong*·da wave (ocean)
onde *ong*·de where
ontem *ong*·teng yesterday
operário/operária (m)/(f) o·pe·*raa*·ryoo/o·pe·*raa*·rya factory worker
opinião (f) o·pee·nee·*owng* opinion
oportunidade (f) o·poor·too·nee·*daa*·de chance
oposto/oposta (m)/(f) o·*posh*·too/o·*posh*·ta opposite
óptimo/óptima (m)/(f) *o*·tee·moo/*o*·tee·ma great (fantastic)
oração (f) o·ra·*sowng* prayer
orçamento (m) or·sa·*meng*·too budget
orelha (f) o·*re*·lya ear
orgasmo (m) or·*gaazh*·moo orgasm
orquestra (f) or·*kesh*·tra orchestra
o senhor/a senhora (m)/(f) oo seng·*yor*/a seng·*yo*·ra you pol sg
os senhores/as senhoras (m)/(f) oosh seng·*yo*·resh/ash seng·*yo*·rash you pol pl
osso (m) *o*·soo bone
ou oh or

ourivesaria ⓕ oh·ree·ve·za·*ree*·a jewellery
ouro ⓜ *oh*·roo gold
outro/outra ⓜ/ⓕ *oh*·troo/*oh*·tra other n&a
ovário ⓜ o·*vaa*·ryoo ovary
ovelha ⓕ oo·*ve*·lya sheep
oxigénio ⓜ ok·see·*zhe*·nyoo oxygen

P

pacote ⓜ pa·*ko*·te packet
padre ⓜ *paa*·dre priest
pagamento ⓜ pa·ga·*meng*·too payment
pagar pa·*gaar* pay
página ⓕ *paa*·zhee·na page
pai ⓜ pai father
país ⓜ pa·*eesh* country
pais ⓜ pl paish parents
palácio ⓜ pa·*laa*·syoo palace
palavra ⓕ pa·*laa*·vra word
palito ⓜ pa·*lee*·too toothpick
panela ⓕ pa·*ne*·la pan • pot (cooking)
papeira ⓕ pa·*pay*·ra mumps
papel ⓜ pa·*pel* paper
— higiénico ee·zhee·e·nee·koo toilet paper
papelada ⓕ pa·pe·*laa*·da paperwork
papelaria ⓕ pa·pe·la·*ree*·a stationery shop
para baixo *pa*·ra *bai*·shoo downhill
parabéns ⓜ pl pa·ra·*bengzh* congratulations
pára-brisas ⓜ pl *pa*·ra·*bree*·zash windscreen (windshield)
para cima *pa*·ra *see*·ma up
paragem de autocarros ⓕ pa·*raa*·zheng de ow·to·*kaa*·rroosh bus station/stop
parapeito ⓜ pa·ra·*pay*·too ledge
parar pa·*raar* stop
para sempre *pa*·ra *seng*·pre forever
parecido/parecida ⓜ/ⓕ pa·re·*see*·doo/pa·re·*see*·da similar
parede ⓕ pa·*re*·de wall (outer)
parlamento ⓜ par·la·*meng*·too parliament

parque ⓜ *paar*·ke park
— de campismo de kang·*peezh*·moo campsite
— de estacionamento de shta·syoo·na·*meng*·too car park
— nacional na·syoo·*naal* national park
parte ⓕ *paar*·te part (component)
partida ⓕ par·*tee*·da departure • match (sport)
partidário/partidária ⓜ/ⓕ par·tee·*daa*·ryoo/par·tee·*daa*·rya supporter (politics)
partido ⓜ par·*tee*·doo party (politics)
partilhar par·tee·*lyaar* share (a room)
partir par·*teer* depart (leave)
Páscoa ⓕ *paash*·kwa Easter
passado ⓜ pa·*saa*·doo past
passado/passada ⓜ/ⓕ pa·*saa*·doo/pa·*saa*·da last (previous)
passageiro/passageira ⓜ/ⓕ pa·sa·*zhay*·roo/pa·sa·*zhay*·ra passenger
passar pa·*saar* pass (kick/throw)
— por poor pass (go by)
pássaro ⓜ *paa*·sa·roo bird
passo ⓜ *paa*·soo step
pasta ⓕ *pash*·ta briefcase
pasta de dentes ⓕ *paash*·ta de *deng*·tesh toothpaste
patinar pa·tee·*naar* skate
patins em linha ⓜ pl pa·*teengzh* eng *lee*·nya rollerblading
pato/pata ⓜ/ⓕ *paa*·too/*paa*·ta duck
patrão/patroa ⓜ/ⓕ pa·*trowng*/pa·*tro*·a employer
paz ⓕ pash peace
pé ⓜ pe foot (body)
peão ⓜ pee·*owng* pedestrian
peça ⓕ *pe*·sa play (theatre)
pedaço ⓜ pe·*daa*·soo piece
pedido ⓜ pe·*dee*·doo order
pedinte ⓜ&ⓕ pe·*deeng*·te beggar
pedir pe·*deer* ask (for something) • order
— emprestado eng·presh·*taa*·doo borrow
pedra ⓕ *pe*·dra stone

P

peito ⓜ *pay*·too breast • chest (body)
peixe ⓜ *pay*·she fish
pele ⓕ *pe*·le skin
penhasco ⓜ pe·*nyaash*·koo cliff
Península Ibérica ⓕ pe·*neeng*·soo·la ee·*be*·ree·ka Iberian Peninsula
pénis ⓜ *pe*·neesh penis
pensar peng·*saar* think
penso ⓜ *peng*·soo Band-Aid
— higiénico ee·zhee·e·nee·koo panty liner • sanitary napkin
pente ⓜ *peng*·te comb
pequeno/pequena ⓜ/ⓕ pe·*ke*·noo/ pe·*ke*·na small
pequeno almoço ⓜ pe·*ke*·noo aal·*mo*·soo breakfast
perder per·*der* lose • miss (lose/ overlook)
perdido/perdida ⓜ/ⓕ per·*dee*·doo/ per·*dee*·da lost
perdidos e achados ⓜ pl per·*dee*·doosh ee aa·*shaa*·doosh left luggage
perdoar per·doo·*aar* forgive
perfeito/perfeita ⓜ/ⓕ per·*fay*·too/ per·*fay*·ta perfect
perfume ⓜ per·*foo*·me perfume
pergunta ⓕ per·*goong*·ta question
perguntar per·goong·*taar* ask (a question)
perigoso/perigosa ⓜ/ⓕ pe·ree·*go*·zoo/pe·ree·*go*·za dangerous
perna ⓕ *per*·na leg (body)
perto *per*·too close • near
pesado/pesada ⓜ/ⓕ pe·*zaa*·doo/ pe·*zaa*·da heavy (weight)
pesca ⓕ *pesh*·ka fishing
pescoço ⓜ pesh·*ko*·soo neck
peso ⓜ pe·*zoo* weight
pessoa ⓕ pe·*so*·a person
pessoas ⓕ pl pe·*so*·ash people
petróleo ⓜ pe·*tro*·lyoo petrol (gas)
piada ⓕ pee·*aa*·da joke
picareta ⓕ pee·ka·*re*·ta pickaxe
pico ⓜ *pee*·koo mountain peak
pilar ⓜ pee·*laar* pillory (column)
pilha ⓕ *pee*·lya battery
pílula ⓕ *pee*·loo·la the pill
— para dormir *pa*·ra door·*meer* sleeping pills
pinça ⓕ *peeng*·sa tweezers
pintor/pintora ⓜ/ⓕ peeng·*tor*/ peeng·*to*·ra painter
pintura ⓕ peeng·*too*·ra painting
piolhos ⓜ pl pee·o·lyoosh lice
piscina ⓕ pesh·*see*·na swimming pool
pista ⓕ *peesh*·ta track (sport)
pistola ⓕ peesh·*to*·la gun
placar ⓜ pla·*kaar* scoreboard
planalto ⓜ pla·*naal*·too plateau
plano/plana ⓜ/ⓕ *pla*·noo/*pla*·na flat
planta ⓕ *plang*·ta plant
plástico/plástica ⓜ/ⓕ *plash*·tee·koo/*plash*·tee·ka plastic
plataforma ⓕ pla·ta·*for*·ma platform
pneu ⓜ pe·*ne*·oo tyre (tire)
pó ⓜ po powder
— de talco de *taal*·koo baby powder
pobre *po*·bre poor (wealth)
pobreza ⓕ poo·*bre*·za poverty
poder ⓜ poo·*der* power
poder poo·*der* can
poesia ⓕ po·ee·*zee*·a poetry
pólen ⓜ *po*·leng pollen
polícia ⓕ poo·*lee*·sya police (officer)
política ⓕ poo·*lee*·tee·ka policy • politics
político/política ⓜ/ⓕ poo·*lee*·tee·koo/poo·*lee*·tee·ka politician
poluição ⓕ poo·loo·ee·*sowng* pollution
ponte ⓕ *pong*·te bridge (structure)
ponto ⓜ *pong*·too point
— de controle de kong·*tro*·le checkpoint
popular poo·poo·*laar* popular
por poor per (day)
— cento *seng*·too per cent
— cima de *see*·ma de above
— perto *per*·too nearby
pôr do sol ⓜ por doo sol sunset
porco/porca ⓜ/ⓕ *por*·koo/*por*·ka pig

DICTIONARY

porquê poor·*ke* why
porta de partida ⓕ *por*·ta de par·*tee*·da departure gate
portão/porta ⓜ/ⓕ por·*towng*/ *por*·ta gate (airport)
porto ⓜ *por*·too harbour • port
Portugal ⓜ poor·too·*gaal* Portugal
português ⓜ poor·too·*gesh* Portuguese
positivo/positiva ⓜ/ⓕ poo·zee·*tee*·voo/poo·zee·*tee*·vaa positive
possível poo·*see*·vel possible
pouco/pouca ⓜ/ⓕ *poh*·koo/*poh*·ka little (quantity)
pousada de juventude ⓕ poh·*zaa*·da de zhoo·veng·*too*·de youth hostel
praça ⓕ *praa*·sa square (town)
— de táxis de *taak*·seesh taxi stand
— de touros de *toh*·roosh bullring
praia ⓕ *prai*·a beach
prancha de surf ⓕ *prang*·sha de sarf surfboard
prata ⓕ *praa*·ta silver
prateleira ⓕ pra·te·*lay*·ra shelf
prato ⓜ *praa*·too dish • plate
precisar pre·see·*zaar* need
preço ⓜ *pre*·soo price
— da passagem da pa·*saa*·zheng fare
prédio ⓜ *pre*·dyoo building
preferir pre·fe·*reer* prefer
preguiçoso/preguiçosa ⓜ/ⓕ pre·gee·*so*·zoo/pre·gee·*so*·za lazy
prender preng·*der* arrest
preocupado/preocupada ⓜ/ⓕ pree·o·koo·*paa*·doo/ pree·o·koo·*paa*·da worried
preparar pre·pa·*raar* prepare
presente ⓜ pre·*zeng*·te gift • present (time)
preservativo ⓜ pre·zer·va·*tee*·voo condom
presidente ⓜ&ⓕ pre·zee·*deng*·te president
— da câmara da *ka*·ma·ra mayor
pressão ⓕ pre·*sowng* pressure (tyre)
preto/preta ⓜ/ⓕ *pre*·too/*pre*·ta black
preto e branco *pre*·too e *brang*·koo B&W (film)
primeiro/primeira ⓜ/ⓕ pree·*may*·roo/pree·*may*·ra first
primeiro ministro/primeira ministra ⓜ/ⓕ pree·*may*·roo mee·*nee*·shtroo/pree·*may*·ra mee·*nee*·shtra prime minister
primeiro nome ⓜ pree·*may*·roo *no*·me Christian name
principal preeng·see·*paal* main
prisão ⓕ pree·*zowng* jail (prison)
— de ventre pree·*zowng* de *ven*·tre constipation
prisioneiro/prisioneira pree·zyoo·*nay*·roo/pree·zyoo·*nay*·ra prisoner
privado/privada ⓜ/ⓕ pree·*vaa*·doo/pree·*vaa*·da private
problema de coração ⓜ proo·*ble*·ma de koo·ra·*sowng* heart condition
procurar pro·koo·*raar* look for
produzir proo·doo·*zeer* produce
professor/professora ⓜ/ⓕ proo·fe·*sor*/proo·fe·*so*·ra teacher
profundo/profunda ⓜ/ⓕ proo·*foong*·doo/proo·*foong*·da deep
programa ⓜ proo·*gra*·ma program
projector ⓜ proo·zhe·*tor* projector
prometer proo·me·*ter* promise
pronto/pronta ⓜ/ⓕ *prong*·too/ *prong*·ta ready
prostituto/prostituta ⓜ/ⓕ proosh·tee·*too*·too/proosh·tee·*too*·ta prostitute
protecção anti-solar ⓕ proo·te·*sowng* ang·tee·soo·*laar* sunblock
protector de borracha ⓜ proo·te·*tor* de boo·*rraa*·sha dental dam
proteger proo·te·*zher* protect
protegido/protegida ⓜ/ⓕ proo·te·*zhee*·doo/proo·te·*zhee*·da protected (species)

protestar proo·tesh·*taar* protest
provisões ⓕ pl proo·vee·*zoyngsh* provisions
próximo/próxima ⓜ/ⓕ *pro*·see·moo/*pro*·see·ma nearby • next
pulga ⓕ *pool*·ga flea
pulmão ⓜ pool·*mowng* lung
pulso ⓜ *pool*·soo wrist
puro/pura ⓜ/ⓕ *poo*·roo/*poo*·ra pure
puxar poo·*shaar* pull

Q

qual kwaal which
qualidade ⓕ kwa·lee·*daa*·de quality
qualificações ⓕ pl kwa·lee·fee·ka·*soyngsh* qualifications
qualquer kwaal·*ker* any
quando *kwang*·doo when
quarentena ⓕ kwa·reng·*te*·na quarantine
quarto ⓜ *kwaar*·too bedroom • room
— de casal de ka·*zaal* double room
— de solteiro de sol·*tay*·roo single room
quase *kwaa*·ze almost
que ke what
quebrado/quebrada ⓜ/ⓕ ke·*braa*·doo/ke·*braa*·da broken
quebrar ke·*braar* break
queimadura ⓕ kay·ma·*doo*·ra burn
quem keng who
quente *keng*·te hot
querer ke·*rer* want
quilograma ⓜ kee·loo·*graa*·ma kilogram
quilómetro ⓜ kee·*lo*·me·troo kilometre
quinta ⓕ *keeng*·ta farm
quinzena ⓕ keeng·*ze*·na fortnight
quiosque ⓜ kee·*osh*·ke kiosk • newsstand

R

racismo ⓜ rra·*seezh*·moo racism
radiador ⓜ rra·dee·a·*dor* radiator
rádio *rraa*·dyoo radio
rainha ⓕ rra·*ee*·nya queen
raio de roda ⓜ *rraa*·yoo de *rro*·da spoke (wheel)
rápido/rápida ⓜ/ⓕ *rraa*·pee·doo/*rraa*·pee·da fast
raquete ⓕ rra·*ke*·te racquet
raro/rara ⓜ/ⓕ *rraa*·roo/*rraa*·ra rare (uncommon)
ratazana ⓜ&ⓕ rra·ta·*za*·na rat
rato ⓜ *rraa*·too mouse
rave ⓕ rrayv rave (party)
razão ⓕ rra·*zowng* reason
razoável rra·zoo·*aa*·vel sensible
realista rree·a·*leesh*·ta realistic
recarregador de bateria ⓜ rre·ka·rre·ga·*dor* de ba·te·*ree*·a jumper leads
receber rre·se·*ber* welcome
receita médica ⓕ rre·*say*·ta *me*·dee·ka prescription
recentemente rre·seng·te·*meng*·te recently
recibo ⓜ rre·*see*·boo receipt
reciclar rre·see·*klaar* recycle
reciclável rre·see·*klaa*·vel recyclable
reclamação ⓕ rre·kla·ma·*sowng* complaint
reclamar rre·kla·*maar* complain
recomendar rre·koo·meng·*daar* recommend
recursos humanos ⓜ pl rre·*koor*·soosh oo·*ma*·noosh human resources
recusar rre·koo·*zaar* refuse
rede ⓕ *rre*·de net • network (phone)
redondo/redonda ⓜ/ⓕ rre·*dong*·doo/rre·*dong*·da round
reembolso ⓜ rre·eng·*bol*·soo refund
refeição ⓕ rre·fay·*sowng* meal
— ligeira lee·*zhay*·ra snack
referência ⓕ rre·fe·*reng*·sya reference
refrigerante ⓜ rre·free·zhe·*rang*·te soft drink
regional rre·zhyoo·*naal* regional
registo automóvel ⓜ rre·*zheesh*·too ow·too·*mo*·vel car registration
regra ⓕ *rre*·gra rule

regressar rre·gre·*saar* return
rei ⓜ rray king
elacionamento ⓜ
re·la·syoo·na·*meng*·too relationship
elações públicas ⓕ pl rre·la·*soyngsh*
oo·blee·kash public relations
elaxar rre·laa·*shaar* relax
eligião ⓕ rre·lee·zhee·*owng* religion
eligioso/religiosa ⓜ/ⓕ
re·lee·zhee·*o*·zoo/rre·lee·zhee·*o*·za
eligious
elíquia ⓕ rre·*lee*·kya relic
elógio ⓜ rre·*lo*·zhyoo clock • watch
elva ⓕ *rrel*·va grass (lawn)
emoto/remota ⓜ/ⓕ rre·*mo*·too/
re·*mo*·ta remote
enda ⓕ *rreng*·da lace
epelente ⓜ rre·pe·*leng*·te insect
epellant
– em espiral eng shpee·*raal*
nosquito coil
eserva ⓕ rre·*zer*·va reservation
eservar rre·zer·*vaar* book (reserve)
espirar rresh·pee·*raar* breathe
esposta ⓕ rresh·*posh*·ta answer
estaurante ⓜ rresh·tow·*rang*·te
estaurant
everenciar rre·ve·reng·see·*aar*
vorship
evisão ⓕ rre·vee·*zowng* review
evista ⓕ rre·*veesh*·ta magazine
ibeiro ⓜ rree·*bay*·roo stream
ico/rica ⓜ/ⓕ *rree*·koo/*rree*·ka rich
im ⓜ rreeng kidney
io ⓜ *rree*·oo river
ir rreer laugh
isco ⓜ *rreesh*·koo risk
itmo ⓜ *rreet*·moo rhythm
oda ⓕ *rro*·da wheel
omântico/romântica ⓜ/ⓕ
oo·*maang*·tee·koo/
oo·*maang*·tee·ka romantic
osto ⓜ *rrosh*·too face
ota ⓕ *rro*·ta route
- de caminhada de ka·mee·*nyaa*·da
iking route
otunda ⓕ rroo·*toong*·da roundabout

roubado/roubada ⓜ/ⓕ
rroh·*baa*·doo/rroh·*baa*·da stolen
roubar rroh·*baar* steal
roubo ⓜ *rroh*·boo rip-off
roupa interior ⓕ *rroh*·pa
eeng·te·ree·*or* underwear
roupas ⓕ pl *rroh*·pash clothing
roxo/roxa ⓜ/ⓕ *rro*·shoo/*rro*·sha
purple
rua ⓕ *rroo*·a street
— principal preeng·see·*paal* main
road
rubéola ⓕ rroo·*be*·o·la rubella
ruínas ⓕ pl rroo·*ee*·nash ruins

S

saber sa·*ber* know
sabonete ⓜ sa·boo·*ne*·te soap
saca-rolhas ⓜ *saa*·ka·*rro*·lyash
bottle opener • corkscrew
saco ⓜ *saa*·koo bag
— de dormir de dor·*meer* sleeping
bag
— saco de fatos de *faa*·toosh suit bag
saia ⓕ *sai*·a skirt
saída ⓕ saa·*ee*·da exit
— à noite aa *noy*·te night out
sair sa·*eer* go out
sais de hidratação ⓜ pl saish de
ee·dra·ta·*sowng* rehydration salts
sala ⓕ *saa*·la room
— de espera de *shpe*·ra waiting room
— de estar de shtaar foyer
— de provas de *pro*·vash change room
— de trânsito de *trang*·zee·too
transit lounge
salão de beleza ⓜ sa·*lowng* de
be·*le*·za beauty salon
saldo ⓜ *saal*·doo balance (account)
saltar saal·*taar* jump
sandália ⓕ sang·*daa*·lya sandal
sangue ⓜ *sang*·ge blood
santo/santa ⓜ/ⓕ *sang*·too/*sang*·ta
saint
santuário ⓜ sang·too·*aa*·ryoo shrine
sapato ⓜ sa·*paa*·too shoe
sarampo ⓜ sa·*rang*·poo measles

saúde ⓕ sa·*oo*·de health
se se if
secar se·*kaar* dry
seco/seca ⓜ/ⓕ *se*·koo/*se*·ka dried • dry • stale
seda ⓕ *se*·da silk
sedento/sedenta ⓜ/ⓕ se·*deng*·too/se·*deng*·ta thirsty
seguir se·*geer* follow
segundo ⓜ se·*goong*·doo second (time)
segundo/segunda ⓜ/ⓕ se·*goong*·doo/se·*goong*·da second
seguro ⓜ se·*goo*·roo insurance
— social soo·see·*aal* welfare
seguro/segura se·*goo*·roo/se·*goo*·ra safe
seios ⓜ pl *say*·oosh breasts
selo ⓜ *se*·loo stamp (postage)
sem seng without
semáforo ⓜ se·*maa*·foo·roo traffic light
semana ⓕ se·*ma*·na week
sempre *seng*·pre always
Senhor se·*nyor* Mr
Senhora se·*nyo*·ra Mrs • Ms
senhoria se·nyoo·*ree*·a landlady
senhorio se·nyoo·*ree*·oo landlord
sensação ⓕ seng·sa·*sowng* feeling (physical)
sensível seng·*see*·vel emotional
sensual seng·soo·*aal* sensual
sentar seng·*taar* sit
sentimentos ⓜ pl seng·tee·*meng*·toosh feelings
separado/separada ⓜ/ⓕ se·pa·*raa*·doo/se·pa·*raa*·da separate
ser ser be (ongoing)
seringa ⓕ se·*reeng*·ga needle (syringe)
sério/séria ⓜ/ⓕ *se*·ryoo/*se*·rya serious
serviço ⓜ ser·*vee*·soo service
sexo ⓜ *sek*·soo sex
— protegido proo·te·*zhee*·doo safe sex
SIDA ⓕ *see*·da AIDS
sim seeng yes
simpático/simpática ⓜ/ⓕ seeng·*paa*·tee·koo/seeng·*paa*·tee·ka nice
simples *seeng*·plesh simple
sinal ⓜ see·*naal* sign
— da linha telefónica da *lee*·nya te·le·*fo*·nee·ka dial tone
sintético/sintética ⓜ/ⓕ seeng·*te*·tee·koo/seeng·*te*·tee·ka synthetic
sobre *so*·bre on
sobremesa ⓕ soo·bre·*me*·za dessert
sobretudo ⓜ soo·bre·*too*·doo overcoat
só de ida so de *ee*·da one-way (ticket)
sogra ⓕ *so*·gra mother-in-law
sogro ⓜ *so*·groo father-in-law
sol ⓜ sol sun
solteiro/solteira ⓜ/ⓕ sol·*tay*·roo/sol·*tay*·ra single (person)
solto/solta ⓜ/ⓕ *sol*·too/*sol*·ta loose
sombra ⓕ *song*·bra shadow
somente so·*meng*·te only
sonho ⓜ *so*·nyoo dream
sonolento/sonolenta ⓜ/ⓕ soo·noo·*leng*·too/soo·noo·*leng*·ta sleepy
sorrir so·*rreer* smile
sorte ⓕ *sor*·te luck
soutien ⓜ soo·tee·*eng* bra
sozinho/sozinha ⓜ/ⓕ so·*zee*·nyoo/so·*zee*·nya alone
subir soo·*beer* climb
— a bordo a *bor*·doo board
suborno ⓜ soo·*bor*·noo bribe
suficiente soo·fee·see·*eng*·te enough
sujo/suja ⓜ/ⓕ *soo*·zhoo/*soo*·zha dirty
superstição ⓕ soo·persh·tee·*sowng* superstition
surdo/surda ⓜ/ⓕ *soor*·doo/*soor*·da deaf
surpresa ⓕ soor·*pre*·za surprise

T

tabacaria ⓕ ta·ba·ka·*ree*·a tobacconist
tabaco ⓜ ta·*baa*·koo tobacco
talheres ⓜ pl ta·*lye*·resh cutlery
talvez tal·*vesh* maybe
tamanho ⓜ ta·*ma*·nyoo size
também tang·*beng* also
tampão ⓜ tang·*powng* plug (bath) • tampon
tampões para os ouvidos ⓜ pl tang·*poyngsh pa*·ra oosh oh·*vee*·doosh earplugs
tapete ⓜ ta·*pe*·te rug
tarde ⓕ *taar*·de afternoon
tarifa postal ⓕ ta·*ree*·fa poosh·*taal* postage
taxa ⓕ *taa*·sha fee • tax
— de aeroporto de a·e·ro·*por*·too airport tax
— de câmbio de *kang*·byoo exchange rate
— de serviço de ser·*vee*·soo service charge
teatro ⓜ te·*aa*·troo theatre
tecido ⓜ te·*see*·doo fabric
teclado ⓜ te·*klaa*·doo keyboard
técnica ⓕ *tek*·nee·ka technique
teimoso/teimosa ⓜ/ⓕ tay·*mo*·zoo/tay·*mo*·za stubborn
teleférico ⓜ te·le·*fe*·ree·koo chairlift (skiing)
telefonar te·le·foo·*naar* telephone
telefone ⓜ te·le·*fo*·ne telephone
— público *poo*·blee·koo public phone
telemóvel ⓜ te·le·*mo*·vel cell/mobile phone
telescópio ⓜ te·lesh·*ko*·pyoo telescope
televisão ⓕ te·le·vee·*zowng* television
temperatura ⓕ teng·pe·ra·*too*·ra temperature (weather)
tempestade ⓕ teng·pesh·*taa*·de storm
tempo ⓜ *teng*·poo time • weather
— inteiro eeng·*tay*·roo full-time
tenda ⓕ *teng*·da tent
ténis ⓜ *te*·neesh tennis
— de mesa de *me*·za table tennis
tensão arterial ⓕ teng·*sowng* ar·te·ree·*aal* blood pressure
tensão pré-menstrual ⓕ teng·*sowng* pre·meng·shtroo·*aal* premenstrual tension
tentar teng·*taar* try (attempt)
ter ter have
— saudades sow·*daa*·desh miss (feel absence of)
terminar ter·mee·*naar* finish
terra ⓕ *te*·rra land
terramoto ⓜ te·rra·*mo*·too earthquake
terrível te·*rree*·vel terrible
terrorismo ⓜ te·rroo·*reezh*·moo terrorism
tesoura ⓕ sg te·*zoh*·ra scissors
teste ⓜ *tesh*·te test
— de gravidez de gra·vee·*desh* pregnancy test kit
— nuclear noo·klee·*aar* nuclear testing
teu/tua ⓜ/ⓕ *te*·oo/*too*·a your (one thing) inf sg
teus/tuas ⓜ/ⓕ *te*·oosh/*too*·ash your (more than one thing) inf sg
tia ⓕ *tee*·a aunt
tigela ⓕ tee·*zhe*·la bowl
tímido/tímida ⓜ/ⓕ *tee*·mee·doo/*tee*·mee·da shy
típico/típica ⓜ/ⓕ *tee*·pee·koo/*tee*·pee·ka typical
tipo ⓜ *tee*·poo type
título de registo do automóvel ⓜ *tee*·too·loo de rre·*zheesh*·too doo ow·too·*mo*·vel car owner's title
toalha ⓕ *twaa*·lya towel
— de mesa de *me*·za tablecloth
— de rosto de *rrosh*·too face cloth
tocar too·*kaar* feel (touch) • play (guitar, etc) • touch
todo/toda ⓜ/ⓕ *to*·doo/*to*·da all • every
todos/todas ⓜ/ⓕ *to*·doosh/*to*·dash everyone

tomada ⓕ too·*maa*·da plug (electricity)
tonto/tonta ⓜ/ⓕ *tong*·too/*tong*·ta dizzy
torneira ⓕ toor·*nay*·ra faucet • tap (sink)
tornozelo ⓜ toor·noo·*ze*·loo ankle
torre ⓕ *to*·rre tower
tossir too·*seer* cough
tourada ⓕ toh·*raa*·da bullfight
touro ⓜ *toh*·roo bull
toxicodependente *tok*·see·ko·de·peng·*deng*·te drug user
trabalhador/trabalhadora ⓜ/ⓕ tra·ba·lya·*dor*/tra·ba·lya·*do*·ra labourer
trabalhar tra·ba·*lyaar* work
trabalho ⓜ tra·*baa*·lyoo work
— num bar noong baar bar work
— doméstico doo·*mesh*·tee·koo housework
— temporário teng·poo·*raa*·ryoo casual work
traduzir tra·doo·*zeer* translate
tráfico ⓜ *traa*·fee·koo traffic
— de drogas de *dro*·gash drug trafficking
traição ⓕ tra·ee·*sowng* cheat
tranca ⓕ *trang*·ka lock
trancado/trancada ⓜ/ⓕ trang·*kaa*·doo/trang·*kaa*·da locked
traseiro/traseira ⓜ/ⓕ tra·*zay*·roo/tra·*zay*·ra rear (location)
travão ⓜ tra·*vowng* brake (car)
trazer tra·*zer* bring
treinador/treinadora ⓜ/ⓕ tray·na·*dor*/tray·na·*do*·ra coach • manager (sport)
treinamento ⓜ tre·na·*meng*·too workout
tribunal ⓜ tree·boo·*naal* court (legal)
trilho de montanha ⓜ *tree*·lyoo de mong·*ta*·nya mountain path
triste *treesh*·te sad
trocar troo·*kaar* change (money) • exchange
trocos ⓜ pl *tro*·koosh loose change
trombose ⓕ trong·*bo*·ze stroke (health)
trovoada ⓕ troo·voo·*aa*·da thunderstorm
tu too you inf sg
tudo ⓜ *too*·doo everything
tumor ⓜ too·*mor* tumour
túmulo ⓜ *too*·moo·loo grave
tuna ⓜ *too*·na (university) music group
turista ⓜ&ⓕ too·*reesh*·ta tourist

U

último/última ⓜ/ⓕ *ool*·tee·moo/*ool*·tee·ma last (final)
ultrasom ⓜ ool·tra·*song* ultrasound
uma vez *oo*·ma vezh once
um outro/uma outra ⓜ/ⓕ oong *oh*·troo/*oo*·ma *oh*·tra another
universidade ⓕ oo·nee·ver·see·*daa*·de university
universo ⓜ oo·nee·*ver*·soo universe
urgente oor·*zheng*·te urgent
usar oo·*zaar* wear
útil *oo*·teel useful

V

vaca ⓕ *vaa*·ka cow
vacina ⓕ va·*see*·na vaccination
vaga ⓕ *vaa*·ga vacancy
vagão cama ⓜ va·*gowng* *ka*·ma sleeping car
vagão restaurante ⓜ va·*gowng* rresh·tow·*rang*·te dining car
vagarosamente va·ga·ro·za·*meng*·te slowly
vagina ⓕ va·*zhee*·na vagina
vago/vaga ⓜ/ⓕ *vaa*·goo/*vaa*·ga vacant
validar va·lee·*daar* validate
valioso/valiosa ⓜ/ⓕ va·lee·*o*·zoo/va·lee·*o*·za valuable
valor ⓜ va·*lor* value
varanda ⓕ va·*rang*·da balcony
vários/várias ⓜ/ⓕ *vaa*·ryoosh/*vaa*·ryash many • several

vazio/vazia ⓜ/ⓕ va·*zee*·oo/va·*zee*·a empty
vegetariano/vegetariana ⓜ/ⓕ ve·zhe·ta·ree·*a*·noo/ve·zhe·ta·ree·*a*·na vegetarian n&a
veia ⓕ *vey*·a vein
vela ⓕ *ve*·la candle
velho/velha ⓜ/ⓕ *ve*·lyoo/*ve*·lya old (age)
velocidade ⓕ ve·loo·see·*daa*·de speed (velocity)
— do filme doo *feel*·me film speed
vencedor/vencedora ⓜ/ⓕ veng·se·*dor*/veng·se·*do*·ra winner
vender veng·*der* sell
venenoso/venenosa ⓜ/ⓕ ve·ne·*no*·zoo/ve·ne·*no*·za poisonous
vento ⓜ *veng*·too wind
ventoínha ⓕ veng·too·*ee*·nya fan (machine)
ver ver see • watch (television)
verão ⓜ ve·*rowng* summer
verde *ver*·de green
verificar ve·ree·fee·*kaar* check
vermelho/vermelha ⓜ/ⓕ ver·*me*·lyoo/ver·*me*·lya red
vestido ⓜ vesh·*tee*·doo dress
via aérea ⓕ *vee*·a a·e·ree·a airmail
viagem ⓕ vee·*aa*·zheng journey
— de negócios de ne·*go*·syoosh business trip
viajar vee·a·*zhaar* travel
vício ⓜ *vee*·syoo addiction
— da droga da *dro*·ga drug addiction
vida ⓕ *vee*·da life
vigiar vee·zhee·*aar* watch (look after)
VIH ⓜ ve ee a·*gaa* HIV
vinha ⓕ *vee*·nya vineyard
vinho ⓜ *vee*·nyoo wine
violação ⓕ vee·oo·la·*sowng* rape
vir veer come
virar vee·*raar* turn
vírus ⓜ *vee*·roosh virus
visitar vee·zee·*taar* visit
vista ⓕ *veesh*·ta view
visto ⓜ *veesh*·too visa
vitamina ⓕ vee·ta·*mee*·na vitamin
voar voo·*aar* fly
vocês vo·*sesh* you inf pl
vóleibol ⓜ *vo*·lay·bol volleyball (sport)
— de praia de *prai*·a beach volleyball
voltar vol·*taar* return
voo ⓜ *vo*·oo flight
vosso/vossa ⓜ/ⓕ *vo*·soo/*vo*·sa your (one thing) inf pl
vossos/vossas ⓜ/ⓕ *vo*·soosh/*vo*·sash your (more than one thing) inf pl
votar voo·*taar* vote
voz ⓕ vosh voice

X

xadrez ⓜ sha·*dresh* chess

Z

zangado/zangada ⓜ/ⓕ zang·*gaa*·doo/zang·*gaa*·da angry
zona ⓕ *zo*·na shingles (illness)

Index

For topics that are covered in several sections of this book, we've indicated the most relevant page number in bold.

A

B

C

10 Ways to Start a Sentence

When's (the next bus)?	Quando é que sai (o próximo autocarro)?	*kwang*·doo e ke sai (oo *pro*·see·moo ow·to·*kaa*·rroo)
Where's (the station)?	Onde é (a estação)?	*ong*·de e (a shta·*sowng*)
Where do I (buy a ticket)?	Onde é que eu (compro o bilhete)?	*ong*·de e ke e·oo (*kong*·proo oo bee·*lye*·te)
How much is (a room)?	Quanto custa por (um quarto)?	*kwang*·too *koosh*·ta poor (oong *kwaar*·too)
Do you have (a map)?	Tem (um mapa)?	teng (oong *maa*·pa)
Please bring (the bill).	Pode-me trazer (a conta).	*po*·de·me tra·*zer* (a *kong*·ta)
I'd like (the menu).	Queria (um menu).	ke·*ree*·a (oong me·*noo*)
I have (a reservation).	Eu tenho (uma reserva).	e·oo *ta*·nyoo (*oo*·ma rre·*zer*·va)
Could you please (help)?	Pode (ajudar), por favor?	*po*·de (a·zhoo·*daar*) poor fa·*vor*
Do I need (a visa)?	Preciso de (um visto)?	pre·*see*·zoo de (oong *veesh*·too)